END OF THE RAINBOW

END OF THE RAINBOW

Oliver Holt

First published in Great Britain in 2010 by Hodder & Stoughton
An Hachette UK company

1

A CIP catalogue record for this title is available from the British Library

ISBN 978 1 444 71595 8

Typeset in Minion by Ellipsis Books Limited, Glasgow

Printed and bound by Clays Ltd, St Ives plc

Hodder & Stoughton policy is to use papers that are natural,
renewable and recyclable products and made from wood grown
in sustainable forests. The logging and manufacturing processes
are expected to conform to the environmental regulations
of the country of origin.

Hodder & Stoughton Ltd
338 Euston Road
London NW1 3BH

www.hodder.co.uk

To Sarah

Contents

Acknowledgements

I could not have written this book without the help of my English newspaper colleagues who covered the World Cup in South Africa. I owe a particular debt to friends like Paul Hayward, Matt Dickinson, Andy Dunn, Martin Samuel, Charlie Sale, John Dillon, Jim Lawton, Michael Walker and Martin Lipton for filling in some of the many gaps in my knowledge but I also feel it is important to acknowledge the debt I owe to all my English newspaper colleagues in South Africa. Sometimes, it feels as if newspapers are under siege but being a newspaper man is still the best job in the world and a big part of the reason for that is the company and the conversation of the other writers.

I also owe a debt to my friends Matshelane Mamabolo and Jermaine Craig, who have helped me to understand and love South Africa; to England players like John Terry, Frank Lampard, David Beckham, Steven Gerrard, David James, Jamie Carragher, Theo Walcott, Joe Cole and Rio Ferdinand who always stop to talk to the press after England matches; to Adrian Bevington and Mark Whittle at the FA; to Joanne Budd, who did such a brilliant job creating the England media centre at the Royal Bafokeng Sports Campus; to Trish Burgess and Phil Shaw, who spotted all the errors I made in writing this book; to Roddy Bloomfield, for asking me to do this book in the first place and for helping to make writing for Hodder such an enjoyable experience; to Sarah Hammond and David Luxton. Finally, I owe a great debt to my bosses at the *Daily Mirror* for many things but, most recently, for sending me to South Africa in the first place.

Photographic Acknowledgements

The author and publisher would like to thank the following for permission to reproduce photographs:

AFP/Getty Images, Barry Aldworth/Sports Inc/PA, Bernat Armangue/AP/PA, Darko Bandic/AP/PA, Adam Davy/PA, Mike Egerton/PA, FIFA via Getty Images, Eugene Hoshiko/AP/PA, David Klein/Landov/PA, Hussein Malla/AP/PA, Rebecca Naden/PA, Martin Rickett/PA, RTL/AP/PA, Michael Sohn/AP/PA.

1 DOWN AND OUT IN BADEN-BADEN

BADEN-BADEN was where it all began. That was where England's Fabio Capello era really started. It may have been June 2006, 18 months before Capello took over as England coach, when England's footballers and their families descended on the small German town on the edge of the Black Forest that was to be their base for that summer's World Cup, but by the time they left a month later as figures of ridicule, it had become clear that the management of the national team needed to be taken in a radically different direction.

Under England's Swedish manager, Sven-Goran Eriksson, the culture of celebrity that surrounded the England team had been allowed to run wild. England's experience in Baden-Baden exposed once and for all the folly of appointing an indulgent manager and permitting the players too much power. The England players needed boundaries, and Eriksson did not give them any. By the end of England's involvement in the tournament, the English public had grown disillusioned with the behaviour of their players and their players' wives and girlfriends, and even though Steve McClaren had already been anointed Eriksson's successor, what happened in Baden-Baden left England supporters yearning for a more disciplinarian manager.

Baden-Baden is a beautiful spa town in southwest Germany. It is a genteel, reserved kind of place with narrow, winding pedestrian streets, elegant shops, a handsome opera house and a lavishly appointed spa complex. The elderly, the affluent and the Russians come to take the waters, seeking a cure for their ills. In the 19th century it was one of the stops on the Grand Tour, a place where the European nobility were fond of spending their summers. In the summer of 2006, though, it was conquered by new foreign invaders. For a month, it was overrun by the English and, in particular, by Wags.

The Wags – a tabloid acronym for the wives and girlfriends of England footballers, invented in the build-up to that year's World Cup – owed their high profile that summer to the willingness of Eriksson to encourage and indulge their fondness for publicity and self-promotion by agreeing to arrangements for them to travel en masse to Baden-Baden and set up camp there.

By that summer, it had been clear for some time that Eriksson was in thrall to his players, certainly the more famous among them. At the start of his tenure in 2000 he had asked David Beckham to autograph a shirt for his daughter. It was a sign of things to come. When Eriksson was manager he gave the team talks and picked the side, but in most other aspects of organisation the players ran the show. So when England sealed their qualification for Germany, the most influential players decided it would be best if their families went too. Plans were put in place.

The Football Association organised a package tour for the Wags and any parents willing to pay the £20,000-a-head asking price. The cost included accommodation at the stately Brenner's Park Hotel, a landmark of luxury and old-style sophistication that stood in its own gardens on the banks of the babbling Oosbach River, coach transfers to and from each England match and match tickets. Nancy dell'Olio, Eriksson's long-time girlfriend, most recently seen appearing on *Marco's Kitchen Burnout*, acted as the group's social secretary. She was busy.

So was the FA. It had run into a problem it could not fix when it discovered that at least 15 football writers from English newspapers had reserved rooms at Brenner's Park for the duration of the World Cup before they had. It explored the idea of cancelling the journalists' reservations, but hotel executives refused to countenance it. At a time when the relationship between press and players was uneasy at best, the scene was set for a most unlikely cohabitation.

There were some mutual benefits. Contact between press and players had become progressively more limited during the 1990s and into the new century. Glenn Hoddle, who was paranoid about secrecy and leaks, had stopped the practice of the press travelling on the same plane as England in the run-up to the 1998 World Cup, and journalists had been discouraged from staying in the same hotel as the players even longer ago than that.

It was the trend of the age. The press had been in retreat in sport for some time, desperately trying to protect its previous hegemony against the march of the broadcast media and the incursions of club websites and club television channels. The press weren't part of the family any more. They were kept at arm's length. They still travelled on the plane with club sides on Champions League away trips, but often the management went to bizarre lengths to make sure the players were hermetically sealed in terms of contact with journalists.

When Manchester United travelled abroad, the players assembled in a special lounge near the gate. The press boarded the plane first and filed through the cabin to the seats in the rear section. Sponsors and their guests would get on next, and they sat in the middle of the plane, forming a cordon sanitaire so that when the players boarded, there was no prospect of them being remotely near a reporter. When the plane reached its destination, the players disembarked first and were out of the airport and on the bus before the journalists even got to the luggage carousels.

Most journalists only came into contact with England players after international matches in the mixed-zone areas set up between the changing rooms and the car park, where the team coach waited, engine running. The journalists were herded behind metal crowd-control barriers, while selected players were brought over to where they stood. After big games there was often a shoving match resembling a rugby scrum in the mixed zone, as journalists tried to work themselves into a position where they could hear or at least thrust their tape recorder close enough to pick up the player's voice.

At Premier League matches contact was even more limited. Manchester United, for instance, did not allow any press access to the players' tunnel at Old Trafford. Most other clubs allowed one or two press men into the tunnel area after games on the understanding that the quotes they picked up from the players were shared with the rest of their daily or Sunday newspaper colleagues.

Social contact between press and players was all but extinct, but in Baden-Baden, to the surprise of everyone, the starvation diet came to an abrupt end. The press and the players' families were suddenly living side by side, observing each other in the hotel gardens, its restaurant, its television room and, most of all, its bar. It was difficult to say which group was the more disconcerted.

Despite the FA's misgivings and the occasional contretemps, the players' parents and the press got on well. As an experiment in social engineering, it was a success. Some of the players' parents had demonised journalists who had written less than complimentary things about their sons, and now at least had the opportunity to express their resentment and talk the issues through. For many of the journalists, talking to the players' families made them think more carefully about how easily a mother or a father can be upset by unkind appraisals of their boy.

Some journalists shared a train ride from Baden-Baden to Cologne with Peter Crouch's parents, Bruce and Jane, on the way to England's group game with Sweden. The Crouches are amiable, intelligent and articulate people, and they made several small observations about the coverage aimed at their son. They pointed out, in particular, that they found it hurtful when Peter was referred to as a 'beanpole' or a 'walking lamp-post'. They felt the press had grown obsessed with his height and sometimes referred to him as if he were a freak, not one of England's first-choice strikers.

Gary Neville's dad, Neville Neville, was also a popular figure. In the early days at Brenner's Park, Neville acted as a bridge between the families who were most suspicious of the press and the journalists. There were several heated exchanges, but when Neville intervened, most of them were resolved amicably. David Beckham's mum, Sandra, had more reason than most to harbour grudges about a number of her son's media tormentors, but most of the time she managed to keep her feelings to herself.

Don Walcott, Theo's dad, was the only parent not staying at Brenner's. His 17-year-old son had signed for Arsenal six months earlier, and the Walcotts baulked at the price the FA were demanding for the Brenner's-based package. He stayed around the corner at a more modest hotel called Der Kleine Prinz, but made a few appearances in the Brenner's bar. Don was another who enjoyed talking through the football issues of the day with the sports journalists. The same went for Joe Cole's dad, George.

Only once did the temptation of modest revenge emerge. After England had been knocked out in the quarter-finals, a group of players' parents had a farewell lunch in the Wintergarten restaurant at Brenner's Park and let the wine flow. Someone signed the bill before they left and stuck a room number on the bottom of it. A couple of weeks later, Steven Howard, the *Sun*'s fearlessly inflammatory chief sports writer, was studying his bill as he prepared to check out and noticed a rather large lunch charge he couldn't remember incurring.

The stay in Baden-Baden was the first time most of the press had made the acquaintance of Jamie Carragher's extended family. The

Carraghers – Jamie's dad, Philly, plus various other relatives and friends who seemed to come and go – announced their arrival in style at Brenner's Park, embarking on a bender that ended one morning just as several journalists were gathering in the foyer to drive to England's training session.

The liveried doormen at Brenner's, more used to dealing with heads of state than the well-refreshed relatives of England footballers, made a half-hearted attempt to deny a couple of the Carragher clan access, and there followed a rolling maul before the lads forced their way to the lifts and up to their room. The doormen looked more stunned than angry. They had never seen anything like this before. They weren't trained for Carraghers.

But after a couple of early misunderstandings, the Carraghers and the English sports journalists got on swimmingly. In fact, the Carragher family became cult figures among the press corps. One journalist was summoned to their room to face the music after the *Sunday Mirror* printed a grainy picture of Philly larking around on the terrace of Brenner's Park and apparently performing a Hitler salute. The elegant first-floor suite had been converted into a crash pad with mattresses strewn across it wall to wall. The journalist got a half-hearted dressing down and ended up staying for a drink.

The Carraghers' stay at Brenner's Park ended rather suddenly one afternoon when a bucket of water was thrown down on to the terrace from a guest room, narrowly missing diners who were having lunch. The Carraghers protested their innocence, but it was obvious by now that Brenner's was cramping their style, so they moved out. They decamped a few hundred yards down the road towards the centre of town to a bar with rooms above it, and stayed there for the rest of the tournament. The journalists christened it 'The House of Scouse'.

Brenner's wasn't the same without them, but it didn't diminish the sense that the English sports journalists got on a lot better with the players' parents than they did with the players. Maybe it was a generational thing. Many of the journalists were closer in age to the parents than they were to the players. Maybe it was just that the players had been burnt too many times by stories they believed encroached upon their personal lives to be comfortable in the presence of journalists.

It wasn't all sweetness and light. After one particularly energetic exchange of views in the Brenner's bar, one of the journalists suggested England would be knocked out well before the final. 'Don't worry,' he said, 'we'll be at this hotel long after you've gone home.' That was not received well. England goalkeeper Paul Robinson's wife, Rebecca, grew upset one evening when she confronted journalists in the bar about the criticism that had been aimed at her husband. And when Victoria Beckham, who kept a lower profile than most of the wives and girlfriends, started chatting to a couple of the journalists from the press corps at the bar one evening, Cheryl Tweedy got the wrong idea and marched to her defence.

This was in the days before Miss Tweedy had reinvented herself as the down-to-earth darling of the nation on *X Factor*, and she made it perfectly plain to the journalists that she was ready to rumble. 'Are these two bothering you?' she asked Mrs Beckham. When Mrs Beckham assured her everything was OK, Miss Tweedy, soon to become Mrs Ashley Cole, backed away reluctantly. 'Just as long as you know I've got your back,' she said.

It was when the Wags arrived in force at Brenner's that the pantomime began in earnest. The players' families strolled around the gardens and set up camp on the sun loungers at the bottom of the steps that led up to the indoor swimming pool. The sightseers, rubberneckers and paparazzi arranged themselves on the opposite bank of the Oosbach, 50 metres away. Long lenses were trained on the Wags all day long, and they did not flinch from the cameras' glare. One day, the *Daily Mail* reported, Joe Cole's then girlfriend, Carly Zucker, changed her sunbathing outfit three times.

The management at Brenner's, worried that their guests might feel violated by this attention from the paparazzi, erected cloth screens around the sunbathing area to block the photographers' view. Some of the Wags were said to be furious. But the screens stayed. The paparazzi were not too dismayed. They had plenty of other photo opportunities.

When they were not sunbathing, the Wags shopped or partied. The leading Wags – Miss Zucker, Frank Lampard's fiancée Elen Rives, Steven Gerrard's wife Alex Curran, Wayne Rooney's girlfriend Coleen McLoughlin – usually opted for safety in numbers on shopping expeditions. Dressed in designer gear from top to bottom, including big sunglasses, they turned left out of the main entrance to Brenner's Park and took the brief stroll to the town centre side by side, forming a mobile blockade across the narrow streets.

It was as if their afternoon stroll had been choreographed. They were a dramatic vision of moneyed womanhood on the move. Passers-by stopped to stare when they walked past, a slavering pack of paparazzi retreating in front of them, snapping away for all they were worth. The Wags were quite a sight and they knew it. The *Guardian*'s Marina Hyde, for whom these displays were manna from heaven, labelled them the Reservoir Wags.

At night the Wags switched into party mode. They colonised a bar-restaurant called Garibaldi's in the centre of Baden-Baden, which became paparazzi nirvana. Miss Rives distinguished herself early on by dancing on a table and belting out her own version of 'I Will Survive'. Her antics were reported in the English newspapers the next day.

The Wags soon became a media phenomenon. Every national newspaper sent news reporters as well as sports writers to World Cups, and by 2006 their duties had changed. For the previous 30 years, the job of news reporters at major football tournaments mainly involved charting the desecration of European cities by English hooligans. There were problems at the 1988 European Championships in West Germany and at the 1990 World Cup in Italy. At the 1992 European Championships in Sweden, English hooligans caused widespread destruction in Stockholm and Malmö. At the 1998 World Cup in France, English yobs had clashed with Tunisian fans before their first group game in Marseille and set the city alight. At Euro 2000 they had laid waste to Charleroi in Belgium.

And then, abruptly, the trouble stopped. The banning orders obtained by the FA and the government prevented the worst troublemakers from travelling abroad. Many hooligans were also discouraged from travelling to the World Cup in Japan and South Korea in 2002 because of the cost and the fearsome reputation of the police force in both countries. That tournament was the year when real England supporters reclaimed the right to follow the national team in peace.

The new trend was confirmed when there were no problems involving England fans at the 2004 European Championships in Portugal. So when the 2006 World Cup came around and it seemed likely that all would still be quiet, it grew increasingly obvious the news reporters would not be able to fill the paper by sticking to their traditional 'hooli-watch' beat. They needed a new agenda. Enter the Wags.

So every English newspaper had at least one news reporter in Baden-Baden. Most had more. One, who had embedded herself at Brenner's Park and tried to befriend the Wags by posing as an ordinary tourist, aroused their suspicions and was asked to leave by the management. Most journalists contented themselves by hanging around Garibaldi's or documenting how much the Wags had spent in the local boutiques.

The truth is that the Wags did not behave particularly badly. They enjoyed themselves on their nights out and had a few drinks. They spent some money on their shopping trips and pampered themselves during the day, lying in the sunshine, swimming in the pool, going to the spa and having lunch on the terrace. They did exactly what most affluent young women on holiday would do.

But it was what they represented rather than what they did that seemed to cause so much offence. To many, their displays of conspicuous consumption symbolised the worst excesses of empty celebrity. They were characterised as young women with no talent of their own, gorging themselves daily on the trappings of their husbands' success. 'Not even the stores of Vuitton and Gucci can keep up with the daily attack of the hooligans with Visas,' one German-based writer for the Spanish paper *ABC* observed. 'The Moët & Chandon doesn't last the night since the team from Albion arrived at this aristocratic health resort.'

The Wags had sprung from the soil moistened by the tears shed at the death of Diana, Princess of Wales, in 1997. The blanket coverage of Diana's life and death had taken the obsession with celebrity in England to new heights, and soon publications devoted to the lives of the famous began to appear and multiply. *Hello!* was the forerunner, *OK!* went weekly in 1996, *Now* was launched in 1997, then *Heat* in 1999 and *Closer* in 2002. There was an insatiable appetite for celebrity: either for reading about one, marrying one or even becoming one.

Some English newspapers were horrified by the monster they had created. Stephen Glover of the *Daily Mail* was particularly appalled. 'Not very long ago, English women were held up on the Continent as the acme of style and elegance,' he wrote. 'Now the world looks at the Wags and sees young women with a lot of money and no style, who behave as though they are enjoying a hen night in Ibiza. It seems not remotely to occur to the Wags, nor to the Football Association executives who, I suppose, are ultimately responsible for them, what a tawdry spectacle and what a shaming role model they present.'

Glover and other conservative commentators interpreted the

behaviour of the Wags as indicative of the dysfunctionality of English society. For others it was merely a symbol of everything that was wrong with Sven-Goran Eriksson's England. Eriksson had come to stand for the triumph of style over substance, reputation over ability, and celebrity over talent. The highly visible presence of the Wags in Baden-Baden and the amount of time the players were allowed to spend with them in the midst of the tournament was confirmation, for many, that Eriksson was in thrall to celebrity.

Eriksson was not a dictator-manager. He listened to players' wishes and did his best to accommodate them. He was a consensus boss, someone who believed that if he kept the players happy off the pitch, they would perform better on it. Austerity was definitely not his thing. The players' hotel, the Schlosshotel Bühlerhöhe, which was occupied solely by the England squad and its support staff, was a spectacular building set on top of a mountain about half an hour's drive outside Baden-Baden. Because the public had been banned, it felt cavernous and half-deserted to the players. Indulged by Eriksson, they quickly settled into a routine of being driven down the winding mountain road to visit their families several times a week.

So a new pantomime began. This time it wasn't just the Wags wandering through the streets of Baden-Baden, but the Wags and their partners. It all seemed the wrong way around, as though the Wags were the stars of the show and the players were their escorts. On visiting days, the photographers camped on the opposite side of the Oosbach were especially busy. They might not be able to train their lenses on the sunbathing area any more, but there were no screens around the conservatory that housed the Wintergarten restaurant, where they could see David eating with Victoria, Ashley hand in hand with Cheryl, and Michael Owen gambolling in the garden with his kids. Wayne Bridge and his pregnant girlfriend Vanessa Perroncel did not get as much attention. They would later . . .

Some of the players saw the bad publicity coming. Gary Neville gave his fiancée Emma such strict instructions about not giving anyone a chance to portray her as a spendthrift party animal that she was nervous about even leaving the hotel with her mum, who was staying with her, in case the paparazzi got a picture of her looking in a shop window or having a soft drink. A few others kept their distance too, but they were in the minority. Their families' trip had not just been sanctioned by the FA, it had been encouraged by the manager. In those circumstances, it was difficult for these players to tell their families that they would be staying in their own hotel rather than coming to visit like the rest of the squad.

Sometimes the players came to Brenner's Park to watch World Cup matches with their families in the television room there. The journalists sat on one side of the semi-circles of chairs and the players on the other. It would be an exaggeration to say they spent more time at Brenner's Park than they did at the Schlosshotel Bühlerhöhe, but it was a close-run thing.

Again, it looked worse than it was. The players were with their families, going on gentle walks or relaxing in the grounds of a hotel. But it left them open to censure and ridicule. It gave the impression that they were in Germany for a family holiday, not for the most important football tournament of their lives, a tournament over which the whole of England had worked itself into a frenzy.

Most of the players who were in that England squad admitted later that the balance between work and leisure was wrong. Even Rio Ferdinand, who had set the tone for the players' attitude to the tournament by filming a programme for ITV called *Rio's World Cup Wind-Ups*, which was based on the US show *Punk'd* and featured unsuspecting squad members, such as Gary Neville, Beckham and Rooney, becoming the victims of pranks, accepted that the players had been caught up in the whirl of attention that greeted them in Baden-Baden.

'There was a big show around the whole England squad,' Ferdinand said. 'It was like a theatre unfolding, and football became a secondary element. People were worrying more about what people were wearing than the games. We were in the bubble ourselves. In Baden-Baden, looking back, it was like a circus. We probably had too much contact with families. That's just my opinion. You're in a tournament and you don't get many tournaments in your career. You have to be focused. Not just the Wags, but families being really close, us being close to you guys in the media, the paparazzi situation; it wasn't really separated from the football.'

Jamie Carragher was even more damning, particularly about Eriksson's laissez-faire attitude. 'I was never sure if Eriksson was an international manager or international playboy,' Carragher wrote in his autobiography. 'I know what he was best at. The longer he spent in the job, the worse his status became as a football coach and the better he became a Casanova.'

That was why, even though England reached the quarter-finals at the 2006 World Cup, and even then lost only on penalties to Portugal, the tournament was seen as a miserable failure by the country's fans and created widespread disillusion with the national team. England's exit prompted a ferocious backlash against the culture of excess that the Wags had showcased in Baden-Baden, and left Eriksson's credibility seriously damaged.

The FA was by then committed to handing the job to McClaren, but even if the Wags never again attained the prominence they enjoyed in Baden-Baden, McClaren was just as much in thrall to the players as Eriksson had been. He referred to them by their first names, even their nicknames. He gave the impression of wanting to be their buddy, not their manager. He never escaped the shadow of what had happened in Baden-Baden.

Nobody knew it then, but Baden-Baden was where England started to turn towards Fabio Capello. Baden-Baden created the conditions for his appointment 18 months later. England fans were sick of player-power and of managers who bowed to it. They wanted the old order restored. They wanted a manager who managed, and they wanted players who would go to a World Cup to play football rather than to wander through the streets of a German spa town gazing into shop windows at designer handbags with their wives and girlfriends. They wanted everything that Eriksson was not, and when they appointed Capello, that was what they got.

Baden-Baden breathed a sigh of relief when the Wags, the England players and the paparazzi departed. The Carraghers were among the last to leave. They paid one final visit to Brenner's Park to collect their belongings from their room and then made an unconventional exit. Rather than use the front door, they strode out through the hotel gardens, their cases under their arms, and past the journalists lying on the deckchairs that the Wags had vacated.

The gate on the pedestrian bridge over the Oosbach was still locked, so they paused on the banks of the little river, rolled up their socks and waded through the water to the other side.

'Tally-ho, boys,' Philly Carragher shouted across at the journalists as he turned to go. 'Tally-ho.'

2 NO MORE MR NICE GUYS

THE first time James Milner was named in an England squad, he arrived at the team hotel carrying illicit cargo. It was February 2009 and Fabio Capello had been in charge for just over a year. Some of the older professionals had regaled Milner with tales of woe about the level of control Capello exercised over them during England get-togethers. In particular, they had told him that the food was miserable and bland, that there was not enough of it and that most players sneaked in a few extras to relieve the monotony. So when Milner showed up at The Grove near Watford, ahead of England's friendly in Spain, he had stashed a couple of bars of chocolate in his case.

When he got down to dinner he told some of the other players what he had done and, as players often do, they sensed the opportunity for a wind-up. They asked Milner, who is one of the most professional and conscientious of modern players, where he had left the chocolate and when he said it was still in his case, expressions of alarm spread across their faces. They lied and told Milner that Capello was such a control freak that he made a point of rifling through the bags of new arrivals to check whether they had smuggled anything in. They said it was only a matter of time until Capello discovered his stash. They said he might even be in his room right that minute. Milner shot back up the stairs and got rid of the chocolate. As he disappeared from view, the other players roared with laughter. There were other occasions under Capello when players got so desperate for some variety in their diet that they arranged for surreptitious fast-food deliveries to be made to the team hotel. One said that when his order arrived at The Grove, which was the team's regular base, he was so worried about being caught red-handed by Capello that he was almost too scared to eat it.

Things had changed since the days of Eriksson and McClaren. McClaren's reign had been short-lived and ill-fated. It had ended one wet winter's night in November 2007 when England lost 3–2 to Croatia at Wembley and failed to qualify for the European Championships in Austria and Switzerland the following summer. In the midst of what was at times a shambolic performance, McClaren had stood on the touchline, sheltering from the pouring rain under an umbrella. It was said later that he did it out of vanity because he was sensitive about his thinning hair being plastered to his scalp, but it was the image that came to define him. Watching at home, the wife of television pundit and *Daily Mail* columnist Andy Townsend said, 'Look at the wally with the brolly.' Townsend mentioned it to the *Daily Mail* sports desk and one of the most famous sports headlines of recent years was born. Even now, after rebuilding his career and his reputation by winning the Dutch title with Twente Enschede, it is a moniker that McClaren has been unable to shake off.

McClaren was sacked the day after the defeat to Croatia, and by mid-December, after the FA had tried and failed to recruit Jose Mourinho, they turned to Capello. Capello was one of the greatest managers of his generation. At 61 years old, he was in the autumn of his career and had been out of work since he was dismissed by Real Madrid in the summer of 2007, but he had won multiple Serie A titles with AC Milan, Roma and Juventus, as well as two Primera Liga titles with Madrid, and he had masterminded one of the most emphatic Champions League Final victories of all when his Milan side crushed Barcelona 4–0 in Athens in 1994. He might have been close to retirement age, but he was still one of the biggest names in world football. After the way McClaren's reign had worked out, there was no great appetite for another English manager to take charge of the national team. Abject failure can do funny things to patriotism. Capello, most agreed, would represent quite a catch if England could snare him.

Capello was interested too. He was attracted by the history of English football and the country's great craving to repeat the yellowing triumph of World Cup victory in 1966. 'My dream is managing England,' Capello had said in a March 2006 interview with the Italian magazine *L'Espresso*. 'It's something I have carried inside me for my entire life. In three years I am going to quit club football, and I would love for my dream to come true. After that, I'll be ready to quit for good.' The FA and its then chief executive, Brian Barwick, were encouraged. Barwick also knew that Capello had been working as an expert summariser for Italian television on the night England lost to Croatia. Capello was in Modena as an analyst at the Italy–Faroe Islands qualifier when the commentator told him the latest score from Wembley and asked him if he would be interested in taking the England job if it became available. 'That would be quite a challenge, eh,' Capello said.

On Friday, 14 December it was announced that Capello had been appointed England manager. He was England's 15th post-war boss and the country's second foreign manager. He had been awarded a four-and-a-half-year contract worth £6 million a year. That made him the best-paid manager in the world. Capello had rejected plans for a bonus system that would have operated on a sliding scale depending on which round England reached in the 2010 World Cup finals. Capello said he wanted a bonus only if England reached the final, which would be played at Soccer City in Johannesburg. He would regard anything else as failure, he told Barwick, and he did not wish to be rewarded for failure. A break clause was included in the contract, which gave both the FA and Capello a two-week window after the World Cup to extricate themselves from the remaining two years of the deal. That meant that if the tournament went badly, the FA could sack Capello without incurring a significant financial penalty. They could save themselves, according to most estimates, about £10 million in potential compensation. But the break clause worked both ways. It also meant that if England did well at the World Cup, other suitors would flock around Capello and he would be able to name his price.

The FA also employed four Italian assistants as part of Capello's team. Franco Baldini, who had worked with Capello at Roma and Real Madrid and was brought in as general manager, was widely respected as a scout and talent-spotter. If Capello was an intimidating presence, Baldini was charming and gregarious. His English was excellent and he had soon struck up a good relationship with many of the football writers in the English press. Paul Hayward, the *Observer*'s chief sports writer, described him as 'a free spirit and all round dude'. Baldini and Capello formed a classic good cop–bad cop combination, both with the press and the players, although by the time the World Cup arrived, some of the England players had come to distrust Baldini and believed he represented a divisive presence.

Then there was 70-year-old Italo Galbiati, who had been a trusted *consiglieri* to Capello for 19 years at Milan, Real Madrid, Roma and Juventus. Galbiati rarely gave interviews, but he did speak to *Gazzetta dello Sport* during the World Cup in South Africa to explain his role. 'If a player makes a mistake, Fabio reprimands him. I reiterate the concept to the player, go again through the mistake, and explain to him how to avoid it in the future,' Galbiati said. 'We joke and we laugh, but we are deadly serious about our work. I just keep a little closer to the players. Our motto is "The day after is another day". We've never rested on our laurels. As a famous Italian song goes, "the party has just started and then is over".'

Capello's team was completed by his fitness coach, Massimo Neri, and his goalkeeping coach, Franco Tancredi. Capello had proposed that each member of his Italian support staff should be mirrored by an Englishman, but this never really happened. Ray Clemence was kept on as a goalkeeping coach, and Stuart Pearce, who was already England Under-21 coach, was hired as an assistant. The job provided valuable experience for Pearce, who was a knowledgeable, enthusiastic coach, because it allowed him to watch Capello in action. But beyond the time-honoured servility of putting the cones out before training sessions, it was often difficult to grasp quite what role Pearce performed for the England senior team.

Capello made his first appearance as England manager on 17 December, when the FA paraded him as the new boss at a press conference at the Royal Lancaster Hotel in London, just north of Hyde Park. Outside, a John Bull character festooned from head to toe in Union Jacks and Crosses of St George, who objected vehemently to the idea of England having a foreign manager and had made occasional placard protests against Sven-Goran Eriksson, held up a banner on which he had written a message that conveyed his feelings about the new appointment: 'Crap-ello'. Inside, in the same cavernous banqueting suite where the Football Writers' Association held its annual awards dinner the Thursday before every FA Cup Final, Capello appeared on the stage. He made his first statement as England manager in English. 'I am very proud and honoured to be the England manager,' he said. 'I have wanted this job for a long time, but at this moment my English is not so well and I prefer to answer in Italian.'

Capello started work at the FA's then headquarters in Soho Square in early January. He moved into an apartment in Chelsea with his wife Laura, and settled into a routine of watching as many Premier League matches as he could in the build-up to his first game in charge, a friendly against Switzerland at Wembley on 6 February. The FA's director of communications, Adrian Bevington, a bright and astute man who got on well with the English media because he was scrupulously fair as well as being as helpful as possible without exceeding the bounds of confidentiality, organised a series of lunches between Capello and various arms of the English media. Bevington had been with the FA since 1997, when he joined the governing body of the English game as a press officer, but he was in a senior position now and rising through the organisation. He understood the workings of the media and their differing demands well. Daily newspaper journalists, Sunday newspaper writers, radio commentators and television broadcasters all met separately with the new England manager in one of the private dining rooms of the Soho Hotel over a period of several weeks.

Almost everyone was impressed with Capello. It was hard not to be. His manner was brusque without being rude, but he was good, entertaining company. The journalists were also struck by his candour. The lunches were off the record, but Capello was still refreshingly honest. Most journalists were struck in particular by how damning he was about Michael Owen at those early lunches. Owen's recent career had been blighted by injury, but under Eriksson and McClaren it had always been assumed that when he was fit he was untouchable. He had been capped 88 times for his country and had scored 40 goals. Only Bobby Charlton, Gary Lineker and Jimmy Greaves had scored more times for England than Owen.

But Capello made it clear that Owen had a lot to do to convince him he was worth a place. Various journalists spoke up on Owen's behalf and pointed out that when he played he usually scored, especially in big games. Capello nodded, but said that when Owen did not score, he contributed nothing to the team. His involvement in build-up play was minimal, his ability to hold the ball up was limited. Capello said that for long periods of matches, Owen was a passenger, and it was obvious from what he said and also from his demeanour that he did not have room for passengers. Owen appeared for Capello only once – in a friendly defeat to France in March 2008, when he appeared as a second-half substitute for Wayne Rooney. He was injured in the build-up to the World Cup, but it was not his hamstring injury that stopped him going to South Africa. Capello would not have picked him anyway.

At one of the lunches Capello was asked if he had read any books by other football managers or coaches from other sports. He mentioned only one: *Sacred Hoops*, a memoir by American basketball legend Phil Jackson, the most successful coach in NBA history, who had guided Michael Jordan at the Chicago Bulls, and Kobe Bryant and Shaquille O'Neal at the Los Angeles Lakers. Capello said he enjoyed *Sacred Hoops* because of the insight it gave him into how Jackson dealt with big stars like Jordan, who Jackson referred to in the book as 'Michelangelo in baggy shorts'. Jackson talked about his battle to make Jordan realise that 'the true measure of a star was his ability to make the people around him look good'.

Capello and his wife had travelled widely, including trips to Tibet and China, and the assorted spiritual references in *Sacred Hoops*, Jackson's use of Taoist principles, and his keenness to draw on the teachings of Native Americans also appealed to Capello. In one passage, Jackson spoke of an initial meeting with Dennis Rodman, the *enfant terrible* of American basketball, whom Jackson was contemplating adding to the Bulls' roster. 'I sat for a long spell in silence with Dennis,' Jackson wrote. 'I felt his presence. To Dennis, words were empty. He had been promised much and been betrayed. He didn't need words. I felt assured that he could and would play and that in the crunch, he would do his part. We had connected by our hearts in a non-verbal way, the way of the spirit.'

It was hard to imagine Capello sitting in meditation with Wayne Rooney and connecting in a non-verbal way, but nevertheless his enthusiasm about Jackson's book seemed to indicate at least a willingness to try to explore ways of dealing with high-maintenance star players. The English press also saw a different side to him when they travelled with him to Maseru in Lesotho in April 2008. Capello had gone to lend his support to an FA-sponsored initiative aimed at encouraging young people to find out their HIV status. He and some of the journalists crowded into a white tent to watch a 14-year-old boy take an Aids test.

Hot tears fell down the boy's face while a doctor explained to him what was happening and what the repercussions might be. Capello watched nervously. The boy's blood was taken and after what seemed like an eternity he was told that his test was negative. He was not HIV positive. Capello admitted that he had been close to tears himself. 'It was a very emotional experience,' Capello said. 'I have taken part in many charitable events to help young people before, but it was never so emotional and so intense as this. There was a lot of tension in the tent. I have children and grandchildren of my own, so I was really afraid and worried. But the happy fact is that, at the end, we scored a goal, so to speak, and it was a very important result.'

Still, when Capello's first England squad met up before the game against Switzerland, the players were met not with spiritualism but with a series of practical demands that Capello saw as ground rules. Most of these so-called Ten Commandments were common sense, but they included the banning of mobile phones and the presence of players' agents at the team hotel. Emile Heskey was the first to fall foul of the mobile phone rule when Capello saw him trying to send text messages while holding his phone under the table when the players were at dinner before a qualifying tie in the Ukraine in October 2009. Capello smashed a tray down on the table in a rage and ordered Heskey to switch his phone off. Nobody used their mobile phone again.

The players were taken aback by what they considered the severity of the conditions that were imposed on them by Capello. After the indulgences of the Eriksson and McClaren years, this was the opposite extreme. Mainly, as Milner had been told, it was the blandness of the food, the boiled chicken and fish, the lack of variety, the lack of anything they considered remotely interesting, that unsettled them. Some of the players found it hard to see the point of effecting dramatic changes in their diet for a couple of days before they went back to the food they ate when they were on duty with their clubs. There was a futility to the ephemerality of it that the players found frustrating, but they put up with it. They also submitted to the new rules about staying in their rooms for long periods of the afternoon. Capello was insistent that they should rest after lunch. Even wandering around the hotel was frowned upon. Again, the players put up with it. It was only for a couple of days at a time.

For his first game in charge against Switzerland, Capello was without John Terry, Ledley King and Frank Lampard through injury. He arranged his team in a 4–1–4–1 formation with David James in goal and a back four of Wes Brown, Rio Ferdinand, Matthew Upson and Ashley Cole. Gareth Barry played in the holding role behind a midfield four of David Bentley, Jermaine Jenas, Steven Gerrard and Joe Cole. Rooney was on his own up front. More than 86,000 fans came to Wembley to witness the start of the new era, and saw England seal a 2–1 win with goals from Jenas and substitute Shaun Wright-Phillips. Considering the last game at Wembley had been the traumatic 3–2 defeat to Croatia, it was a promising beginning.

England lost the next game against France, though, looking lacklustre and unsure, and after summer games against the USA, Trinidad and Tobago and the Czech Republic, they went into their opening back-to-back World Cup qualifiers against Andorra in Barcelona and Croatia in Zagreb with the public still unsure what to make of Capello. England had again been poor against the Czechs, and had salvaged only a 2–2 draw with a 92nd-minute equaliser from Joe Cole. Everyone liked Capello's stance on discipline and had warmed to certain details, such as the fact that he called the players by their surnames, but they knew that the real test of how much had changed would come against Croatia.

The tie against Andorra carried bad memories of the last time England played against them in the Olympic Stadium in Barcelona in March 2007, when McClaren was subjected to vicious barracking from England fans throughout the game. This time, England negotiated the game smoothly enough. The pattern of the match was similar to the one they had played 18 months earlier but the mood was different. England fans had given up on McClaren by the time his team faced what was effectively a side representing a Pyrenean ski resort, but it was still too early to judge Capello. The England manager sprang a surprise by playing the Arsenal prodigy Theo Walcott on the right side of a midfield four instead of David Beckham, but everything else was routine, and England won with two goals in seven minutes from half-time substitute Joe Cole. It was decent preparation for Croatia.

Croatia had never lost a competitive international at the Maksimir Stadium, a run that extended to 35 games, and many had assumed that Capello would recall Beckham so that he could draw on his experience and use him as a steadying influence in the intimidating atmosphere. But Capello kept faith with Walcott in a 4–4–2 system that paired Rooney and Heskey together in attack. Walcott repaid Capello with a hat-trick as England cut loose and destroyed Slaven Bilic's side 4–1. The victory was greeted with wonderment by England fans, who had been expecting another humbling from the Croats to go with the home and away defeats they had inflicted on McClaren in the European Championship qualifiers. The victory in Zagreb was England's best result since the 5–1 victory over Germany in Munich in 2001.

It was the perfect outcome for Capello. It drew a thick line under the McClaren era and vindicated all the changes in tone and mood that Capello had made. Any of the players who might have been harbouring resentments about the Spartan conditions, strict discipline and bland diet they were having to put up with before England matches knew that they would have to keep their mouths firmly shut. Whatever Capello was doing, it was working beautifully. This was not a time for dissent. The mood in the country was totally transformed. Most England fans had been resigned to a miserable World Cup qualifying campaign, and had assumed that Croatia would finish top of the group and England would make the play-offs at best. Now they started dreaming again.

Never mind qualifying for the World Cup. With Capello in charge, anything was possible. In the public mind, England had been reborn, rid of the dead weight of so many years of Eriksson and McClaren and their shared unwillingness to assert authority over their players. Now, finally, England had a manager who was knocking the same players into shape and they were responding. Capello became a national hero overnight, the man who had single-handedly vanquished player-power and made the Premier League's millionaire stars have some respect for authority at last. He described the Wags as 'a virus'. He was hailed as a kind of football vigilante, Charles Bronson in a tracksuit, putting the Baby Bentley Brigade, the drinkers, the brawlers, the partyers, the playboys all back in their place. Capello could do no wrong.

Walcott provided an enthralling insight into Capello's modus operandi off the pitch in an interview he gave to the *Guardian*. He told the newspaper's David Hytner about an incident where he had misread the time of a team meeting on the noticeboard and, belatedly realising his mistake, rushed down to the hotel lobby to be told the meeting was already over. Panicking, Walcott asked where Capello's room was and knocked on the door. Capello opened it and Walcott apologised profusely for his oversight. Capello did not say a word. He smiled at him enigmatically and then pushed the door slowly shut in Walcott's face. 'I was like "Oh, no",' Walcott said. 'I was so scared.' Another player remembered being called up for an away match. It was the first time he had been involved in one of Capello's squads and he was expecting some dialogue with the England coach about his future prospects. Capello did not speak a single word to him from the moment the squad met up to the moment it disbanded.

Nobody cared. The results were all that mattered. Capello's methods seemed infallible. After the win in Zagreb, the rest of the qualifying campaign was gloriously straightforward. England thrashed Kazakhstan 5–1 in their next game and then won away in Belarus. There were no slip-ups, although some pointed out that when England had come up against Spain, the European Champions and one of the world's best sides, in a friendly in Seville in February 2009, they were comfortably outclassed and beaten 2–0. But everything was going too well to allow an inconvenient truth like that to intervene.

Capello had made qualifying seem so simple. He had made everything all right. His solution of how to fit Steven Gerrard and Frank Lampard into the same midfield was to push Gerrard out to the left in the 4–4–2 system that he favoured. Gerrard's admirers still argued that he should be played more centrally and further forward, supporting Rooney, but as the victories kept coming, their voices went unheard. By the time Croatia came to Wembley in September 2009, England had played seven and won seven of their qualifying matches, and they knew another victory would take them to the World Cup with two games to spare. They played even better than they had in Zagreb and demolished their opponents 5–1.

England were playing magnificently. Their confidence was sky-high. If they could have played the World Cup that autumn, they might have won it. But they had to wait. And as they waited, the fortress of Capello's reign began to crumble.

3 | TERRY IN TROUBLE

WHEN Tiger Woods crashed his Cadillac Escalade into a fire hydrant outside his Florida home at the end of November 2009, it set in motion a chain of events that changed the public perception of the world's most famous sports star forever. It turned out that, far from being the very model of a conservative and devoted family man, Woods had had a series of secret affairs. In the days and weeks that followed, he was engulfed by a wave of moral repugnance.

Several of his sponsors deserted him. It was not enough for consultancy giant Accenture that Woods was the best golfer in the world. When he was revealed as a human being with faults and weaknesses like everybody else, not the user-friendly, reassuringly unthreatening, determinedly uncontroversial front man whose false image they had helped to create, they dropped him fast. 'Go on, be a Tiger', the slogan of their advertising ampaign, now carried a rather different resonance. So did 'It's in you', the Gatorade ad built around Woods. Gatorade dumped him too. Gillette pulled the commercials in which he appeared. For nearly five months Woods disappeared from golf. And from public life. When he eventually came back, at the US Masters in Augusta in April 2010, there were still plenty of people saying it was too soon.

The mixture of horror and outrage that greeted the revelations underlined the fact that public tolerance for the excesses of sports stars had disappeared. There is nothing new about sportsmen being involved in extramarital affairs, but where once their sexual adventures were ignored or indulged and accepted as part of the macho culture that dominates sport, even encouraged as a reaffirming extension of a sporting star's prowess on the pitch, increasingly they are interpreted as signs of sport's moral turpitude.

The change can be traced largely to the explosion in player wages and the distance it placed between sportsmen and the fans that support them. In England, the old sepia model of Sir Stanley Matthews travelling to the ground on a public bus with football supporters had been replaced with an unpalatable vision of a young millionaire footballer at the wheel of a Baby Bentley with tinted windows – untouchable, remote, impossibly rich and keen to avoid contact with the people who worshipped his celebrity.

As footballers' wages went up, so did ticket prices. Even with the tens of millions earned for them by increasingly lucrative television deals, many Premier League clubs blew an unhealthy proportion of their budgets on the salaries of their superstars. So even though they were bringing in more money than ever, the clubs were spending more than ever too. In the 1990s and the first decade of the 21st century, ticket prices rose and rose, and English football moved out of the financial reach of its traditional working-class base.

It passed into the hands of a new breed of football fan, emboldened by the demise of the hooliganism that had plagued the 1970s and 1980s, and enriched by the economic boom years of the 1990s. Alongside them came the socio-economic group identified by former Manchester United captain Roy Keane as 'the prawn sandwich brigade'. Also known disparagingly as 'the corporates', these people were the denizens of the new empire of executive boxes and hospitality suites that invaded Premier League grounds.

Football's new middle-class rump of supporters brought with them a sense of entitlement. They expected a certain quality of service and facilities at a football stadium. And they expected the right kind of behaviour from the players they were taking their wide-eyed children to see. They were paying a lot for their tickets and they wanted a lot in return. Football was a more sanitised experience now. No one turned a blind eye to player misbehaviour any more.

The aftermath of the terrible tragedy at Hillsborough in 1989 and the transition to all-seater stadia, enforced by the Taylor Report, started that process of change in football support, and the steep rise in player salaries in the new century finished it. Many older fans felt disenfranchised and deserted. They looked at English football and, for all its success in the Champions League and the fact that it attracted many of the world's best players, they saw a game obsessed with money and caught in a culture of vulgar excess. These abandoned masses were filled with nostalgia for the game they once knew.

The media were too. If the supporters felt as though they were being kept at arm's length, so did many journalists. Some friendships between players and reporters survived, but the days of casual socialising between footballers and journalists disappeared towards the end of the 1980s. There was a breakdown in trust, partly because of the new interest in the players' private lives and the tension that caused, and partly because of the influence of players' agents, who preferred to keep journalists at a distance so as not to dilute their own influence with their client. The result was an increasing dislocation between players and reporters. Less and less contact. At Manchester United the age-old practice of allowing at least one national newspaper reporter into the players' tunnel after games to talk to a couple of members of the team was discontinued several years ago.

Once, after a match between United and Arsenal, Matt Dickinson, then the chief football correspondent of *The Times*, was taken in error up the Old Trafford tunnel by Arsenal press officer Amanda

Docherty. When Sir Alex Ferguson caught sight of Dickinson, he charged towards him and Docherty, shouting in fury. Dickinson beat a hasty retreat.

Every journalist has a story to tell of being abused by Ferguson at one time or another. Most are recounted with wry amusement rather than hurt or reciprocated hostility. Journalists had also become inured to the brooding reluctance of players to speak to them, perhaps because the players feared their words being misrepresented, or they were scared of saying the wrong thing, or they simply couldn't be bothered.

The England striker Emile Heskey helped to pioneer the method of evading questions in the mixed zone, where journalists wait behind barriers to speak to players after England international matches, by wandering out of the dressing room with a mobile phone clamped to his ear, occasionally muttering into it. It worked for years until once, after an England game at the new Wembley stadium, Heskey's phone rang while he was talking into it.

By the time Fabio Capello took over as England manager, many football reporters felt they no longer had much to lose in their dealings with players. As they rarely saw the players they were writing about, no longer had to face them over breakfast or in a hotel corridor, it was easy to feel no longer accountable. English football was high on its own wealth and power. It felt it was untouchable, that it needed no one. So if many supporters felt rejected by football and footballers, so did much of the media.

It was against this backdrop of volatility and uncertainty that John Terry was deposed as England captain at the beginning of February 2010. He was sacked by Capello because he was alleged to have slept with the wrong woman, Vanessa Perroncel, the former girlfriend of Terry's former Chelsea teammate Wayne Bridge. Capello dealt with Terry swiftly and brutally, and made it clear his decision was nothing to do with past controversies and certainly nothing to do with Terry's performance on the pitch. It was purely his private life that had cost Terry the job, Capello said.

Capello was widely applauded for his ruthlessness. In the media we vilified Terry and held him up as all that was wrong, not just with football, but with English society as a whole. Finally, the mob that hounded Terry said, somebody had had the guts to stand up to player-power and put the poster-boy for this generation of brash young millionaires firmly in his place. A few voices worried about the precedent Capello was setting by sacking someone over an issue in his private life, but they were in the minority.

Terry, who had been appointed skipper by Steve McClaren when David Beckham resigned after the 2006 World Cup and then reappointed by Capello after a protracted beauty contest with other candidates, had already been made vulnerable in the eyes of some of his critics by a steady succession of scandals. Most of them fell outside his control, but that did not stop momentum building against his captaincy.

In March 2009 his mother, Sue Terry, and his mother-in-law, Sue Poole, were arrested and cautioned after being caught with £800-worth of clothes and groceries taken from Tesco and Marks & Spencer at an out-of-town shopping centre near Weybridge in Surrey. They did not realise that accepting a caution meant they admitted guilt. The revelations were greeted with astonishment more than anything else. It was not as if the England captain had not been generous to his relatives. He had bought both his mother and his in-laws houses on the same exclusive estate where he lived with his wife Toni and their twins, George and Summer, in Oxshott.

Terry dealt with the matter well. He was embarrassed but he did not hide. That would have been impossible anyway because England were preparing to play a friendly international against Slovakia at the time. But he also took care not to condemn his mother. Terry and his brother Paul, a professional player who has eked out a career in the lower leagues, had had a tough upbringing in London's East End and had seen the sacrifices their parents had made for them in supporting their football endeavours. He was not about to abandon his mum for the sake of a day of positive PR.

Seven months later it was the turn of Terry's father to land with a thud on the front pages. The *News of the World* caught Ted Terry in a sting operation, where he supplied cocaine to one of its undercover reporters. Ted, who had worked as a forklift truck driver when his son was growing up, was filmed handing over three wraps of the drug in the lavatory of a wine bar called Unit 4 near Grays in Essex.

The story was a fresh embarrassment for the England captain, but there were also poignant details in it that proved he was doing everything he could to be a dutiful and loving son. Still unaware that he was talking to an undercover reporter, Ted Terry begged him not to mention to anyone that he was John Terry's dad and told him proudly that his son had bought him a £15,000 Rolex watch as an early birthday present, as well as tickets for holidays to Dubai and Florida.

So why was he dealing drugs in an Essex wine bar? It was obvious he didn't need the money. Why, when he was living in a house that had also been paid for by his son, was he trying to make £40 by selling cocaine to a stranger? Boredom, maybe. An inability to adapt to a new life? Ted Terry was no longer a forklift truck driver. He didn't need to be. His son paid the bills.

But sometimes it is just as difficult for a player's family to adapt to new circumstances as it is for the player himself. They are like lottery winners, catapulted out of their old lives and communities by a huge financial windfall. Maybe they should feel as lucky as everyone tells them they are, but it is hard to turn your back on your old life, your old friends, your old ways. Footballers, men who become millionaires overnight, and their families are among the *déracinés* of our society.

When he was younger and working his way through the ranks at

Chelsea, Terry had got into trouble himself too. His transgressional history was familiar in the context of an English youth culture that places a heavy accent on getting drunk to have fun.

But Terry realised he was putting his career in jeopardy and vowed to change his habits. A court case, in particular, shocked him. He was banned from playing for the England Under-21 side until he was cleared. But thereafter he avoided trouble. He turned his back on aggression in bars and clubs. He knew when to leave, and made sure he went home in a car provided by the club.

There were still stories of excess, of giant bar bills racked up in the VIP areas of fashionable London clubs such as Mahiki and Whisky Mist during victory celebrations, but that was as much about Terry's teammates as it was about him. These were young men, mainly from working-class backgrounds, who suddenly found themselves with vast amounts of disposable income. It was fanciful to expect them to sit at home all day and night avoiding social contact and spending money as thriftily as if they were earning the modest amounts their childhood friends were paid.

Terry's private life came under constant scrutiny. He was the victim of several lurid kiss-and-tell articles in national newspapers, authored by women who claimed to have had a variety of sexual encounters with him. One said he had seduced her in the back of his Bentley. Quite why it was in the public interest to publish their accounts is open to question, but all the reports were couched in strictly disapproving terms about the fact that Terry was cheating on his girlfriend, Toni Poole, whom he had begun dating when he was still in the Chelsea youth team.

Until Vanessa Perroncel happened, none of the rumour or innuendo, none of the dalliances in his private life, affected Terry's career in any way. His managers at Chelsea did not attach any importance to them as far as his value to the team and his ability to lead it was concerned. The only time he had ever been in real trouble was when he was charged for the assault on the doorman at the Wellington Club in 2002, and even on that occasion, a jury had found him innocent of any crime.

Terry had quickly developed into an outstanding player. He had joined the Chelsea youth system at 14 and made his senior debut as a late substitute in a League Cup tie against Aston Villa in October 1998 when he was 17. He had a loan spell at Nottingham Forest and nearly signed for Huddersfield Town before deciding to try and make the grade with Chelsea's first team. He was an established member of the side from the 2000–01 season, making 23 starts. He captained the club for the first time in a Premier League fixture against Charlton Athletic in December 2001.

He learnt from superstar defenders like Marcel Desailly and Frank Leboeuf when they arrived at Chelsea, and was struck by the work ethic of Gianfranco Zola. He was a fixture in the first team under Claudio Ranieri, and by the time Jose Mourinho arrived at Stamford Bridge in 2004, Terry was captain and the man universally recognised as the team's leader on and off the pitch. He was an inspirational figure for the club in the Mourinho era, often playing through pain and refusing to miss a match, even when he was suffering from injuries that would have sidelined most other players. His courage was obvious and unrivalled.

He was dominating in the air and composed and assured on the floor, equally comfortable with both feet. Alan Hansen, once a supremely accomplished defender in the great Liverpool sides of the 1980s and who had become a prominent pundit, praised Terry continually for his reading of the game and his ability to defend the near post when balls were crossed from wide positions. Terry contributed crucial goals, mainly headers from set pieces where he was a commanding and intimidating presence. Together with Frank Lampard, he was the bedrock of the Mourinho team that won back-to-back Premier League titles in 2004–05 and 2005–06.

His club form was mirrored by his performances for his country. He made his international debut in June 2003 and was one of England's best players at the 2004 European Championships. By the 2006 World Cup, he and Rio Ferdinand had established a formidable centre-half pairing, and Terry was named in Fifa's official World Cup All-Tournament Team, the only England player to be given that honour.

When David Beckham quit as England captain after the tournament, the new manager, Steve McClaren, appointed Terry in his place. In June 2007, Terry scored the first England goal at the new Wembley in a 1–1 draw with Brazil, and even though England failed to qualify for the 2008 European Championships, Terry proved his strength of character yet again when, a few days after he had missed the crucial penalty in Chelsea's Champions League Final defeat to Manchester United, he captained the side for the first time under Capello in a friendly against the USA and scored one of England's goals in a 2–0 win.

Capello had deliberated for eight months about who to choose as his permanent captain. He experimented with Ferdinand, Gerrard, Beckham and Gareth Barry in the matches that followed his appointment as manager. Many thought he had decided on Ferdinand. The *Evening Standard* ran a back-page story before the decision was made public, on the eve of an England friendly against the Czech Republic in August 2008, saying that Ferdinand would be the skipper. Even Terry was convinced of it. But when the announcement came, Terry was Capello's choice.

Capello knew all about Terry's history when he made his decision. He knew about the sex scandals he had been involved in. He knew about the court case. He knew about the allegations concerning his behaviour the day after the attacks on the Twin Towers. He knew that Terry had once parked his black Bentley in a disabled parking space in Esher while he went to have lunch at Pizza Express with his family. He knew he had a chequered past, but he also knew that, from everything he had seen in training and in matches, Terry was the best man for the captaincy. He made an informed choice and Terry did not let him down. He played like a giant in the World Cup qualifying campaign and, once again, was the mainstay of the defence.

But after qualification had been secured, Terry was hit by a succession of new scandals. In November 2009, he was accused of trying to cash in on the England captaincy when a PR company, Riviera Entertainment, contacted businesses touting for commercial endorsements. The email advertisement that they produced looked amateurish and was badly spelt – it said Terry had been voted one of the world's most 'influencial' people – and Terry was forced to issue a statement distancing himself from it.

There was some snobbery involved in the reaction to Terry's search for commercial opportunities. The email may have smacked of a small-time operation, but the appalled reaction and the suggestion that Terry was 'for sale' was hypocritical and perverse. Weren't all England players for sale? Didn't they all authorise their agents, either tacitly or actively, to pursue commercial opportunities for them? Didn't they all have boot deals and a range of sponsors who owned them for a couple of days a year each?

Like most of the other players in the England first team, Terry was from a working-class background, but he and his family, more than the rest, were ridiculed as chavs. That term was coined to describe yobs who covet the trappings of wealth, and mimic the rich by spending their money on symbols of affluence, such as Burberry clothing. Many felt threatened by the social mobility of footballers like Terry, and were jealous of the vast wealth that seemed to them to have fallen into their laps.

Terry, with his *OK!* wedding at Blenheim Palace and his country pile in Surrey, was an affront to the values of Middle England. He was a threat to the notions of thrift and hard work and modesty that were the accepted ways of accumulating wealth. When they looked at him, people saw riches easily won. They saw a fortune and a lifestyle that seemed to mock the efforts of normal men and women. They saw, or thought they saw, the undeserving rich at play.

The truth was different. Players like Terry paid a price for what they earned. They had to sacrifice much of their youth to make it in professional football in the 21st century. They had to sacrifice friendships with peers who led normal lives. They had to live in the spotlight, casual relationships seized on and picked apart, nights out frowned upon. Their careers were short and, when they ended, the transition to a new life shorn of adrenalin and adulation was almost invariably painful and often ruinous. Those offended by the vast wealth of men like Terry saw easy money, but they did not see the dedication behind the success.

But Terry was England captain, and Chelsea had made him the best-paid player in the Premier League when they increased his wages to £170,000 a week, so he was an obvious target. In the summer of 2009, after he had been linked with a move to Manchester City, he cut his ties with his long-standing agent, adviser and friend Aaron Lincoln. Lincoln, a former Chelsea kit-man, amiable and decent, fair and open with journalists, was popular in football circles, and his presence in Terry's camp helped prevent damaging stories being written about the England skipper.

When Lincoln was Terry's agent he had also encouraged Terry not to sign for a newspaper as a columnist in its sports pages. Lincoln knew from his friends in journalism how the game worked. He knew his client would receive a generous fee for the columns he agreed to write. He also knew that the deal would be resented by the rest of Fleet Street and that Terry would become even more of a target. Signing a deal with a particular paper is confirmation that you are sleeping with the enemy.

But Terry saw things differently. He worked hard for charities that helped the armed forces, and particularly servicemen and women injured in Iraq and Afghanistan. He attended functions and visited hospitals, and was moved by the suffering and the courage he encountered. He wanted to find more ways to contribute financially. He had been courted by the *Sun* for a long time, and after he split with Lincoln, he signed a deal to write a handful of columns for the paper in the months leading up to the World Cup.

A few days before Christmas Terry was in trouble again. This time undercover reporters from the *Sun*'s sister paper, the *News of the World*, posing as businessmen, were given a tour of the Chelsea training ground in Cobham by Terry and ticket tout Tony Bruce. The businessmen paid £10,000 in cash for the tour, the paper reported, which included watching the players training and eating in the club canteen, and even though Terry told them his share was going to charity, the conversation, which was secretly recorded by the reporters, made it look as though Terry and Bruce were doing something underhand.

For the first time since Capello had appointed him, questions began to be asked about Terry's suitability to be England captain. Newspapers ran polls on the issue. Radio phone-in callers debated it on air. But there was never really any possibility that Terry would be stripped of the captaincy. The training ground affair was embarrassing, particularly for Chelsea, but it was hardly a sackable offence.

The *News of the World* exposé was important because it gave Terry's critics more ammunition and chipped another small piece out of his defences. It began to feel as though he was one more front-page headline away from disciplinary measures. Capello was unimpressed by the events at the Chelsea training ground and the way they had played out in the media. He was getting bored with Terry attracting the wrong kind of news.

4 FABIO CAPELLO'S NEW MORAL ARMY

BY the end of January 2010, rumours had been circulating in Fleet Street for a couple of weeks that the *News of the World* had a story alleging that John Terry had had an affair with Vanessa Perroncel, the former long-term girlfriend of Wayne Bridge and the mother of Bridge's son. After Terry discovered the story was about to be published, his lawyers prevented it appearing by obtaining a so-called super-injunction that also forbade the media mentioning that the injunction even existed.

But the super-injunction served only to galvanise sections of the British press that might otherwise have turned up their noses at the tawdry tale of a football love triangle. The issue suddenly crossed newspaper boundaries. It was a sports story, a news story, a media story and a legal story. It was a cause célèbre now, a case that involved press freedom. The super-injunction was heavily criticised as the latest example of the courts bringing in a privacy law by the back door. The *Daily Telegraph* and the *Guardian* pursued it with zeal.

MPs and lawyers criticised the original decision of High Court judge Mr Justice Tugendhat to impose a super-injunction on the Terry–Bridge story. They pointed to it as another instance of anonymity being granted 'willy nilly' by the courts to enable the rich and powerful to prevent any negative publicity while, at the same time, milking positive publicity when it benefited them financially.

Then things changed for Terry. On 29 January Mr Justice Tugendhat reversed his original decision and relaxed the gagging order. He said an injunction was 'not necessary or proportionate having regard to the level of gravity of interference with the private life of the applicant', adding that 'the nub of the applicant's complaint is to protect his reputation, in particular with sponsors'.

The *News of the World*, which had been due to challenge the initial decision later the same day, had been expected to argue that revealing details of the affair was in the public interest because any fall-out between Terry, Bridge and those players taking sides with one or the other could affect team morale in the England camp, and even influence team selection at the World Cup. They never got the chance to put their argument, but events unfolded much as they had predicted.

The gagging order was overturned on a Friday, so the *News of the World*, which is published on Sunday, lost out on its own story. The Terry scandal was splashed across the front and back of almost every daily paper on Saturday. The *Guardian* was the only exception. With splendid high-minded eccentricity, it chose to run coverage of the Terry–Bridge affair only in its Media section. Everyone else went berserk. The story, particularly a few months away from the World Cup, was a media dream.

Bridge and Miss Perroncel, a lingerie model, had lived together for several years in the same area as Terry and his family, and had a son, Jaydon, who was three when the scandal broke. Their relationship had foundered some time after Bridge was signed by Manchester City in January 2009 and moved to live in the north. Miss Perroncel and their son remained at the family home in Oxshott, and the relationship ended in the summer.

Bridge and Terry were close mates, and their partners had struck up a friendship too. They all went out for meals together. Old pictures of the two couples at Chessington World of Adventures with Jaydon and Terry's twins soon surfaced in the newspapers. But some time after the end of Bridge's relationship with Miss Perroncel, it was reported, Terry had begun an affair with her. Both Terry and Miss Perroncel strongly denied having a physical relationship, but Bridge did not appear to believe them. Although Bridge had had no desire to rekindle his relationship with Miss Perroncel, he was angry and upset when he found out about the alleged affair with Terry, something he considered a betrayal by his former teammate. Bridge was, according to friends, 'in bits'.

Terry was fiercely criticised. He was accused, again, of sullying the England captaincy through his actions. Many expressed their disgust at what they saw as his feral sexual behaviour. There were widespread demands for him to be stripped of the armband. Enough was enough, people said. Bridge was so furious that he was reported to be considering turning his back on the England squad rather than having to share a space with Terry.

Terry's behaviour united the country almost as joyously as winning the World Cup would have done. The English rose up from the blamelessness of their lives and abandoned themselves to what the American author Philip Roth described in his novel *The Human Stain* as 'the ecstasy of sanctimony'. Roth was describing America's reaction to Bill Clinton's affair with Monica Lewinsky, but his words fitted the reaction to Terry too. It seemed strange that February to witness the outpouring of anger and disgust over Terry's behaviour, and to try to reconcile it with the visions of England we see all around us. The chaotic scenes of casual debauchery and nakedness in our city centres on Friday and Saturday nights, the spiralling divorce rate, the dilution of human contact promoted by the computer era, the poll that revealed in the same week that Terry was under siege that nearly half of British men were regular watchers of pornography online. Terry was a product of all that. He had grown from it. He was not an exception. He was the rule. And to pretend otherwise was disingenuous and self-deluding.

Modern England is a country where the future king imagined himself living as a tampon inserted in the vagina of his married mistress, where the corruption of the political elite was exposed by the publication of expenses claims made by Members of Parliament, and where the catastrophic misjudgements of the multi-millionaire 'masters of the universe' in the financial centre of the City of London had driven the nation close to bankruptcy. And yet there were still moral clean-freaks who found it within themselves to pretend that a football player whose performances on the pitch were beyond reproach should be forced to swallow coals and lose the captaincy because he had been unfaithful to his wife.

Terry was excoriated by a new moral army of seething zealots and outraged puritans. Some among them clung to the idea that, even though they might occasionally have strayed from the path themselves, they had never challenged the taboo of sleeping with a teammate's wife or ex-girlfriend. That, the callers to the radio phone-ins said, was what made Terry's crime so heinous. He had breached a male code of honour. He had crossed a line and he could never be trusted again.

The fact that Miss Perroncel wasn't actually Bridge's partner any more, and hadn't been for several months, was conveniently ignored. So the hounding of Terry was based on a peculiarly misogynistic, medieval line of argument. The outrage over Terry's conduct centred on the idea that he had slept with a friend's wife. But he hadn't. Even if the reports of the affair were true, he had slept with a friend's former girlfriend.

The logic used by Terry's critics implied that a woman was a man's chattel long after their relationship had ended. It suggested that even though they had split up, Bridge was still entitled to regard Miss Perroncel as his emotional property. It was, therefore, particularly amusing to see a feminist like Janet Street-Porter, who had admitted to serial infidelities in her own marriage, lining up on *Question Time* a few days after the story broke to condemn Terry and describe him as 'loathsome'.

Some media outlets tried to perform the classic trick of aspiring to rise above the storm while scrabbling around in the detritus of Terry's life as energetically as everyone else. Radio 5 Live was particularly good at it. Several of its presenters mocked the blanket front- and back-page coverage the tabloid newspapers devoted to the affair. Nicky Campbell, the station's breakfast show host, apparently saw nothing contradictory about referring to 'the media's' obsession with the story, seeming to forget he was part of the media. Nor did he appear to notice anything puzzling about marvelling at the newspaper feeding frenzy surrounding Terry and then hosting a phone-in about it a few minutes later.

Amidst it all, no one asked whether Bridge had entered into a new relationship with a woman since his move to Manchester. No one has asked that question to this day. No one seemed to think it important, even relevant. The argument was couched in deeply traditional terms. Bridge could do what he wanted when the relationship ended, but Miss Perroncel had to remain chaste. Or, at the very least, she had to steer clear of forming a romantic attachment to anyone Bridge might ever have known.

The more that was known about the alleged affair between Terry and Miss Perroncel, the more it became obvious that the only person Terry had to answer to was his wife Toni. They had been together for 15 years and their relationship had not been without its difficult moments. Before they married in the lavish ceremony at Blenheim Palace in June 2007, Terry had admitted to infidelities and had said he was determined to change his ways.

Toni had always forgiven him. Some female commentators called her a 'doormat' for doing that, even though, at a similar time, Cheryl Cole was being described as 'courageous' and 'brave' when she forgave her husband, Terry's Chelsea teammate, Ashley Cole, after it was revealed he had seduced a conquest despite first being sick all over her. Mrs Cole forgave him that indiscretion, but when her husband sent another woman pictures of himself in his Y-fronts, it was too much to bear.

Still, the contrasting treatment of Mrs Terry and Mrs Cole was another example of the hostility towards Terry and his family. After the latest scandal involving her husband became public, Toni fled to Dubai with the couple's twins. All manner of pundits and chat show hosts were enraged on her behalf, but it was up to her to judge her husband's conduct. In Dubai she was pictured wearing a top bearing the message: 'I Love the Chaos'.

But there were more and more calls for Capello to judge Terry too. The England manager was convalescing from knee surgery at his holiday home in Lugano, Switzerland, when the storm broke around Terry. He was made aware of the allegations against his captain, and of the *News of the World*'s claim that Miss Perroncel had had an abortion after she became pregnant with Terry's child. Some speculated that Capello might be especially horrified by this revelation because of his staunch Catholicism.

Capello stayed in Lugano and kept his counsel, but in England the cacophony of disapproval surrounding Terry grew and grew. Many assumed he would pull out of Chelsea's Premier League fixture against Burnley at Turf Moor the day after the injunction was lifted, but he travelled north with the team as if nothing had happened and played as well as ever. With the exception of Stoke City's Britannia Stadium, where the crowd generates the best atmosphere in English football, Turf Moor was the last place Terry would have wanted to visit with a scandal hanging over him.

The Burnley fans gave him a predictably rough ride and subjected him to a series of lewd chants. 'Same old Terry, always cheating,' was one of the milder ones. Terry responded by scoring a late winner with a thundering header from a corner. He did not celebrate after the goal, shrugging aside the congratulations of his teammates as he ran back to his own half. He looked angry and emotional. It was the only clue that there was something out of the ordinary about the game for him, but no one could accuse him of lacking the stomach for a fight.

Four days later he played for Chelsea at Hull City's KC Stadium, another venue he might not have chosen as the ideal place to try to continue his rehabilitation. Chelsea could only draw this time, and Terry showed signs of strain when he reacted to some of the home fans' chants. The Hull supporters had been working diligently on their attempts to bait him. 'Chelsea, wherever you may be,' they sang to the tune of 'Lord of the Dance', 'don't leave your wife with John Terry. Cos he likes a shag, he likes a bit of fluff, and he'll get your missus up the duff.'

The next day, Capello flew back into England and was besieged by reporters and camera crews at Heathrow. He looked shaken by the intensity of the interest and the jostling mob that met him. He had been England manager for just over two years, but this was the first time he had been exposed to the full frenzied force of a classic English football scandal. Until now, the results he had achieved had ensured a relatively quiet life. This was the first real test of his judgement in a crisis. He summoned Terry to a meeting at his Wembley office the next day, Friday 5 February.

Many of those urging Capello to sack Terry as captain were acting on the basis that it was the right thing to do by Bridge. Bridge, who was represented by Terry's former agent, Aaron Lincoln, had kept a dignified silence since the story broke, but there was much speculation that he would refuse to play for England again while Terry was still captain. Some of Bridge's Manchester City colleagues showed their support for him after a Premier League match against Portsmouth on 31 January. There were other matches that Sunday, and at the Emirates a rumour swept around the ground that Gareth

Barry and Shaun Wright-Phillips were among those who had worn Team Bridge vests underneath their City kit. That would have been a grievous blow to Terry because it would have confirmed talk of a split in the England dressing room. Then it emerged that none of City's England players had been involved. Carlos Tevez, Stephen Ireland and Nigel de Jong had sported the logos on their shirts. Still, their actions added more heat to the debate.

Tevez said that in the neighbourhood he came from in Buenos Aires, Terry would have had his legs cut off for doing what he had done. Or he would have been killed. Others voiced concerns that the unity of the England team would be damaged if Terry were allowed to retain the captaincy. There were suggestions that several England players were appalled by what they saw as Terry's betrayal of Bridge, that they had lost all respect for their captain and that they no longer wanted him as their leader. Terry's critics argued it was wrong that a man who had acted so irresponsibly should still be the figurehead of the England team.

The truth was that most England players cared little about Terry's indiscretions. There was certainly no appetite to confront him about what he had done, nor to agitate for his removal as captain. There was a certain amount of sympathy for Bridge, but most players recognised they were hardly in a position to judge Terry. They regarded the circus surrounding their embattled captain with wry amusement and a degree of relief that he, rather than them, was the focus of the headlines.

Some commentators guessed as much. The *Daily Mail* unleashed one of its star news columnists, Jan Moir, to dissect football. Moir had caused much controversy with a recent finger-wagging piece about the tragic death of gay Boyzone singer Stephen Gately that ended with the observation, 'under the carapace of glittering, hedonistic celebrity, the ooze of a very different and more dangerous lifestyle has seeped out for all to see'. She wrote then of 'dark appetites' and 'private vice', and her view of footballers' lives was similarly bleak. 'It is hard to imagine the rest of the England squad feeling his [Terry's] shame,' Moir wrote. 'Bad luck you got caught, mate, is probably about the height of it. After all, many of them have been or are in the same situation themselves; with the same interchangeable squad of predatory, pumped-up, big-haired tootsies whose sole ambition in life is to storm the sordid citadel of wagdom. They are spray-tanned vultures, these girls, their lipstick beaks forever pick-picking on the rich carrion of goggle-eyed Premier League players. One flash of luscious thong and the poor dumb footy clucks hardly have a chance. Don't they all just deserve each other?'

Moir and other social commentators were not concerned with the footballing repercussions of what Terry had done, but most of those from the world of football who were busy condemning the England skipper stopped short of demanding his exclusion from the England squad. Their moral ire had its limits. Their disgust at Terry's depravity was bounded by pragmatism. Their concern for Bridge stopped short of banishing Terry from the England squad altogether, which was what would have really solved Bridge's problem. But it was obvious that that would damage England's chances of winning the World Cup beyond repair. They wanted Terry to have his wrist slapped, but deep down they knew that the Chelsea defender was far more important to England than Bridge was.

The FA did the right thing. They did nothing. They were the subject of lazy criticism about how their stance was typical of an organisation often paralysed by indecision and infighting. They were accused of poor leadership, of being weak-willed and afraid to act. But this time, doing nothing was the strong course of action. FA chairman Lord Triesman and chief executive Ian Watmore, who would both leave the organisation suddenly a few months later, had agreed that the final decision on Terry's future as captain must lie with Capello. They did not want to second-guess him. Most importantly, they did not want to cause a rift with a manager they admired and valued by making a decision that he felt undermined his authority.

Many thought Terry should resign. They said it would be the honourable way out. Even on the morning of his showdown with Capello, Terry faced more damaging allegations. The *Daily Mail* ran a front-page story that accused him of trying to hire out his 12-seat private box at Wembley, a perk of the captaincy, for £4000 a match. That was against FA rules. Terry denied the accusations immediately and said that the box no longer belonged to him, but the timing was unfortunate.

As he drove from Chelsea's training ground to Wembley, Terry was still adamant that he had nothing to apologise for. He was fiercely proud of being England captain, just as he was of being Chelsea skipper. He believed that resigning would be an admission of guilt. He had never let himself down on the pitch, and he believed that ought to be enough. He did not expect to be fired when he arrived at Wembley and was ushered into Capello's office.

The prospect of Miss Perroncel, who was being represented by the publicity agent Max Clifford, selling her story to the *News of the World* had receded. There were rumours that Terry had done a deal with Miss Perroncel and won her silence. These rumours were firmly denied by both parties. Miss Perroncel explained that her silence was to protect her young son which seemed belated given what had already been published.

There were only three people in the office: Terry, Capello and Baldini. There was some small talk about Capello's knee operation, but Capello had little appetite for pleasantries and the conversation quickly moved on. Terry insisted that the stories about him and Miss Perroncel were not true and that nothing had happened between them. Capello ignored his argument. He had already made his mind up. He had not summoned Terry to his office for a discussion. This was not a time for closing statements. It was a sentencing. Capello told Terry he was no longer England captain. The meeting had lasted 12 minutes.

5 YOUNG BOYS, BUT RICH BOYS

IN the hours after Terry's dismissal, Capello's only attempt at conciliation was to release a brief statement. 'After much thought I have made the decision that it will be best for me to take the captaincy away from John Terry,' it said. 'As a captain with the team, John Terry has displayed extremely positive behaviour. However, I have to take into account other considerations and what is best for all of the England squad. What is best for all of the England team has inspired my choice.'

Terry released an even shorter statement. 'I fully respect Fabio Capello's decision,' it said. 'I will continue to give everything for England.' A piece also appeared on the front page of the *Sun* the next day, quoting Terry as saying he hoped to be England captain again one day. A couple of weeks later Capello said that would never happen while he was England boss.

Capello was lauded for his no-nonsense approach. There was still a novelty value in an England coach displaying this kind of untrammelled authority. After the craven surrender to player-power evident in the Eriksson and McClaren years, large sections of the English public still felt a thrill every time Capello put his players in their place. They saw this urbane, dignified older man's treatment of Terry as an analogy for something wider too. The vilification of the young in England has become an established media position, articulated through the easy characterisation of anybody under the age of 18 as either dependent on drugs or heavily influenced by violent video games unless proven otherwise. When Capello cut Terry down, his approval ratings shot up and he was fêted as if he were a cold-eyed vigilante exacting vengeance on behalf of a wronged generation.

There was also much amusement when it emerged that Capello had not bothered to mention to Rio Ferdinand that he was the new England captain. He didn't see the need. Ferdinand had been vice-captain so, as far as Capello was concerned, when the captain was removed, the vice-captain stepped up automatically. Others would have paraded the new skipper in front of the media to mark the change. Capello didn't even telephone Ferdinand. He said he would talk to him about it the next time he saw him. That played well, too.

Some commentators observed that it had come to something when the English needed to be taught a lesson in morality by an Italian, but many within the FA felt that Capello sacked Terry not because of the player's actions, however much he might have disapproved of them, but for more pragmatic reasons, particularly the realisation that the appetite for Terry's removal had become insatiable and that, if he remained as captain, the negative glare might begin to hijack the squad's preparations for South Africa. Capello was determined to stop that happening.

Publicly, Capello insisted he had sacked Terry purely because of his affair with Miss Perroncel and the fact that another member of the squad, Bridge, was involved, not because of the drip-drip of bad publicity the Chelsea captain had begun to attract. Capello still had links with Spanish journalists because of his time in charge at Real Madrid, and soon after he had sacked Terry, he gave an interview to the Spanish station Gol Television. He was asked if it had been a hard decision to take the captaincy away from Terry.

'No,' Capello said. 'Players and fans want the captain's armband to be worn by an exemplary player. They want the captain to be an example for young children. What happened with Terry wasn't good. I saw him at Wembley and we spoke about the affair and we spoke about football. It was fine. He understood. I explained to him that he could not continue as captain, but I also told him that he would continue to be a leader on the pitch and an important player because a coach needs a player like that.'

Capello's comments exasperated some of his allies, who were aware he was making himself a hostage to fortune by saying he wanted the England captain to be a role model. It might have been what Capello believed, and it might have struck a chord with those in England fed up of seeing footballers splashed across the front pages for varying degrees of outrageous behaviour, but it was a huge risk. It begged the question of what Capello would do the next time an England player stepped out of line. There was bound to be a next time, after all, and probably fairly soon.

If Capello was looking for 'exemplary players' in the England team, he would have to look for a long time. Many of the senior England players had colourful histories of their own. Ferdinand, the new skipper, was scarcely blemish-free. In September 2003 he had precipitated a crisis in English football when he skipped a drugs test at Manchester United's Carrington training ground. Ferdinand was warned he had to take the test, but left the training ground without meeting the testers. He claimed he forgot and went shopping for bed linen in central Manchester instead. Frantically though United tried, they could not reach him because he did not answer his mobile phone. In December that year, an FA commission banned him from football for eight months, and he missed the rest of United's season and England's involvement in Euro 2004. United's lawyer Maurice Watkins made himself look foolish when he said the punishment was 'savage and unprecedented'. Dick Pound, the president of the World Anti-Doping Agency, promptly pointed out that Ferdinand had got lucky; the accepted sentence for skipping a drugs test was two years.

Then there was the new vice-captain, Steven Gerrard. Six months earlier, Gerrard had been involved in an embarrassing court case after he was accused of affray for hitting a man during a brawl in the early hours of the morning at a Southport bar called the Lounge Inn. Gerrard, who had been drinking beer and a liqueur-based shot called a Jammy Donut, admitted pulling a jumper over the head of Marcus McGee and landing three upper-cuts on him after a dispute about who chose the music being played in the bar. Gerrard claimed he had acted in self-defence because he was convinced Mr McGee was about to hit him. The jury at Liverpool Crown Court took just over an hour to acquit him, and the judge assured Gerrard he could walk away from the trial with his reputation intact.

Then, ten days after Capello sacked Terry for his moral lapses, Ashley Cole's private life hit the front pages, when it was revealed he had sent pictures of himself in his underpants and hundreds of suggestive text messages to a secretary. Other messages and pictures of Cole, some sent from the England team hotel before the World Cup qualifying tie against Andorra in June 2009, had been sent to a topless model called Sonia Wild. The latest revelations were too much for Mrs Cole. She walked out.

But Capello did nothing. Cole had just been diagnosed with a broken ankle that would keep him out of football for three months, so Capello could hardly drop him for the next friendly international against Egypt at Wembley on 3 March. But there was no suggestion that he would be punished when he returned to fitness, nor was there any summons to Capello's office for discipline to be administered. Capello's inaction over Cole exposed the flaw in his stance over Terry. He had punished Terry for a moral lapse, but allowed Cole to escape unrebuked.

Capello seemed untypically flustered by the frenzied interest surrounding his sacking of Terry. When he arrived in Warsaw for the draw for the 2012 European Championship qualifying tournament two days after he had dismissed his captain, he was curt with English reporters. 'No questions about John Terry or the captain,' he told them as he stood on a dais after the draw had been made. He brushed away attempts at follow-up questions on the subject.

At a League Managers' Association Dinner at Wembley the following Thursday, he also seemed ill at ease. The published running order was changed so that he did not have to spend as much time on the stage and was not exposed to questions from the audience. It was left to three previous England managers – Graham Taylor, Terry Venables and Sven-Goran Eriksson – to take part in a question and answer session, and even then the subject of Terry appeared to be off limits.

There was much talk among the managers at the dinner that evening about how badly Terry had been treated. Many of them felt Capello had set a worrying precedent. When he sacked Terry, he established a new set of rules. He made it clear that the way players behaved in their personal lives could have repercussions for their England career, and by doing so, he put a price on their heads. He gave legitimacy to newspapers investigating the private lives of Premier League superstars because there was, suddenly, a public-interest justification for doing so. Many of the older managers at the LMA dinner that night laughed at the kind of things they had allowed players from previous eras to get away with. They told stories of one former England skipper in particular, whose behaviour had made Terry look like a shrinking violet and yet had never been reprimanded because his performances on the pitch were unaffected.

It also became clear that Capello had misjudged the situation in several ways. He had assumed that sacking Terry provided him with a guarantee that Bridge would not retire from international football. In other circumstances, Bridge might have been expendable, but, with exquisite timing, Ashley Cole broke his ankle in Chelsea's 2–1 defeat at Everton a few days after Terry's sacking and there were doubts about whether he would be fit for the World Cup. Suddenly,

Bridge was not England's reserve left-back any more. He was the first choice. Actually, he was pretty much the only choice.

When he attended a conference for World Cup coaches in Sun City at the end of February, Capello was bullish about Bridge. He was almost glib, in fact. He said he would include him in the squad for the upcoming Egypt friendly and that he was sure there was no problem with Bridge's state of mind. He was sure he would play. It was obvious he believed that by removing Terry as captain, he had lanced the boil. Perhaps he thought that Bridge wanted Terry punished for what he had done and that Terry's loss of the armband had sated his desire for vengeance.

But Capello read it wrongly. Bridge believed Terry had told other players that he (Bridge) had been parsimonious with the maintenance payments for their son (Miss Perroncel later sued Bridge for improved terms) and that Miss Perroncel could not cope. Bridge was furious. He felt his fitness to be a father was being called into question and that Terry was merely trying to cover his tracks.

It did not matter to Bridge that Terry was not England captain any more. Bridge knew that if he were selected for the World Cup squad, he would still have to spend up to six weeks in Terry's company, that he would have to share dressing rooms and team rooms and dining rooms with him in South Africa, and he could not stomach that idea. He was also fearful that he and Terry would become the focus of a media soap opera, their every move, their every interaction fiercely scrutinised for hints of a snub or a reconciliation. Bridge is a quiet kind of man, a man who does not relish the limelight. The idea of that kind of attention was anathema to him.

If Capello had really wanted to make a moral stand over Terry and ensure that Bridge travelled to South Africa, he would have left him out of the squad altogether. There was a precedent. Steve Sampson, the coach of the USA team at the 1998 World Cup, dropped his captain

John Harkes from the squad when it emerged before the tournament – although not publicly – that he was having an affair with the wife of a teammate, Eric Wynalda. But Capello was not prepared to go that far. Terry was too valuable to him to be left at home.

So a couple of days before Capello was to announce his squad for the game against Egypt, Bridge released a statement. 'I have thought long and hard about my position in the England football team in the light of the reporting and events over the last few weeks,' it said. 'It has always been an honour to play for England. However, after careful thought I believe my position in the squad is now untenable and potentially divisive. Sadly, therefore, I feel for the sake of the team and in order to avoid what will be inevitable distractions, I have decided not to put myself forward for selection. I have today informed the management of this decision. I wish the team all the very best in South Africa.'

Not only had Capello failed to rehabilitate Bridge, but he had also unsettled Terry. Capello was forced to pick the previously uncapped Everton defender, Leighton Baines, as the starting left-back against Egypt. Whatever anyone thought of Terry's morals, everyone was agreed that he was England's most commanding defender. There were problems all over the back four. Most worryingly, there were lingering injury concerns over Terry's central defensive partner, Rio Ferdinand, who missed large chunks of Manchester United's season with chronic back problems. Terry was absolutely crucial to England's hopes of success in South Africa, but now there were signs that stripping him of the captaincy had destabilised him.

Terry is an emotional man and what Capello did to him was an enormous blow to his pride. It also put him under a great deal of pressure when he played for Chelsea in what was left of the 2009–10 Premier League season. Every eye was on him in every game. Many hoped for a mistake as evidence that he was still paying a price for his philandering, but at first he seemed immune. Two days after his sacking, he was Chelsea's man of the match in their 2–0 victory over Arsenal at Stamford Bridge. After the game he walked through the press room where the daily newspaper journalists were writing their match reports and quotes pieces and made a point of stopping to shake hands with several of those who had supported him and several who had not.

But soon the mistakes began to come. Terry made an uncharacteristic error against Everton at Goodison Park three days later, jumping too soon to try to intercept a long ball forward, only to watch it sail over his head and fall to Louis Saha, who took it on his chest and thumped it into the net. He suffered moments of uncertainty at the San Siro near the end of February when Chelsea lost 2–1 to Inter Milan, and he had another difficult game against Manchester City at Stamford Bridge a few days later when City crushed Chelsea 4–2. As the season wore on, he recovered his confidence, but every time he slipped up, as he did against Spurs at White Hart Lane in mid-April when he was sent off for two bookable offences, it was traced back to the day in February when Capello sacked him, and new questions were asked about whether his form was a worry as far as the World Cup was concerned.

Before the game against City, a Saturday lunchtime kick-off on 27 February, Terry and Bridge came face to face for the first time since the scandal broke 30 days earlier. The build-up to the match was dominated by fevered speculation about whether Bridge would shake Terry's hand when offered to him as the teams lined up on the pitch before the match. When the moment came, pubs around the country stilled. It was probably the most dramatic few seconds of even that enthralling season.

The climactic moment of a football soap opera was being beamed into our living rooms, our pubs and our bars. The whole country seemed to be rooting for the underdog, the lovelorn, the betrayed Wayne Bridge, wanting him to stand up to his tormentor. The City players started to walk down the line of Chelsea players. Each shook Terry's hand, although Craig Bellamy turned away as he did so. When it was Bridge's turn, he looked at Terry's outstretched hand and took his away from it, moving on to shake the hand of the next player in line.

The scene was played over and over again in slow motion for the rest of the day and the rest of the night. It was an assassination, a frame-by-frame drive-by in front of more than 40,000 people. Terry didn't crumple when Bridge refused his hand, and kept on walking, but it was a humiliating snub. Some thought Bridge childish and vindictive, others that Terry was getting his just desserts.

When the England players gathered at the Grove hotel near Watford the next day, Bridge was not among them. Neither was the new captain, Ferdinand, who was absent with a recurrence of his back injury, hardly the ideal beginning to the new skipper's new era. Terry was there, but he knew his ordeal was not yet over. Many were predicting that he would be booed at Wembley during the Egypt game, just as Frank Lampard, Ashley Cole, Peter Crouch and Owen Hargreaves had been booed by England fans in the recent past.

Capello gathered his players together before they trained and told them he was sick of seeing their names in the headlines for the wrong reasons. He told them it had to stop. He told them they needed to make sacrifices and that if they didn't, they would suffer the consequences. 'It was short and sweet,' Steven Gerrard said. 'He reiterated that we have responsibilities as players both on and off the pitch.'

On the eve of the match, Capello spoke to the press at Arsenal's training ground at London Colney. He sat at a long table in the room at the end of the media centre where Arsène Wenger usually holds court. It was the first proper chance anyone had had to ask him about his decision to sack Terry, and the questions came thick and fast. After the first three he lost patience. 'Why do we have to speak about this for such a long time? You are interested in the game or the life of the players?' Capello was reminded that he had made the private lives of the players a matter of legitimate interest when he sacked his captain because of his private life. Capello accepted that and the questions continued.

The subject widened from Terry's behaviour to the problems today's footballers face adjusting to the sudden acquisition of fabulous wealth. 'The private life is a big problem for some players, but also a big problem for their clubs and, in the end, for me,' Capello said. 'It will be really important that the players, in this last period before the World Cup, are careful in their own private lives at every moment. These are important players and they have to be an example to the children and all the fans. For that reason, they have to stay careful and sacrifice something in their lives. I am not being unrealistic asking for this. Why? I remember in Spain, players would go to the disco and sometimes drink something, but they did not have big problems with different players, different girls, different women. These are young players, young boys, but rich boys. This is the problem.'

And so, from Capello's broken English, came the sentence that summed up a decade of under-achievement from the so-called golden generation of England footballers who were supposed to take the world by storm. Young boys, but rich boys. It was all there in those five words. All the temptations, the social dislocation that came with the massive financial rewards of being a footballer, the way our players kept getting sucked back into our drinking culture, the leeches that want their money, the reluctance to take personal responsibility for their actions, the complacency that can come with wealth and celebrity.

Suddenly, after a qualifying campaign that had engendered so much hope, the Terry Affair seemed to have drained England of much of its optimism. The season was starting to take its toll too. Injuries were cropping up everywhere. The game against Egypt was not about maintaining momentum any more. It was about trying to staunch the bleeding and gauging just how much hostility there was to Terry. Both Capello and Rooney had issued pleas for clemency on Terry's behalf, but no one knew whether their appeals would be successful.

The realisation of what had happened to him must have finally hit Terry as he stood in the Wembley tunnel waiting to take the field. He was no longer at the head of the side. He was reduced to the ranks, fourth in line, behind Jermain Defoe. The camera lingered on his face. He looked tense and strained. The only armband he was wearing was a black one to mark the death of Macclesfield Town manager Keith Alexander, the league's first black manager, who had died earlier that day.

Most of the hostility engendered by the past month of controversy died in the night air. There were isolated outbreaks of booing when Terry's name was read out. Full of nerves, he hit his first attempt at a pass straight into touch and that brought forth another round of catcalls. But there was nothing like the sustained abuse that Hargreaves and Cole had once suffered. Soon there were chants of support for Terry. There was even a sign in the crowd that said simply, 'We Forgive You'. 'There were a few jeers, but I can handle that,' Terry said afterwards. 'I really appreciated the support most supporters gave to me. It meant a lot.'

Maybe there was an acceptance from the England fans that whatever Terry had done, the team needed him badly. That much was evident midway through the first half when Ferdinand's replacement, Matthew Upson, slipped while he was trying to mark Egypt forward Mohamed Zidan, and Zidan controlled the ball and lashed a shot past Robert Green. For half an hour a sense of gloom enveloped Wembley. After the upheavals of the previous month, it was clear that England desperately needed a victory against the African champions to restore morale.

Even though Rooney was struggling to find the form that had made him so unstoppable for Manchester United, England fought their way back into the game after the interval. Half-time substitute Peter Crouch scored a 56th-minute equaliser, and Shaun Wright-Phillips, a replacement for Theo Walcott, put England ahead with a quarter of an hour left. England found their freedom again and Crouch finished things off with a third England goal ten minutes from the end.

As England moved towards victory, the Terry Affair entered its epilogue. When Gerrard was substituted 17 minutes from the end, he passed the captain's armband to Rooney. When Rooney was in turn replaced with four minutes left, he passed it to Gareth Barry. It was anyone's guess who might have been next if Barry had been substituted too, but whoever it was, it would not have been Terry. For him, the captaincy was a memory. His dream of being the first to lift the World Cup at Soccer City, just as Bobby Moore had done at Wembley 44 years earlier, was over.

6 ONE ICON STUMBLES, ANOTHER FALLS

THERE is a small café on the concourse at Munich Airport called Bar Beleg, and when Fabio Capello saw two English journalists sitting at one of the tables there the morning after Manchester United had lost to Bayern Munich in their Champions League quarter-final first leg at the end of March, he wandered over with the silver Rimowa carry-on suitcase that accompanied him everywhere, sat down and asked them what they knew. It was obvious what he meant. Everyone was talking about one thing, and it wasn't United's 2–1 defeat at the Allianz Arena.

United had lost to an injury-time strike from Ivica Olic, and while the Germans crammed into the stadium might have seen only the goal, the English did not. In their peripheral vision they saw a figure fall to the floor and begin to writhe in pain. Wayne Rooney, who had put United ahead after 64 seconds, had been involved in an innocuous collision with Bayern striker Mario Gomez in the build-up to the Germans' 92nd-minute winner. As Rooney challenged him from behind, Gomez inadvertently stood on Rooney's left foot.

At first it seemed that Rooney might have suffered another broken metatarsal, the same injury that had made him a big doubt for the 2006 World Cup, but replays showed that when he leapt in pain, he landed awkwardly on his right foot and twisted his ankle. Rooney looked as if he was in agony, and he was helped from the pitch by United physios, who removed his right boot straight away. He left the stadium on crutches with his right foot in a protective plastic boot. England held its breath.

After Paul Gascoigne sustained a serious knee injury during the 1991 FA Cup Final, the headline on the back page of the *Sun* the following Monday read, 'Oh God, Please Don't Let Us Lose Gazza'. There were well-founded worries about the effect the injury would have on Gascoigne's career, not just his availability for a tournament. But the reaction in the English press to Rooney's injury was almost as emotional. 'In Roo-ins' was the headline on a couple of the back pages the day after the Bayern game. 'Get Well Soon' was another. Everyone was in a state of barely concealed panic. There were only 72 days until the start of the World Cup.

Rooney's injury was clearly not as bad as Gascoigne's had been, but this was the one thing Capello had feared more than any other. Rooney had been in unstoppable form for United and for England. Liberated by the sale of Cristiano Ronaldo to Real Madrid before the start of the 2009–10 season, he had begun to hit the same heights he reached during the 2004 European Championships in Portugal. He took that tournament by storm, bewildering the best defences in Europe with his power, his hunger and his boldness. Only a broken foot against the hosts in the quarter-finals broke the spell.

With Rooney back in that kind of mood, anything seemed possible for England in South Africa. Whatever England's other deficiencies, a revitalised Rooney could compensate for them. At United he had finally been released from the sacrificial role Sir Alex Ferguson had often asked him to play so that Ronaldo could enjoy free rein. Rooney was the epitome of a team player, and when Ferguson asked him to play wide on the left of a five-man midfield, tracking back and covering the opposing full-back, he did it willingly.

But the role had blunted his attacking verve. Many felt he was wasted in a wider position. Most accepted that he was the most talented English player since Gascoigne, yet the brilliant creative force that was so evident at Euro 2004 had been gradually subsumed by a life of defensive responsibility at Old Trafford. Only when Madrid lured Ronaldo away and Ferguson handed Rooney the main strike role did the extent of Rooney's brilliance become apparent again.

Rooney had everything: pace, power, vision, hunger. He was a playground footballer. It was easy to see the child inside him still, the kid who loved to kick a football around, the player who still adored the game, who had not grown cynical about it or tired of it, but who just wanted to play. He had matured a lot too since he had reacted to the sly provocation of the Portuguese in 2006 and earned himself a red card in the World Cup quarter-final by grinding his boot into the groin of the prone Ricardo Carvalho. There were still moments where he succumbed to his temper, but they were far fewer now, and the loss of control was more modest.

When he collected the Footballer of the Year award at a dinner in central London a few weeks before England left for South Africa, he was even confident enough to poke a little fun at Ferguson, who was sitting near him on the top table, glowering because he thought Rooney's question and answer session with Sky's Jeff Stelling had gone on too long. 'The manager said to me before the season that I needed to score more headers,' Rooney said. 'But I was playing out wide a lot back then. I said: "Do you want me to get on the end of my own crosses?"'

That night, Rooney also pointed out that even when he had been getting into the box the previous season, it was difficult to predict when Ronaldo was going to cross the ball. The arrival of Luis Antonio Valencia had changed that, and Rooney was thriving on the balls the former Wigan player was firing in from the right. Rooney scored 26 league goals in 2009–10, second only to Chelsea's Didier Drogba. The fact that both his fellow professionals and the nation's football writers chose Rooney as the player of the season showed that they valued the England forward's overall contribution to his team more than Drogba's.

Rooney's form was the main reason why United stayed in contention for the title until the last day of the season. They were a weaker team without Ronaldo and Carlos Tevez, who had been sold to Manchester City, but Rooney's goals and all-round play camouflaged that. He was not quite as dominant within the England side, but there was a recognition that he was the team's best player and its talisman. It would be an exaggeration to say his absence would have made England an ordinary side, but it would have been hard to envisage England mounting any sort of realistic challenge to win the World Cup without him.

Capello had left the Allianz Arena by the time Rooney was injured. He was in a car heading back to his hotel in Munich when his mobile phone began to light up with calls and text messages. As he sat sipping his espresso at Bar Beleg, he did not know what to feel. He raised his eyebrows and exhaled when the reporters told him that first estimates said Rooney would be out for two to three weeks. It was not clear whether it was an expression of relief or worry. If the injury was not serious, it might be a blessing in disguise. It might do Rooney good to have an enforced rest. Then again, he was in such a rich vein of form that interrupting it posed a risk that he might not be able to recapture his touch. The worst scenario, of course, was that the injury involved serious ligament damage and would rule him out of the World Cup. England's odds of winning the World Cup had lengthened from 5–1 to 6–1 overnight in the wake of Rooney's injury.

Ferguson, understandably, was in a foul mood after the Bayern game. He was curt when he was asked about Rooney. 'Wayne has hurt his ankle,' he said. 'I don't think it's terribly serious.' But United were notorious for being economical with the truth about injuries, so a certain amount of dread remained. Two days later, Ferguson gave a new update. He said Rooney had not suffered any bone damage or serious ligament damage. 'The nation can stop praying now,' Ferguson said.

Ferguson was not quite right about that. He was adamant that Rooney had 'no chance' of playing in the return leg against Bayern at Old Trafford a week later, but he rushed him back anyway. Rooney made an impact in the first half, but faded fast and was substituted ten minutes after the interval. He missed the next match away at Blackburn Rovers, a draw that swung the balance in the title race decisively towards Chelsea. Then he appeared tentative and frustrated in the narrow victory over Manchester City, was absent for the penultimate home game, and walked off the pitch with a mixture of ankle and groin complaints 13 minutes from the end of United's final game of the season, against Stoke at Old Trafford. He had not been able to stop scoring before he hurt himself against Bayern, but now the knack had left him. His form had disappeared. His face wore a look of surly exasperation, as though he could not understand what was happening. If he had just been able to avoid injury for another couple of months, if he had kept rattling in goals and boosting his confidence to even greater heights, if Gomez had not trodden on his foot, if Rooney had not tracked back to try to stifle that final Bayern attack, maybe the whole complexion of England's World Cup campaign would have been different.

As Capello sat at Bar Beleg, he was already fighting the feeling that things were starting to get away from him. Stripping John Terry of the captaincy had been a big upheaval, there was uncertainty about when Ashley Cole would return to full fitness, and Capello must have been furious about Wayne Bridge's decision to turn his back on England because he could not bear to spend time with Terry. A fortnight before Rooney was injured, the England coach had also had to come to terms with the news that David Beckham had been ruled out of the World Cup after rupturing his Achilles tendon.

Beckham was playing for AC Milan against Chievo at San Siro when he was hurt. The game was 87 minutes old when he came to collect the ball in the centre circle. He controlled the pass with his left foot, turned and planted the foot behind him. Then, as he prepared to play a pass with his right foot, Beckham hesitated and winced in pain. He knew immediately something was seriously wrong. He touched the ball to his nearest teammate and then began to hop on his right foot, keeping the weight off the left. He signalled to Milan coach Leonardo and the bench that he needed to be substituted. He bent down to feel his heel and realised what had happened. He crumpled to the floor and after he had been helped to the sideline, he was covered in blue blankets and carried away on a stretcher. 'It's broken, it's broken,' he told the team physios, weeping.

Beckham flew to Turku in Finland the next day, where Achilles specialist Sakari Orava repaired the tendon. Most estimates said he would need three or four months of rehabilitation before he could even start kicking a football again. Beckham was distraught. Some thought it was the end of his career. He was 34, and rupturing an Achilles tendon was a serious injury. The older a player got, the more difficult it became to recover from setbacks like that. It was harder and harder to regain fitness and return to the level he had been playing at before. Beckham said immediately that he would not retire. But even though he had made miraculous comebacks before, he accepted that his chances of playing in South Africa were over.

It was a desperately cruel blow for Beckham. Steve McClaren, who was keen to make a gesture that distanced him from the discredited regime of Eriksson, had dropped Beckham from the England squad after the 2006 World Cup and made it plain he considered it the end of his England career. At Real Madrid, Beckham had often been overlooked by new boss Fabio Capello, and it was beginning to look increasingly unlikely that Beckham and the Madrid hierarchy would be able to reach agreement on a new contract when his existing deal ran out at the end of the 2006–07 season. Although the former England skipper was mulling over offers to join AC Milan and Everton, he did not want to disrupt his sons' education more than he had to by moving them to Italy for a couple of years, and he was dubious about diluting his popularity with Manchester United supporters by joining a rival club in the northwest of England.

So he began to turn his thoughts to a future on the other side of the Atlantic. The idea of ending his career in the USA, where Major League Soccer (MLS) was increasing in popularity, had appealed to him for some time, and he knew the lifestyle would suit his children and give his wife, Victoria, a chance to pursue new career opportunities in Los Angeles. Beckham already had links with the LA Galaxy, which was owned by sports and entertainment giants AEG, who were partners in Beckham's soccer academy in Los Angeles, so it was a natural fit. The move was announced in January 2007. It was said that the Galaxy would pay him £128 million over five years, although the money included sponsorship contracts, a share of shirt sales and club profits, as well as his salary. AEG president Tim Leiweke did not employ understatement when announcing Beckham's arrival: 'David Beckham will have a greater impact on soccer in America than any athlete has ever had on a sport globally,' he said. 'David is truly the only individual that can build the bridge between soccer in America and the rest of the world.'

The standard in the MLS was improving all the time, but it was not close to being on a par with the Premier League, La Primera Liga or Serie A. In Europe it was still regarded as a joke league. The names of some of its stadia – Pizza Hut Park, Dick's Sporting Goods Park and Rio Tinto Stadium – did little to dispel that impression. English fans were still resistant to the idea of clubs selling stadium naming rights, even though they were beginning to creep into the Premier League. Lower down the pyramid, York City's Bootham Crescent stadium had been renamed KitKat Crescent for five years as part of a sponsorship deal with Nestlé, and to the English ear,

Dick's Sporting Goods Park fitted more into that category than Arsenal's decision to sell the name of its new stadium to the Emirates airline. Beckham's move did not quite amount to going to Hollywood to be a film star, which was the scornful way Capello described it. But moving to America did seem to be an admission from Beckham that he felt his England career was over. His manager, Terry Byrne, was careful to make sure Beckham did not express any bitterness towards McClaren about his exile just in case he should come to regret it. Neither of them thought there was any way back but it was sage advice.

By the spring, things had changed dramatically. Beckham won over Capello at the Bernabeu, forced his way back into the Real Madrid side and helped them snatch the league title from Barcelona. At the same time, McClaren was coming under intense pressure following a string of disappointing qualifying results. In March 2007, England contested a dull goalless draw with Israel in Tel Aviv, and then endured 90 minutes of being booed and jeered by their own travelling supporters when they played Andorra in Barcelona a few days later. England won 3–0, but there were ugly scenes at the Olympic Stadium in Montjuic. The England squad members who had not made the team or the substitutes' bench were chased from the stands by angry England fans. McClaren was thoroughly rattled. He answered two questions in the post-match press conference and then walked out.

McClaren needed to do something to breathe new life into the team and deflect the criticism that was raining down on him. So in May he performed a spectacular volte-face and recalled Beckham for a friendly international against Brazil and a qualifier against Estonia. Beckham was back on the inside, but when he joined the Galaxy that summer, he was confronted with the dilemma of how to hang on to his England place while playing in a second-rate league and living on the Pacific coast of the USA. There was also the issue of the 11-hour journeys back and forth to England every time he was called up. Beckham made the commitment eagerly, but his return to the England camp placed strains on his nascent relationship with the Galaxy.

The strain increased when Capello took over as England boss in December 2007. He awarded Beckham his 100th cap when he played him against France at the Stade de France in March 2008, but Capello had already made it clear that he would not pick him if his only club football was played with the Galaxy. He said he didn't believe Beckham would be able to retain his fitness if he merely trained with another club during the MLS close season, which extended from November to April. He also made it plain that he believed Beckham needed to be playing at least some of the year at a higher level than the MLS could offer. Beckham realised that he had either to act on Capello's advice or abandon his dream of becoming the first Englishman to play in four World Cups. That autumn, it was announced that Beckham would join AC Milan on loan for two months at the start of 2009.

The loan went so well that Beckham was desperate to extend it. He loved life in Milan and relished the chance to play with players such as Ronaldinho, Kaka and Andrea Pirlo. It was an escape from the mediocrity of the MLS. He also knew that being an active member of the Milan squad was keeping him in Capello's thoughts. By now Beckham had realised that playing in South Africa, a prize he once thought had been denied him by McClaren, was now firmly within his grasp, and he was determined not to let it slip away again. Later that spring the Galaxy were paid $10 million to allow Beckham to stay at San Siro until the end of the Serie A season in May. It was never made clear how much of that fee Milan had paid and how much Beckham had contributed himself, but it was obvious that he was keen to do everything in his power to further his ambitions of playing in one last World Cup.

Beckham paid a price with the Galaxy fans too. They felt belittled and rejected by his desire to stay in Italy. When he returned to play for the Galaxy in July 2009, he was heckled and jeered by angry home fans during a friendly match against Milan at the club's Home Depot Stadium. It did not help that the club captain, Landon Donovan, had accused Beckham of being disloyal. Some fans held up a banner that read 'Go Home Fraud', and at half-time, Beckham was involved in an angry altercation with Galaxy supporters. But the resentment diminished as the Galaxy season progressed. Beckham won the crowd over and led the team to the season finale, the MLS Cup Final, which they lost to Real Salt Lake.

Capello rewarded Beckham's commitment to the England cause by picking him regularly. He had played in 16 of Capello's 22 games in charge, and had reached 115 caps before he was injured against Chievo. But he had started only six of those games, and Capello's use of him as a cameo substitute prompted a heated and long-running debate. Because each one of Beckham's caps took him closer to, or past, a series of England appearance landmarks, his contribution to every international was fiercely scrutinised. Many argued that his truncated involvement in matches devalued his caps total. In one World Cup qualifying tie, away to Belarus in Minsk in October 2008, he won his 107th cap when he was brought off the bench one minute from the end. In one run of four England cameos, he clocked up a total of less than half an hour on the pitch. Many felt aggrieved that Beckham passed Bobby Moore's famous landmark of 108 caps by amassing appearances in such a way. They treated every new cap Beckham won as an affront to the memory of Moore and the majesty of men like Bobby Charlton and Billy Wright.

Some of his detractors seemed to have forgotten that, in his prime, Beckham was recognised as one of the best players in the world, probably the best crosser of a ball this country has ever had. Twice he was runner-up for the World Player of the Year Award, once to Rivaldo, once to Luis Figo. He was measured against the elite of the world game. He had won six league titles in England and one in Spain. He had won the Champions League too, and became the first English player to make 100 appearances in that competition. His achievements in an England shirt might not have come close to matching Moore's, but neither was he an impostor. And those who poured scorn on the way that Beckham won his caps usually neglected to mention that Moore made more than a quarter of his England appearances in games against Wales, Scotland and Northern Ireland in the old annual Home International tournament.

Beckham's caps record was a product of a new football era when national teams played more often and the substitute system, introduced only late in Moore's career, allowed more players to win caps every time a team played. But, despite the angry accusing tone of much that was said and written about Beckham's career, he could not be blamed for the fact that England managers kept picking him. There was also a contradiction at the heart of much of the criticism aimed at him. Many commentators bemoaned the indifference of the modern player to appearing for his country. They lamented the fact that club football had usurped international football in their loyalties, and eviscerated men such as David Bentley for turning their back on playing for England in an Under-21 summer tournament. Yet when someone like Beckham put his England career ahead of everything else in his life, his critics said it was just a vanity project.

The subtext of much of the criticism about Beckham had always been that England managers allowed their judgement of his footballing worth to be swayed by his celebrity. They were blinded by the stardust, the argument went. But that argument stilled when Capello kept picking him too. The Italian was seen as the ultimate unsentimental manager. He hated celebrity. He hated the trappings of celebrity. Yet even when he could have made all sorts of excuses to leave him out – his age, the air miles, the MLS, the circus around him and so on – Capello included Beckham in the England squad time after time. 'This manager doesn't hand out caps to people so they can reach milestones,' Rio Ferdinand said before Beckham equalled Moore's caps record in a friendly against Spain in February 2009.

By the beginning of 2010, when Beckham returned to AC Milan for a second loan spell, it had become obvious that Capello had already made up his mind to include him in his 23-man squad for South Africa. If he decided that Theo Walcott and Aaron Lennon were his first choice right-sided midfielders, then he would shoehorn Beckham into the World Cup party somewhere else. But he was going to go no matter what. Capello valued him for his experience and technique. He knew he would be a good tourist during weeks of near-confinement at the team camp that were bound to test the patience of some of the other players, and Beckham was still the most technically able player in the England squad. The ball didn't bounce off him as it did off many of the rest of them, particularly in pressure situations. If Capello wanted to protect a lead near the end of a game, he knew he could bring Beckham on to help keep possession and run the clock down. He also knew that his delivery at set pieces was invaluable.

Beckham sat out the game against Egypt at Wembley at the beginning of March on the substitutes' bench, but by then Capello did not need him to prove anything. He knew everything he needed to know about Beckham, and he had already allocated him a seat on the plane to Johannesburg. He started with Walcott on the right and brought Shaun Wright-Phillips on in the second half. It meant Beckham stayed on 115 caps, which provided some succour to those who were already dreading the moment he reached the final frontier and drew level with Peter Shilton's England record of 125 appearances. Even if Beckham played in both England's World Cup warm-up games and then England went all the way to the World Cup final and he played in all seven group and knock-out matches, he could reach only 124.

All those calculations became irrelevant on the night of 14 March when Beckham struggled to the sideline at San Siro and was carried away on a stretcher, his head in his hands, his face a mask of despair. All his sacrifices, all the hundreds of thousands of miles he had flown, all the time he had spent away from his family, all the wrath he had faced at the LA Galaxy, all the criticism he had continued to face in England, everything he had endured in pursuit of his last great career goal of playing in the 2010 World Cup and finally doing himself justice at a major tournament suddenly counted for nothing.

Capello blinked it all back as he sat at Bar Beleg. He was sanguine about the setbacks that had suddenly afflicted his squad. He was also remarkably honest about some of the limitations he faced as he wrestled with his squad selection for South Africa. On occasions like that, he impressed journalists with his candour about the quality of some of the England players. Sometimes it had been made clear beforehand that the comments were off the record. On other occasions like this one, Capello either trusted the journalists not to print his comments in their newspapers, or was confident enough in his opinions not to care whether they did or not.

This time it was obvious that he had deep misgivings about Gary Neville's late bid to force his way back into the squad. Neville had missed much of Manchester United's season through injury, but right back was a problematic position for Capello. Liverpool's Glen Johnson was the obvious candidate to start there in England's opening game, but there was a vacancy for his back-up, and many believed a fit Neville, with his strong character and his organisational abilities, would be a valuable asset. Capello was not convinced. He pointed to the way Neville's lack of pace had been exposed by

Franck Ribery against Bayern. He said Neville had only been comfortable when Nani was double-teaming Ribery with him. He also pointed out it was Neville's misjudgement and handball that had led to the free kick from which Ribery had scored the Bayern equaliser.

But Capello was even more damning about England's goalkeeping situation. 'The goalkeepers,' he said, shaking his head. Then he mentioned Joe Hart and shook his head even more vigorously. He seemed worried about Theo Walcott. He said he had been 'bad' for Arsenal against Birmingham the previous week, but it was also clear that he wanted to give Walcott the benefit of the doubt. He said he hoped he would play against Barcelona that night. Walcott did play. In fact, after Arsenal had been utterly outplayed in the first half, Walcott came off the bench when they were 2–0 down and rescued the game. He scored one goal and set up the equaliser.

The flight to Heathrow was called, and as Capello and the journalists walked to the gate, his mind turned to the great English obsession: penalties. He said he had read an interview with Roberto Baggio recently, where Baggio talked about the penalty he had missed in the shoot-out at the end of the 1994 World Cup Final and said it was the first time he had ever put a spot-kick over the bar. Capello pointed out that even great penalty-takers, such as Baggio and Marco Van Basten, missed at important times in their careers.

'There are two things the English worry too much about,' Capello said. 'Penalties and the captain.'

One of the journalists asked him why he had not dampened the English obsession with the captaincy and handed it to the oldest player in the team, or the one who had the most caps, as was the custom in Italy and Spain and several other countries.

Capello smiled and shrugged his shoulders. 'I cannot change everything at once,' he said.

7 THE CAPELLO INDEX

THE reasons why Fabio Capello was so popular with England's fans and its media were as much to do with the things he had *not* done as with the things he had. He had never been caught having secret talks with the Chelsea chief executive, he had never given the impression that the England job was a bonus when it came to helping him chase skirt, and he had never been stung by a fake sheikh offering him the chance to join Aston Villa.

Unlike Sven-Goran Eriksson, he had never behaved as if the England job were a halt in the wilderness until something better or more lucrative came along. He did not bat his eyelashes at other suitors. When he was linked with the Juventus job at the end of April, the story was dismissed immediately. There was no flirtation. There was no hint he might try to use the interest as a lever to force up his wages at the FA.

Nor had he tried to use the England job as a device to attract financial offers from elsewhere. Eriksson was the king of that. His pre-World Cup tie-ups included Cirio Del Monte pasta sauces, a box CD of soothing classical favourites and two PlayStation games: Sven-Goran Eriksson's World Cup Challenge and Sven-Goran Eriksson's World Cup Manager. Neither of which was any good, according to the industry.

The English public had grown bored and exasperated with Eriksson's opportunism. There were still many who felt deeply uneasy about the national team being managed by a foreigner, so everything Eriksson did to suggest that he did not see the job as the pinnacle of his career exacerbated those misgivings. An idea of Eriksson took hold in the public consciousness: he was a nice man, but he was weak.

Capello was different. With him, everything was clean. Everything was neat. Capello was all straight lines, smart suits and barked commands. No junk food, no mobiles, no World Cup song, no distractions, no bowing to celebrity, no *World Cup Wind-Ups*. There was no blurring around the edges, no room for misinterpretation. He had his eye on only one prize. He was scrupulously dedicated to the England job. It all added to the idea that, in Capello, England had found a man who was a throwback to a time when honour was more important than money.

So it came as a rude shock when reporters were invited to an upstairs auditorium at London's Stock Exchange on Monday 10 May, the day before Capello was to announce his initial 30-man World Cup squad, and found themselves being handed press releases to announce the launch of a private commercial venture called the Capello Index. Even the football writers assigned to cover the England team, writers who were used to the sport's money-driven culture, were surprised that Capello had seen the need to lend his name to the project. He had gone more than two years in the job without making a significant error and now, just when England most needed to be free of upheaval, he had slipped up. The same thought occurred to everyone: it was what Sven would have done.

The journalists had not gone to the Stock Exchange expecting controversy. They had expected the Capello Index to be a database the England manager would keep for his own use. The main purpose of attending was to speak to Capello about the squad announcement the next day and the selection dilemmas he was facing over Owen Hargreaves and Gareth Barry. But as they scanned the press release and listened to introductions, a sense of astonishment took over.

The compère for the event was the Sky Sports presenter Ed Chamberlin. As he spoke, Capello sat at a table flanked by Internet entrepreneur Chicco Merighi, the chief executive of the Capello Index, and Francesco Bof, an Italian professor of sport management. Some of the journalists were aware of Adrian Bevington shifting uncomfortably in his seat a few rows further back in the auditorium.

The press release said Capello was unveiling a new formula for rating players. It was a new football index for the fans, it said. It was based on a model he had developed himself over the previous two years for measuring a player's performance. 'The Capello Index will create an international player ranking system as well as providing the scoring mechanism for a new fantasy football game, the Capello XI,' the release said. The fantasy game was to be launched at the World Cup.

The Capello Index had been tested during the previous month and applied to games in the Premier League, La Primera Liga, Serie A and others. It marked players out of 100 and tried to reward their impact on games in every area of the pitch. For instance, if a player scored the only goal of a game, he would receive a higher mark for that goal than a player who scored the fifth goal in a 5–0 victory. The importance of the game was also taken into account.

Cristiano Ronaldo was at the top of the initial Capello Index, with an average score of 70.8, followed by Dani Alves in second place and Lionel Messi in third. In Capello's list of the world's leading defenders, Ledley King, Michael Dawson, Sol Campbell and Gary Neville were all in the top ten. But none of England's first-choice back four – Glen Johnson, John Terry, Rio Ferdinand and Ashley Cole – made the cut.

It was obvious immediately that the scheme was fraught with problems. The Capello Index would mark England players after every England World Cup match, and those marks would be available to the public within two hours of the final whistle. Even though, technically, it was the system devised by Capello that would mark the players rather than Capello himself, the danger was clear: the marks would be interpreted as Capello's judgement on an England player's individual performance.

Footballers are sensitive enough to those kinds of judgement anyway. They hate the marks out of ten so beloved of national newspapers. Reporters can write stinging criticism of a player, often without repercussions, but nothing is more likely to attract a barbed comment from a player, even an angry phone call, than a low mark in the ratings. Suddenly, England players were about to be confronted by a scenario where it was their manager who was doing the ratings.

It was also clear that those ratings would become one of the main talking points of the coverage of England every time they were published during the World Cup. After each England game, there would be a new burst of controversy. If the Capello Index awarded a player a bad mark, speculation would rage that he might be dropped for the next game. It would give a direct insight into Capello's thinking on each member of the team. It would be like being privy to one of his team talks. Or, even worse, being privy to what he said to his assistants, the kind of stuff he didn't want the players to hear.

The potential for division and dissension was obvious too. What if Frank Lampard scored a considerably lower mark than Steven Gerrard? What if Wayne Rooney's ratings compared unfavourably to Emile Heskey's? What if England were due to play Brazil and every single Brazil player rated higher than any England player on the Capello Index? How would Capello try to talk up England's chances to his players before that game?

And all this was set against the great football mantra that what goes on in the dressing room stays in the dressing room. Glenn Hoddle, a distant predecessor of Capello, was castigated for writing a diary that spilt details of, among other things, Paul Gascoigne's traumatised reaction to being left out of England's 1998 World Cup squad. His authority never recovered, and he was sacked soon after it was published, even though he administered the final blow to his credibility himself by musing on the sins the disabled had committed in former lives.

What Capello was threatening to do was shatter that dressing-room code on a weekly basis – not after the tournament, but during it. It begged the question: how could Capello demand confidentiality and discretion from his players when a ratings system bearing his name was beaming his opinion about his players around the world after every match?

Then there was the issue of whether Capello would profit from the index. He said he had no financial motive for committing himself to the scheme, but the entry fee for Capello XI, the online fantasy league game based on analysis from the Capello Index, varied between £29.99 and £199.99, with cash prizes for the most successful selections. It also emerged that Merighi, Capello's business partner, was chairman of Goal Ventures Ltd, a company that owns goaltipwin.com, an online sports betting website that advertises itself as 'the punter's ultimate tool'.

Capello had told the FA about his involvement in the scheme several weeks earlier, and Bevington, anticipating the media reaction, had urged Capello to withdraw from it. But the FA was going through one of its habitual periods of upheaval. Its chief executive, Ian Watmore, had resigned several weeks earlier over frustrations at obstacles to progress within the organisation, and its then chairman, Lord Triesman, was distracted by his workload as chairman of England's bid to host the 2018 World Cup. All the people with real authority were too busy to give it the attention it needed.

Nor did the FA want to alienate their manager on the eve of the World Cup. Capello was in a powerful position. He had delivered a near-flawless qualifying campaign and the media and the public loved him. He was a stubborn man, not easily dissuaded, so when he persisted with the Capello Index, perhaps the FA did not feel able to press the point.

It became clear even before he had left the Stock Exchange that Capello had made a serious error of judgement. After the initial announcement of the scheme, the England manager went into another room to conduct interviews with radio journalists, and then returned to speak to the press. He was not given an easy ride. Some of the best football and sports politics journalists in the country were in the room. The tone of the questions from men such as Charlie Sale of the *Daily Mail*, Shaun Custis of the *Sun*, and John Cross of the *Daily Mirror* left Capello in little doubt that the FA advice had been right.

Capello did his best to protest. He said he had not been paid in advance for his involvement and would only make money if the Capello Index was successful. 'It's not only for money,' he said. 'It is for the fans. Because of my interest in football. It's good for the fans and for me it's good. No problem, no pressure. It will be easy to speak with the players about their performances. I can say: "Look, your index is no good, you'll have to train more."'

Nobody was mollified by that explanation. In fact, the feeling of astonishment only grew. It was difficult to understand how Capello had walked into this without heeding the warnings of the FA. Worse, it was difficult to understand why he should have needed any warnings in the first place. It was not feasible for a manager of a leading international side to put his name to a scheme like this and preside over it during a World Cup if he wanted to keep his job. It was Capello's naivety that was as shocking as anything else. It was obvious that the reaction in the next day's newspapers would be hostile. Emails were sent to the FA hierarchy to warn them that, for the first time during Capello's tenure, the manager was about to attract heavy criticism.

The backlash was fierce. The country was wrestling with the issue of a hung parliament and the protracted and increasingly desperate negotiations of the leading parties as they tried to form a coalition. It was a time of great uncertainty and disillusionment with the political system and the party leaders. That Tuesday morning the country was still effectively without a prime minister. The front pages were occupied, but suddenly the back pages found themselves dealing with a power vacuum in the management of the England football team too.

The *Daily Mail* back page headline was typical. 'Rank Stupidity' it said. Most articles contained a mixture of disbelief that Capello, who had exercised such unswervingly good judgement until then, could have made such a crass mistake. Some had questioned whether he made the right call when he sacked John Terry as captain, but they were in a minority. This time, Capello's critics did not meet any opposition.

Capello was paid £6 million a year by the FA as part of a four-year deal that ran until 2012. That made him one of the best-rewarded coaches in the world. And yet he had allowed himself to become embroiled in a scheme that had links to online gaming and that cheapened his reputation. Suddenly, England supporters began to wonder if he was the antithesis of Eriksson after all or whether he too had succumbed to the temptation to try to cash in on the England job.

It was only a few months earlier that Terry had been pilloried by the media for using the England captaincy to advertise himself as a marketing weapon for leading companies. It was one of the reasons Terry's detractors said he was not fit to wear the armband. It was one of the reasons they applauded Capello for sacking him. Now the man they had looked to in order to set an example to the players had let them down as well.

The morning after the Stock Exchange launch, Capello met with several senior members of the FA at Wembley. Reluctantly, he accepted that the outcry meant it was impossible for him to be associated with the Capello Index during the World Cup. He conceded that his continued involvement would become a damaging distraction and, to the great relief of the FA representatives, he agreed to suspend his commitment to the project until after the tournament.

The FA and Capello's representatives began a damage limitation exercise. 'Fabio Capello's involvement has been purely as a technical expert to establish statistical criteria for the index,' a spokesman for Capello said. 'However, he wants to ensure that all appropriate protocols are in place before the project proceeds and has therefore decided to postpone it.'

But Capello's discomfort was not over yet. That afternoon he had to face the press again to discuss the 30 players he had selected for his provisional World Cup squad. The England coach was, as ever, immaculately dressed when he walked into the Wembley media auditorium, but his sharp blue suit could not hide the fact that he looked uncharacteristically vulnerable and unsure. It was the media's first chance to question him about his retreat from the Capello Index.

Because he was flustered, his grasp of the English language was worse than usual. Now and again the press conference lurched towards farce. When Capello was discussing the ankle ligament injury sustained by Barry, he said there would be an update on his progress on the 34th of May. It was pointed out to him that he probably meant the 24th. He nodded.

When he was asked about the Capello Index and whether he accepted he had made an error of judgement, Capello tried to deflect the question. 'This is a press conference for the 30 players I have chosen,' he said, before turning to Bevington, who was sitting beside him, for help. Bevington backed him up. 'We discussed it with Fabio over the last 24 hours and Fabio has made a decision to postpone it until after the World Cup,' Bevington said. 'That ends the debate.'

But Capello's air of invincibility had gone, and questions that journalists might have considered impertinent to ask a week earlier, questions they might have shrunk from for fear of alienating the great man, now seemed fair and reasonable. To their credit, Custis and Matt Lawton of the *Daily Mail* challenged his refusal to discuss the matter.

Capello grew impatient. He refused to admit he had made a mistake or even that his involvement with the Capello Index during the tournament could send out an unfortunate message. 'I think this, for me, is a press conference about these players,' he said. 'I read what you wrote. I know what you have to do. We decided what we have to do. That's it, finished, from me.'

It *was* finished too. There were some more critical headlines the next day. 'Slap Down' was the *Daily Mail*'s take on the fact that the FA had prevailed in their wish for Capello to distance himself from his marking system. But that was the end of it. If Capello had dithered, if he had refused to act, the story could have become his 'fake sheikh' moment. It could have created a serious problem. But his decision to withdraw from the scheme until after the World Cup denied the story the momentum it needed and it fizzled out. There was no evidence that his relationship with the England players had been damaged. Many of them were surprised when they heard about the Capello Index, but the furore was over almost before it had begun. Far from being scandalised, they were generally uninterested.

To the players, it was a distant prospect that had never become a reality. They never had to answer questions about it. They never had to suffer the awkwardness of being asked why they thought Capello had given them a bad mark. It did not get to the point where it could have affected their respect for their manager or undermined his ability to rule the squad as a dictator.

But it sowed a seed of doubt about Capello's judgement where before there had been none. And as the details began to emerge of how Capello had selected his squad of 30, the doubts grew.

8 | CHAOS MULTIPLIED BY 30

ABOUT the same time that Fabio Capello was unveiling the ill-fated Capello Index at the Stock Exchange, Paul Scholes answered the phone at his home on Saddleworth Moor, north of Manchester. Franco Baldini, Capello's assistant, was on the other end of the line. 'Hello, Paul,' Baldini said. 'How would you like to play in the World Cup?'

Scholes is a phlegmatic character but even he was taken aback by the offer. He did not know what to say. He was astonished. He was 35 years old and had made the last of his 66 appearances for England almost six years earlier in England's Euro 2004 quarter-final exit at the hands of hosts Portugal. He had got bored of being asked to play out of position on the left side of midfield by Sven-Goran Eriksson to accommodate Frank Lampard and Steven Gerrard, and he didn't enjoy being away from his wife and young children. So he retired from international football.

He was not the type of man to retire because he wanted to make a dramatic gesture. He hated attention. He didn't want to attract any more than was strictly necessary. He didn't retire in the hope that a manager would persuade him to return. He retired because he wanted to retire. Playing for Manchester United was what gave him most enjoyment, and he wanted to prolong his career at Old Trafford. Steve McClaren had tried to coax him back when he took over from Eriksson in 2006, but Scholes had told him he wouldn't change his mind.

Now, without any warning, and just 24 hours before Capello was to announce his provisional World Cup squad of 30 players, Baldini was on the phone. Maybe Scholes should have anticipated the call. A couple of weeks earlier, it had emerged that Jamie Carragher, the Liverpool defender who had turned his back on England duty in June 2007, had accepted the chance to return to play in South Africa. Carragher had had a miserable season with Liverpool, who had finished seventh in the Premier League, and decided Capello's offer would give him an opportunity of gaining some fulfilment from a hitherto barren year. He said he was relishing the chance to work with a man of Capello's stature.

Carragher's views on playing for his country made him a curious choice as a man for Capello to pursue. In an enthralling autobiography released after his international retirement, he had admitted that 'defeats wearing an England shirt never hurt me in the same way as losing with my club'. After he had missed a crucial penalty in the England World Cup quarter-final shoot-out against Portugal, he recalled, he sent a text message to former Liverpool boss Kenny Dalglish. 'I would rather miss for England than LFC,' it read.

Carragher wrote how, for him, civic pride was more important than nationality. He said he felt a huge weight lifting from his shoulders when he stopped playing for England. He criticised England fans, and said that although he had experienced instances where the Liverpool supporters had helped their side achieve a result, he could not recall the same happening when he had played for the national team.

Despite those sentiments, most people were instinctively pleased to see Carragher back in the squad. They accepted that he was articulating his love of Liverpool rather than distaste for England. And he had taken care to stress that he had never given less than his all in any form of football he had ever played. He was engaging, honest company, a man who would be a good tourist during the long weeks away in South Africa, and a player who could fill several roles in defence. In extremis, he might even be pressed into service as a holding midfield player. Capello's squad of 30 would be whittled down to a final 23 by 1 June, but everyone knew Carragher would be on the plane to South Africa. He wasn't coming out of international retirement just for ten days' training in Austria.

Encouraged by that success and panicked by the late realisation that both Gareth Barry and long-term injury absentee Owen Hargreaves were unlikely to be fit for the tournament, Capello decided to make one final attempt to persuade Scholes to play for England again. Scholes asked if he could think it over. Baldini told him he had until ten o'clock the next morning to make up his mind.

After two and a half years of steady planning, two and a half years of dogma about how players must be fit and in form to be selected, two and a half years of establishing a meritocracy within the squad, Capello had ripped up all his rules. First Carragher received an SOS, and now Scholes was called, out of the blue, and told he had less than 24 hours to make up his mind whether he wanted to play for England in the World Cup after six years in international retirement. Scholes was still a fine player, but this smacked of utter desperation.

Capello had panicked at the thought of losing Barry. The Manchester City midfielder was not a spectacular performer, but he had become one of Capello's most important players. He was a calm, efficient holding player, and his positional sense made him the key to allowing Frank Lampard and Steven Gerrard to play together successfully in the same midfield unit. The balance of the side was not as good without him.

But the approach to Scholes also betrayed a fundamental lack of understanding of the United veteran's personality. Scholes loves the game, but he hates the baggage that comes with being a star player. His loathing of interviews had become legendary. He only ever spoke to the media if he absolutely had to. He never, ever did one-on-one interviews with national newspapers. He didn't have an agent. He didn't get involved in sponsor commitments. His negotiations for a new contract once lasted 27 seconds – as long as it took for him to walk into the room, sit down and sign it.

So even if playing in the 2010 World Cup represented a football challenge for Scholes, the mania that would accompany England to Rustenburg would have been anathema to him. At his last major tournament in Portugal, he had been persuaded to do an interview with a group of newspaper chief sports writers before the group game against France on the basis that their reports were likely to be less inflammatory than others might be. But Scholes made a couple of jokey remarks about how Thierry Henry liked to talk a lot, and the headlines the next day were not quite what he had been expecting. 'Shut It,' the back page of the *Sun* proclaimed. It was the last England interview Scholes ever gave.

As he mulled over Capello's offer, the United midfielder also realised that if he walked straight back into the squad, he would feel as if he had cheated fellow professionals who had toiled for years to win the chance to go to a World Cup. He called Baldini the next morning and told him he was staying retired.

Later, Capello tried to pass off Scholes's decision as a simple matter of the player preferring to spend the summer with his family. He also tried to give the impression that Scholes had been aware of his intentions for some time. But Scholes gave a rare interview to his local newspaper, the *Oldham Evening Chronicle*, when he attended the opening of new changing rooms at a nearby club, Chadderton Park, and said that was not quite accurate. 'It was a big decision and I wasn't really given enough time to think about it, so I decided not to take up the offer,' he said. 'If they'd asked me earlier I probably would have accepted.

'There are players in the squad who have spent nearly two years flying all around the world helping England qualify for the World

Cup, whereas I haven't been involved for a long time. It wasn't a case of wanting to go on holiday, it was the fact that I got the call so close to the tournament, and also I didn't want to take the place of someone who helped get England to South Africa. The idea just didn't sit comfortably with me.'

The sense of order and discipline that Capello had built up in such painstaking fashion was collapsing around him. When he should have been putting the finishing touches to his squad that morning, he was locked in meetings with FA officials about the Capello Index. The man who preached no distractions could not help but be distracted.

The news of Capello's desperate offer and Scholes's rejection of it had been leaked by the time Capello walked into the press auditorium at Wembley on Tuesday afternoon. Already on the defensive about being forced to withdraw from the Capello Index, he now found himself having to try to justify a selection process for his initial 30-man World Cup squad that had descended into chaos.

There were also other issues, apart from the desperate late call to Scholes, that chipped away at the manager's hard shell. Capello had told journalists in his press conference at the Stock Exchange the day before that there was no way Barry would recover from his ankle ligament injury. 'Too long, too long,' he had said dismissively. But when the list of 30 names was released the next morning, Barry's was among them. The press were furious that they had been misled. For the first time under Capello's tenure as England manager, the mood was hostile and confrontational when he walked into the Wembley auditorium.

Like most other people, football writers have an aversion to being made to look stupid. After Capello's guidance about Barry, many had written stories suggesting that not only was Barry out, but that Owen Hargreaves, who had suffered chronic knee problems and had not kicked a ball for England since appearing in a friendly against the

USA in May 2008, was to be handed a dramatic recall. When the list of names was announced, Barry was in and Hargreaves was out.

There were other glaring problems with the squad that looked like mistakes a novice would make. There were three left-backs and only one right-back, Glen Johnson. Johnson was injury-prone, and his first-choice back-up appeared to be Carragher, who didn't like playing right-back. In fact, one of the reasons Carragher had retired from international football in the first place was because he had been asked to fill in as a full-back instead of playing in his preferred role in the centre of defence.

The logic for including three left-backs was flawed too. Capello said he had picked both Leighton Baines and Stephen Warnock, who had two caps between them, because Ashley Cole was still recovering from injury. But Cole had been fully fit for several weeks and was fresh from a fine 90-minute performance for Chelsea in the previous Sunday's 8–0 demolition of Wigan Athletic, which had sealed the Premier League title for Carlo Ancelotti's side. In those circumstances, including both Baines and Warnock and leaving out right-sided cover like Gary Neville made little sense.

Neville's omission was puzzling too. Despite the reservations Capello had expressed about him after the first leg of United's Champions League tie against Bayern Munich, Neville had looked as if he was recovering his form and fitness as the season drew to a close. His experience would have been invaluable in South Africa too. The way Capello's mind seemed to be working, maybe Neville would have had a better chance of making the squad if he had retired from international football a couple of years before.

Things got stranger. Having had more than two years to hone his choice, Capello picked five players – Carragher, Michael Dawson, Ledley King, Adam Johnson and Scott Parker – who had never appeared in one of his sides before. It would have been six if the Fulham forward Bobby Zamora had responded positively to

Capello's overtures, but the England boss apparently did not realise that Zamora was about to have an operation for an Achilles' injury. Zamora told Capello he would love to go to South Africa but he couldn't. If he had known he was under consideration for a place in the party, something Capello had never intimated, he would have had the operation earlier in the season.

Anarchy had swamped Capello when everyone least expected it. The selection process was a shambles. It soon emerged that Hargreaves, who had played 30 seconds of league football for United in the 2009–10 season, had only been left out of the squad after the England manager had spoken to Sir Alex Ferguson at the League Managers' Association dinner at the London Marriott Hotel in Grosvenor Square the previous night. Ferguson had told Capello that Hargreaves was nowhere near ready to return to international football. Joe Cole, who would have been left out of the 30, was hurriedly pencilled back in.

Amid more confusion, Capello was then told that there was a chance Barry might recover from his ankle ligament injury in time to play in the tournament after all. England's medical team had been informed that Barry's next assessment on the injury was due to be undertaken on 30 May, which would have been too late for Barry to merit consideration. But at the Wembley press conference, Capello said it now seemed he would get an update on Barry's condition on 24 May.

Again, the logic for Barry's inclusion seemed questionable. Capello might have been desperate for him to make it, but Barry had told friends there was no way he would be fit for the World Cup. Even though initial estimates had put his recovery time at one month, the suggestion was that his injury was similar to the one Robin Van Persie had sustained playing for Holland against Italy in November 2009. Van Persie said he would be out for six weeks. He didn't come back for six months.

So a selection process that had promised to be straightforward was anything but. There was nothing that smacked of recklessness in the way that Eriksson's selection of Theo Walcott had done four years earlier, but there was both unease and surprise at the way Capello's assuredness and authority had unravelled when the late injury to Barry had disrupted his planning. The desperation calls to Carragher and Scholes were his Walcott moments.

Some good players had missed out. Paul Robinson, the Blackburn Rovers goalkeeper, did not make the 30. Neither did Gary and Phil Neville, nor Wes Brown, the Manchester United defender. The Aston Villa forwards Ashley Young and Gabriel Agbonlahor, who had once seemed strong candidates to be in the final squad, had fallen from favour. So had their teammate Stewart Downing, and the West Ham striker Carlton Cole. Nor was there a place for Phil Jagielka, the Everton defender who had recovered from a serious knee injury.

Those omissions underlined the fact that England would still be taking a strong squad to South Africa. If uncertainty had characterised some of his selections, Capello had also been true to his word about picking players in form when it came to others. Adam Johnson made the 30. That was a bold choice. So was the inclusion of Michael Dawson. And Scott Parker's selection was a reward for the way he had helped drag West Ham clear of relegation.

Joe Cole made it – just. So did Darren Bent and Shaun Wright-Phillips, although it was hard to see Wright-Phillips ousting Walcott or Aaron Lennon when it came to the final 23. Michael Carrick had sneaked in too, but it was a measure of how far his stock had fallen that there were suggestions that if Barry did not make it, Capello would turn to Huddlestone to fill the role of holding midfielder in his starting line-up rather than the United player.

Seven players were to be cut from the list after England's final international warm-up match against Japan in Graz. The favourites for that cull were Warnock, Dawson, Parker, Barry (because of his injury), Wright-Phillips, Joe Cole and Bent. The squad of 30 was due to leave the following Monday for a fortnight of training in Austria, punctuated by a Wembley friendly against Mexico on 24 May and the game against the Japanese on 30 May.

But the chaos was not quite over yet for Capello. The day after the announcement of his provisional squad, John Terry, who was training with Chelsea at Cobham in the run-up to the FA Cup Final, collided with Daniel Sturridge as Terry was running back towards goal. The two men fell to the ground and Terry's right foot was trapped underneath Sturridge's body. Terry usually shrugs off the kind of knocks that cause other players to writhe on the floor in pain, but this time he was in obvious distress.

He was helped off the training pitch and taken to hospital. He thought he had broken a metatarsal, and the news was relayed to Capello that his former captain appeared to be out of the World Cup. For a player who had suffered so much adversity already, it seemed like a particularly cruel blow. It had been bad enough to be denied the dream of lifting the World Cup as skipper, and now this. It felt as though he had been cursed.

All sorts of thoughts must have been rushing through Capello's mind. If Terry was out, that was probably the end of any lingering hopes England had of winning the World Cup. Ferdinand, Terry's central defensive partner, was an injury worry. So was King, the first choice to step in for Terry. Upson was struggling for form, Dawson was untested, Carragher had not played international football for three years. Capello knew Terry's absence would be a blow that would be hard to overcome.

Terry had a CT scan at the hospital. He had convinced himself he was out of the World Cup, but the scan appeared to show that he had suffered only bad bruising. He left with his foot in a protective boot and released a statement saying he had suffered a 'minor knock' in training. He said that not only would he be available for the World Cup, he intended to play in the Cup Final for Chelsea against Portsmouth that Saturday.

Worries persisted, though. Nobody was quite sure Terry was really injury-free. He was desperate to lead Chelsea to the first Double in their history, desperate to win another trophy to keep wiping away the memory of everything that had befallen him earlier in the season. If he were injured, he would not show it or admit it until after the final.

The game soothed the fears. Terry was superb in Chelsea's 1–0 victory. One soaring leap in the first half, when he planted a header against the Portsmouth bar, calmed any concerns about his ability to put his full weight on his right foot. Portsmouth did their best to rough Chelsea up, and Terry did not shirk any physical challenges. He was fine. Capello breathed a sigh of relief. But as Terry was lifting the trophy above his head, another crisis was unfolding.

9 | THE WIRE

TWO hours before the FA Cup Final, Adrian Bevington received a text message on his mobile phone. He read it and frowned. He was hosting a table in the FA Club on one of the upper levels of Wembley Stadium and had invited a few journalists, colleagues, the Sky presenter Chris Kamara and Darren Bent's father, Mervyn, to eat with him. Bevington got up from the table and made his apologies. He said he would be gone for some time.

He had just been warned that the *Mail on Sunday* was planning to run a story the next day about Lord Triesman, whose posts included FA chairman and chairman of England's bid to host the 2018 World Cup. Triesman had been secretly taped by Melissa Jacobs, a woman he considered a friend, airing conspiracy theories about rival 2018 bidders Spain and Russia.

During a lunch and gossip at London patisserie Paul in Marylebone High Street, Triesman had told Miss Jacobs, who had fitted herself with a wire and secret microphone, that he had heard Spain was enlisting the help of Russia to bribe referees at the World Cup in South Africa in return for Spain withdrawing its candidature for 2018 and supporting Russia's bid.

It was obvious immediately that it would be impossible for Triesman to remain in positions of authority at the FA. It was a clear case of entrapment by Miss Jacobs, and it was questionable whether the publication of Triesman's views during a private conversation were in the public interest. But once they had found their way on to the front page of a national newspaper, the resulting furore made his position as a senior FA executive untenable.

It was unclear quite what Miss Jacobs' motivation was for duping Lord Triesman. She claimed that she and the 66-year-old peer had had a six-month affair some time earlier, which she had subsequently ended when she grew to feel guilty about conducting a relationship with a married man who also had a young child. She had kept scores of flirtatious text messages from Triesman. It was also reported that she had been paid £75,000 by the *Mail on Sunday*.

The matter was concluded quickly. Bid chief executive Andy Anson and his team worked through the night to try to limit the damage. Letters of apology were faxed to the football associations of Spain and Russia. England's bid leaders distanced themselves from Triesman and stressed that the opinions he had expressed were not representative of the bid as a whole. By Sunday afternoon, Triesman had resigned as chairman of the bid and as chairman of the FA.

On Monday morning the daily papers fell upon the story with a mixture of glee, grief and *schadenfreude*. Many in football found Triesman smug and self-satisfied. The award-winning *Daily Mail* columnist Martin Samuel, one of football's most influential voices, had referred to him unswervingly as 'Lord PleasedMan' in his columns. Triesman had also made enemies at the Premier League for having the impertinence to criticise the level of debt its clubs had run up.

The *Sun*'s front page accused Triesman of ruining England's chances of hosting the 2018 World Cup. 'Lord Treason' its banner headline said. Others were just as unforgiving. Most agreed that Triesman's remarks had caused England's bid serious embarrassment at the very least. The more pessimistic said that his gossiping had done irreparable damage and that England's chances of success were effectively over.

In fact, once Triesman had resigned, it was evident that there was little real cause for further displeasure to be visited on England's 2018 candidature. Unless Fifa wanted to use Triesman's embarrassment as a stick to beat England with, what he had said was an irrelevance. It was hardly as if Triesman's views were germane to the English bid. What he said about Spain and Russia did not alter the fact that England could offer superb stadia and passionate fans. Nor did his claims threaten any impact on the huge profits the England bid was promising it could deliver for Fifa after pioneering tournaments in South Africa and Brazil in 2014. Fifa said its ethics committee would have to investigate. Some said a Fifa ethics committee was an oxymoron.

The Triesman story prompted two wider debates. The first was whether there was any truth in what he had said about Spain, Russia and bribery. The initial suggestion recorded in Triesman's conversation with Miss Jacobs, that Spain would try to influence referees in South Africa, seemed outlandish. For a start, if there was one team that did not need the help of officials, it was the Spanish. They were good enough to win without help. It sounded like a conspiracy too far.

But Triesman was far from being the first high-ranking football official to voice fears about the influence of Russian money in football's decision-making processes. Most journalists who covered the politics of sport had had conversations with Fifa officials or Uefa apparatchiks or executives from national football associations that had involved references, joking or otherwise, to Russians bearing brown paper bags stuffed with money.

Rightly or wrongly, many believed Russia had already bought the right to host the 2018 World Cup. The vote to decide the host country was not due to be held until December 2010 in Zurich, but there were plenty who believed the competition was already over. There was no proof, certainly no evidence, that anyone was willing to corroborate, and it might have been that the idea of Russia corrupting the system was just a lazy stereotype. But Triesman was merely repeating theories others had expounded.

If England's bid team had not been so desperate to move on from the Triesman affair and wipe his words from history, they might have suggested that instead of investigating England 2018 on the tenuous grounds it could have broken rules forbidding commenting on rival bids, maybe Fifa should turn its attention to Triesman's allegations and make a proper effort to establish whether they had any substance. That never happened.

A second debate raged more fiercely. It centred on the destructive tendencies of the English media, particularly the press, in the build-up to important sporting events and decisions. The *Mail on Sunday*'s decision to publish the details of the private conversation between Lord Triesman and Miss Jacobs, which she had presented to the paper, attracted furious and immediate criticism.

The *Mail*'s own website was deluged with comments at the bottom of the Triesman story that accused the newspaper of engaging in the most unscrupulous and unprincipled form of journalism, and, in the process, damaging England's hopes of staging a tournament that millions of the country's football fans were looking forward to as a landmark in their lives.

Callers to the many and varied phone-ins on the BBC radio station 5 Live sent out the same message. They were angrier with the *Mail on Sunday* than they were with Lord Triesman. Some said they would boycott the paper and its daily counterpart. The *Guardian*'s media commentator, Roy Greenslade, said the *Mail on Sunday*'s decision to publish the story was starting to look like a huge mistake. 'I'm beginning to wonder,' Greenslade wrote, 'whether it could lead to a boycott of *Sun*–Hillsborough proportions because of growing outrage from all manner of people.'

There was still some confusion over exactly how the *Mail on Sunday* had procured the story. One version was that they had fitted

Miss Jacobs with her recording equipment and sent her into battle at the Paul patisserie, expecting a mere kiss-and-tell involving the dirty old man at the top of the FA and his middle-aged mistress. Instead, when they listened to the tape, they found they had a highly significant sports story on their hands.

The *Mail on Sunday* denied that. 'We would also like to make it clear,' the newspaper said in a statement, 'that Melissa Jacobs put details of her relationship with Lord Triesman on the Internet, and made her recording of her conversation with him without the knowledge or involvement of the *Mail on Sunday*. There is no question of entrapment, the paper was simply reporting events that had already taken place.'

Miss Jacobs had indeed put some details of her relationship with Triesman on the Internet, albeit referring to him in code as Mr T. It made uncomfortable reading including intimate descriptions of trysts in her Pimlico flat and revelations that she had mental health issues.

Those details cast further doubt on the wisdom of the *Mail on Sunday*'s readiness to publish her secretly recorded conversation with Lord Triesman, but it was disingenuous of other media outlets to criticise the newspaper too harshly. There were suggestions that the story had been turned down by the *News of the World* and the *Sunday Mirror*. Other newspapers that had been supporting England's 2018 bid for some time would also have been squeamish about purchasing Miss Jacobs' recording.

These were murky waters. It was a shabby form of journalism, certainly, but the *Mail on Sunday* was hardly alone in espousing it. Miss Jacobs deserved opprobrium for her treachery, but if her account of an affair with Lord Triesman were true – he insisted their relationship amounted to nothing more than the odd peck on the cheek on parting – he was hardly to be lionised either.

Some argued that the repercussions alone of the story justified the decision to print it. The FA chairman resigned his post over it. The rest of the 2018 bid leaders considered his comments, whether they were made in private or not, irresponsible enough to cut Triesman loose with indecent haste. The FA, English football's governing body, was plunged into chaos. In terms of setting the agenda, the story was a spectacular success.

But the *Mail on Sunday* appeared to be deeply unsettled by the hostile reaction to its decision to publish the conversation between Triesman and Miss Jacobs. Triesman's observations on a variety of other matters, including, it is believed, unflattering opinions of some of his adversaries at the Premier League, had been held back for publication the following Sunday. But this time the *Mail on Sunday* lost its nerve and shrank from printing them. It was interpreted as an admission of error.

In the furore that enveloped football on that FA Cup Final weekend, it went almost unnoticed that Miss Jacobs was represented in her negotiations with the *Mail on Sunday* by the publicity agent Max Clifford, the same man who had advised Vanessa Perroncel when the story broke about her alleged affair with John Terry. Clifford is a go-to guy in cases like this, but his involvement with Miss Jacobs nevertheless begged the question of whether there were other links between the two cases.

The fear when Fabio Capello stripped Terry of the England captaincy was that it would make other players more vulnerable to kiss-and-tell stings in the run-up to the World Cup. In some ways, Lord Triesman was distinctly B-list compared to the England skipper, but in terms of tabloid exposés, he was still a trophy. Maybe Miss Jacobs had felt empowered when she saw the havoc Miss Perroncel wrought. Maybe she felt encouraged by the stories of the sums Miss Perroncel was supposed to have earned from the whole affair.

Others certainly saw a link between the two stories. Gary Lineker,

England's second-highest goal-scorer and the BBC's football anchor man, said he would no longer be writing his regular column in the *Mail on Sunday* in protest at the paper's decision to print Lord Triesman's unguarded comments. Lineker, an ambassador for England's 2018 bid, said he could no longer work for a paper that had damaged that bid. Then he opened a new front in the battle over the story. He said that sometimes it seemed as if the press was hell-bent on destroying the reputation of England players in the run-up to World Cups rather than supporting them.

Lineker, who wrote for the *Sunday Telegraph* before moving to the *Mail on Sunday*, claimed there was 'some sort of thirst for negative stories' before a major football competition, and called on the country at large to encourage newspapers to behave more responsibly. 'They all seem to champion the national side and show patriotism, but when push comes to shove and they have the opportunity of selling an extra few newspapers, at times I think they will make errors of judgement in stories that are basically just private issues. It can affect their confidence and the overall performance of the national team on the pitch, let alone the bid to actually stage the competition.'

The relationship between the English press and the English players before major tournaments is a familiar theme in recent football history. Most of Bobby Robson's team refused to speak to journalists at the 1990 World Cup in Italy because of allegations about some players' sex lives that had surfaced in the build-up to the tournament. Before Euro '96, the players made the front pages again after a wild night out during their pre-tournament trip to Hong Kong, when they participated in a drinking game that involved sitting in a dentist's chair and having shots poured down their throats. Before the 1998 World Cup, Teddy Sheringham was pilloried when he was pictured smoking a cigarette on a night out in Portugal, and Paul Gascoigne sealed his exclusion from Glenn Hoddle's final squad when a photographer snapped him eating a kebab after a drunken evening in Soho.

Many fans agreed with Lineker. Mark Perryman, one of the leaders of the London England Fans group, said patience with the English press was wearing thin among supporters. 'Most fans are rather fed up with a press that is out to gun our captain, our manager, and now the chairman of the FA,' Perryman told the BBC. 'The front page of one of the newspapers was "Lord Treason". I'd actually say "Daily Treason", that's how I would name one of our papers.'

As one of the new wave of England fans who helped to transform the image of the country's travelling supporters, Perryman's views deserved to be heard. After the dark days of England fans laying waste to countries they visited in the 1980s and 1990s, and at Euro 2000, Perryman had helped to ensure that the voice of the majority of decent fans drowned out the screams of the minority of hooligans.

He organised cultural exchanges during journeys to away games. England fans visited schools in countries where England were playing to swap football memorabilia and try to reassure local children that their hooligan reputation was no longer warranted. Perryman was also an articulate front-man for fans' groups when supporter-related issues were in the news.

But the attitude of the press towards the England team is not as destructive as Perryman and Lineker suggested. The reason, for instance, that there are more stories about the country's star footballers in the run-up to a tournament is the same reason that Tesco plastered giant Cross of St George stickers across the floors of their stores a few weeks before the World Cup in South Africa began, and the same reason why Nike released an advert featuring its leading football icons in the last week of May.

The point is that public interest in football and footballers is at its height in the build-up to the World Cup, and commercial organisations react accordingly. An overwhelming percentage of the stories about the England team in the English newspapers in the weeks before the tournament are positive. Even the day after Capello gave his shambolic performance at the press conference to discuss his 30-man squad, the main headline on the *Daily Mail*'s sports coverage was 'Fabio's Pride of Lions'.

Capello had had two and a half years of uninterrupted good publicity until the blip of the Capello Index. None of the papers wanted to ruin him. They wanted the opposite. He had met most newspaper editors and sports editors since he had taken charge, some of them several times, and all had been impressed. The football writers liked him too. He didn't treat one better than another, he didn't give an interview to *The Times* but not the *Guardian*. He was fair and matter-of-fact, the players seemed to respect him, and he achieved superb results in qualifying. For everyone in newspapers that was more than enough. In fact, English newspaper journalists are often accused of being jingoistic fantasists too. Those who tipped England to win the World Cup in South Africa were castigated for raising expectations to unrealistic levels and heaping pressure on the players.

But although newspaper journalists and sports editors are sometimes cheerleaders when it comes to the England team, they do not wear blinkers. So when they were confronted with the Capello Index, a scheme that in both its timing and conception was manifestly idiotic, they criticised Capello's involvement in it. To do otherwise, to have tried to hush it up or pretend it didn't exist or that Capello had no interest in it, would have been wrong and dishonest.

It would also have been to neglect their duty. At its best, the press keeps football's players and managers honest. In a football era where greed is king, there are not many checks and balances. A free press is one. If the English press had turned a blind eye to the Capello Index, if they had been too obsequious to write about it and it had been allowed to proceed, it would have caused disharmony in the England camp and damaged morale during the World Cup. The intervention of the newspapers stopped that happening by forcing Capello to abandon his part in the venture.

The same logic applies to pre-tournament stories about players. The vast majority are positive. The week after the FA Cup Final, Capello took his 30-man squad to Austria to train at altitude in the mountains. A day was set aside for the media to visit the training camp at Irdning, a two-hour coach journey from Graz, and they were allowed to speak to Jamie Carragher, Rio Ferdinand, Peter Crouch and Steven Gerrard. The interviews appeared in the daily papers throughout the week and they were uniformly supportive of the players and Capello.

The press does not set out deliberately to damage an individual player. It certainly does not aim to undermine squad morale. In fact, after the angst caused by the John Terry–Wayne Bridge affair, one reporter at a News International title was told to forget about a story he had got that reflected badly on another England player. Even then, several months before the tournament, some newspapers were growing nervous about carrying negative England pieces.

There are other problems with the Lineker theory of press damage. The most inconvenient is that the press is neither as critical nor as destructive as England fans. Frank Lampard is a darling of the media, always helpful, always courteous and a world-class midfielder as well, yet there was a period when he was singled out for abuse by England fans. The same applied to Peter Crouch and Owen Hargreaves.

At Premier League grounds it is common for supporters to walk past the press box and berate journalists for being consistently critical of their team. 'Are you going to write something nice about us today?' is the most popular form of query. Fans of every club are convinced the press hates their side, but the truth is just that journalists don't love the club as much as the fans do. They can't. It's their job to be objective, not subjective.

Some journalists can be vindictive. So can some supporters. A couple of seasons ago, when Arsenal fans booed Emmanuel Eboue so lustily that Arsène Wenger took pity and substituted him, even though he had come on as a substitute himself, the same fans used their next breaths to turn their anger on the press box for not being supportive enough of their team.

Journalists write nice things about Manchester United, Chelsea, Arsenal and other leading clubs every day because, most of the time, those clubs are playing fine football and winning matches. Journalists respond to what they see. Most of them do not have hidden agendas. The media might make plenty of mistakes, but it also acts as a useful scapegoat for supporters in times of adversity. Some fans cloak their frustrations with their side in resentment of the media.

But it is absurd to suggest that if an England player is involved in a high-profile incident away from the football pitch and it is brought to the attention of a newspaper that that newspaper should ignore it because it would somehow help the England team win the World Cup. English newspapers would like nothing more than for England to win the World Cup. Their circulations, which get a massive boost during football tournaments anyway, stay buoyant as long as England are in the tournament. England actually winning the thing is every newspaper executive's dream. Still, however much an England World Cup victory might boost flagging circulations, it is not the job of newspapers to help England win the World Cup. It is the job of newspapers to report the news, and England footballers are, most definitely, news.

They are as newsworthy now as film stars and pop idols. They are A-list celebrities. They live in the biggest houses and eat at the best restaurants and party at the trendiest West End discos with Prince Harry. The post-Taylor Report English football boom of the 1990s created them, and they have survived and prospered in the Premier League limelight. They have profited handsomely from newspaper coverage and the interest of glossy magazines such as

Hello! and *OK!* They have encouraged that coverage. They have coveted it. They have been complicit in it. So when they make the headlines for the wrong reasons, they are not victims of a newspaper vendetta, but simply working inhabitants of the lucrative and narcissistic world they fell in love with.

Some of them accepted that they have to take the rough with the smooth. David Beckham always did. But others found it more difficult. Ashley Cole raged against it. He posed with his wife Cheryl in a white shirt unbuttoned to the waist to advertise the National Lottery in 2006, and collected half a million pounds from *OK!* for their wedding pictures. But when his marriage fell apart after allegations that he had been unfaithful, he turned on the photographers who were jostling for pictures of him in his misery. 'You ruined my life,' he told them as he convalesced from an ankle injury in the south of France. He forgot that they had played a part in constructing his life too.

Sometimes the justification for printing stories about footballers' private lives is flimsy, but when a player has constructed an image of himself that is false and that has made him millions of pounds, it is possible to argue that it is in the public interest to reveal details about the player if those details show that he is, in fact, an entirely different man from the one his publicity suggested.

Tiger Woods proved that point. Woods made tens of millions of dollars from endorsements on the basis of a clean-cut, wholesome, business-like image that had been painstakingly constructed and aggressively protected. When it became obvious that Woods was not quite what advertisers and, more importantly, consumers had thought him to be, many of his sponsors dropped him. They felt the real Woods was not worthy of their patronage, thus justifying the *National Enquirer*'s exposure of his double life at a stroke.

In the two weeks before the World Cup, the celebrities whose private lives were most under scrutiny were not England footballers, but the pop singer Ronan Keating and Sarah, Duchess of York, for various misdemeanours, sexual and financial. It is part of the modern psyche to search for instant judgements; the pre-eminence of the entertainment mogul Simon Cowell, whose appeal is based on his cruelty, is evidence of that. Footballers are not singled out for special treatment; they are just the same as every other celebrity – fed into the grinder when they screw up.

10 THE FINAL COUNTDOWN

WHEN the England squad left for their pre-World Cup training camp in Austria the Monday after the FA Cup Final, there were two groups of notable absentees. The first was the five Chelsea and Portsmouth players in the 30-man party, who were granted a couple of extra days' rest. The second was the Wags. Under previous regimes, the players' families had accompanied them on pre-tournament visits to Dubai, Sardinia and Vale do Lobo to cushion the blow of their impending separation. Fabio Capello dispensed with that tradition, as everyone knew he would. The Wags stayed at home.

Austria might not have been their scene anyway. This was not a sunshine break at a beach resort. Capello took the squad to Irdning, high in the Austrian Alps, as a form of altitude training to prepare them for the conditions they might experience during the tournament. Two of England's three group games – against Algeria in Cape Town and against Slovenia in Port Elizabeth – were at sea level, but the opening match against the USA in Rustenburg was at altitude, and if England progressed, there was a good chance they would play in Johannesburg, also at altitude, in the quarter-finals.

The media were allowed a brief visit. They flew to Graz on the Wednesday evening, took the two-hour coach journey to Irdning on Thursday morning, were given access to four players, and then embarked on the journey home. The press were particularly interested in Jamie Carragher and his reasons for abandoning international retirement. He spoke of the chance of playing under a manager of Capello's stature and the opportunity to compete in another World Cup. And he admitted that after everything he had written about playing for England in his autobiography, he was expecting a rough ride from the fans at Wembley when England played against Mexico in their final home game before the tournament the following Monday.

Capello worked the players hard in Irdning. England were to play friendlies against Mexico at Wembley on 24 May, and Japan in Graz on 30 May, before they left for South Africa. Training was more intense than at previous pre-tournament get-togethers, and Capello took an active, hands-on approach to the sessions at the small town's tiny ATV Arena. The squad stayed at a handsome five-star resort, the Hotel Schloss Pichlarn, but discipline was strict there too. The players were not allowed as much time socialising with each other as they were accustomed to. The height of Capello's indulgence in the week leading up to the Mexico game was to permit them nine holes of golf on the hotel course.

As the weekend grew nearer, speculation about Capello's line-up against Mexico increased. The England coach was notoriously hard to read in terms of his team selections, partly because his habit of telling his players who was in the team only two hours before a game prevented the chance of it being leaked to the newspapers the night before. But the side he picked against Mexico was bound to give some clues about who was likely to make his final 23, which was to be announced on 1 June, and who would be in his starting line-up for the first World Cup game against the USA on 12 June.

Many assumed Carragher would start at right-back. Others were confident Wayne Rooney would be left out because Capello was worried about him aggravating the niggling injuries he was carrying on Wembley's notoriously treacherous pitch. Some argued that Theo Walcott would start on the right and Aaron Lennon on the left as Capello experimented with using the blistering pace of both in the same side. And, whether Rooney played or not, no one was quite sure whether Peter Crouch or Emile Heskey, would play in attack. Or whether they would play at all.

Initially, most interest centred on the international return of King after such a long absence. Some thought Capello would deploy him as a holding midfielder in the absence of Gareth Barry, who had stayed in England for treatment rather than fly to Austria with the rest of the squad, but when the team sheets were released to the media an hour before kick-off, it was clear that he would play alongside Rio Ferdinand, hardly a picture of health himself, in the centre of defence.

Great things were expected of the Spurs centre-half. England supporters had grown familiar with the lapses of Rio Ferdinand, and some were worried about John Terry's form, but confidence in King seemed to have grown in inverse proportion to the number of games he played. There were nagging concerns about England's defence, and the excellence of King's occasional performances for Tottenham had persuaded many that he could be the saviour of the back four.

But King was a disappointment against Mexico. He looked exactly what he was: a defender with bad knees. He was one-paced. He was ponderous. So was Ferdinand. King scored England's opening goal with a header from a corner, but at the back he looked out of place. He was fooled early on by a sweet turn from the former West Ham United forward Guillermo Franco, who had hardly injected fear into Premier League defences, and King found it hard to recover. He said afterwards that he needed more time to get fit. The former England manager Terry Venables, writing in the *Sun*, said the match had persuaded him that King didn't deserve to be in the final 23.

King's return was an anti-climax. So was the game. It had been billed as a big send-off for the England squad, their last home game before they left for South Africa nine days later, and David Beckham, who had been offered an unspecified coaching role by Capello, was sitting behind the dug-out wearing an England blazer, but still the atmosphere was muted. Capello's stern face gazing down on the fans from a massive poster as they walked to the stadium set the tone. The England manager's expression seemed to be a warning that this was no time for celebration. Every supporter found a red or white T-shirt on their seat so that they could wear it and form a giant St George's Cross for the cameras in the air, but that was the limit of the pomp on offer.

England won the match 3–1 with goals from King, Crouch and Glen Johnson, who had a superb game at right-back and was named the man-of-the-match. But England's performance raised more questions than it answered. Capello was grateful to Robert Green for two good one-on-one saves from Carlos Vela, the Arsenal winger. Better, more experienced players, would have scored. The stadium announcer's decision to play 'Rule the World' by Take That as England embarked on an awkward lap of honour in front of a half-empty stadium after the match attracted much wry comment the next morning. England might have won, but their fellow finalists, Mexico, had played the better football.

England's performance did nothing to ease worries about who would replace Barry if his desperate battle to regain fitness was unsuccessful. Capello had to choose between Michael Carrick, Tom Huddlestone and Scott Parker to audition for Barry's place against Mexico. Huddlestone and Parker had both finished the season strongly for their club sides, Spurs and West Ham, and Huddlestone in particular had attracted a growing band of admirers who felt he was ready to claim a position in the starting line-up. But Capello went for Carrick.

Carrick was a fine midfielder, a brilliant passer of the ball, a clever reader of the game, and the provider of the occasional crucial goal. But he had also developed a tendency to go missing on the big occasions, and there were rumours that Sir Alex Ferguson blamed him more than any other player for Manchester United's dismal showing in the 2009 Champions League final against Barcelona in Rome, when United were overwhelmed by the Catalans. The way Carrick played for United in the 2009–10 season suggested he was still haunted by that failure.

There was some surprise that Capello had even included him in the squad of 30, so Carrick needed to have a big night against Mexico to strengthen his chances of making the final 23. But the big night never came. Playing alongside James Milner, who was deputising for Frank Lampard, Carrick had a poor game. His passing was awry, his confidence diminished every time he wasted possession, and gradually he disappeared from the game. When he was substituted after an hour, many believed he had blown his chance.

Huddlestone did not do a lot better, and Parker didn't even get off the bench. It was a measure of the concern about the balance of the central midfield that Capello was asked after the game whether he would consider playing Lampard and Steven Gerrard together again at the heart of the team. Capello evaded the question a couple of times, but eventually he made it clear he did not believe the two players could form an effective partnership in the middle of the pitch.

Eriksson and McClaren had both persevered with Lampard and Gerrard, refusing to believe that two such talented players could not work out a way of producing an effective blend. But both men rarely reproduced their club form when they played together for England. Their inability to form a partnership became one of England's great unresolved dilemmas. Capello showed no inclination to go back to a system that had failed before. It was obvious that Gerrard, who had been forced to play in a wider position on the left-hand side by Capello, would have relished a return to the centre, but Capello appeared to rule that out.

He preferred to see Gerrard further forward, he said, and believed that he had limited effectiveness as a deeper-lying player. His comments hinted at sympathy with those who argued that Gerrard did not possess the necessary discipline to play as a holding midfielder. Playing Lampard and Gerrard together in the centre, he felt, would leave England too exposed to an opponent's counter-attack.

And so, over the next few days, the spotlight returned to Barry. The day after the Mexico game, the Manchester City midfielder had more tests on his injured ankle, and the FA announced that the results had been encouraging enough to persuade Capello to wait right up until 1 June before he made a decision about him. England had another of its World Cup injury fights on its hands, but there was a sharp contrast between the low-key coverage allotted to Barry's efforts and the stop-the-clocks attitude that had characterised the obsession over whether David Beckham and Wayne Rooney were going to recover in time for previous tournaments.

The nation was not urged to pray for the Barry ankle in the way it had been begged to for the Beckham foot in 2002. There were no life-size cut-outs of Barry's ankle in the newspapers so that supporters could rub them in an attempt at the kind of mass-healing that had been advocated with Rooney's foot in 2006. Uri Geller did not appear on GMTV calling on all England to unleash its powers of restoration on Barry's damaged ligaments.

Nor was there a squadron of news helicopters flying above Barry's car on the way to the hospital where he had his tests. The 24-hour rolling news channels had turned Rooney's journey to a private hospital in Manchester in 2006 into an event imbued with all the drama of O.J. Simpson's flight from Los Angeles in his white Ford Bronco. But no one even knew where Barry's tests were being conducted. Or, if they did, they didn't bother saying. Nor were there batteries of television cameras to film him emerging from the hospital.

Yet there was an argument that Barry was as important to England's chances of success in 2010 as Beckham and Rooney had been in Japan and Germany. Barry did not have the same charisma as Beckham or Rooney. He was not the star of the new Nike World

Cup advert like Rooney was. He could not change a game with a moment of breathtaking brilliance like Rooney could.

There was nothing spectacular about Barry. He had only broken into the side in the first place because the career of Owen Hargreaves, the country's leading holding player, had been affected by injury for more than two years. But England's defensive vulnerability against Mexico had proved what we already knew: without Barry, Capello's England side lacked balance. England had badly missed Terry, Lampard and Ashley Cole at Wembley too, but the more Carrick had given the ball away and the more Mexico had launched attacks through the centre of England's midfield, the more obvious it became that Barry's presence was crucial.

Barry had a talent for holding the team together and, in particular, allowing Lampard and Gerrard to function together in midfield. In a football era where so many players' abilities were compromised by their egos, by their desire to show off, Barry was immune. He was a fine player, but the ambition in his performances was limited to doing simple things well. His distribution was unfussy. He rarely wasted possession. His tackling was good. His reading of the game was even better. And when Lampard raced forward, trying to get ahead of his centre-forward, Barry had the discipline not to be sucked into the attack too. He did not allow himself to be dragged out of position. Others might have been more talented than him, but Barry was the side's pivot.

So Capello decided to do what he had vowed he would not do. He decided to wait for a player until the last minute and risk taking him to South Africa, even though he could not possibly be fully fit. Similar decisions had cost England dearly in 2002 and 2006. Beckham had scored a crucial penalty against Argentina in Japan after he recovered from his broken metatarsal, but his detractors pointed out that he had also jumped out of a tackle in the quarter-final defeat to Brazil, a moment that led to England conceding an equaliser. In Germany, Rooney's lack of match fitness was exacerbated by the fact that Eriksson asked him to play alone up front. His growing frustration was a contributory factor to his sending-off during England's draw with Portugal, which led to their defeat on penalties.

But when England returned to their Austrian training base the Wednesday after the Mexico game, Capello was keen to talk up Barry's chances of making the final 23. By the weekend, he was saying it was a formality that Barry would be fit. It was just a matter of the doctors giving the player the all-clear. The England manager was talking like a man who had realised just how much he needed the City midfielder and was trying to persuade himself that everything would be all right.

He had one fall-back option: Fifa rules stipulated that if a player in the final 23 was ruled out through injury before the tournament began, he could be replaced. The replacement need not necessarily be drawn from the original 30-man squad, so if Barry was named in the 23 and it then broke down, Capello could go back to a player he had left out altogether. Or he could make one last desperate attempt to persuade Scholes to emerge from retirement. Or he could take the most reckless gamble of all and go back to Hargreaves.

There were other fitness worries as England prepared for the game against Japan. Even though the media had not been given any access to the England camp when the players had returned from the friendly against Mexico, the training pitch in Irdning was in a small stadium that was not surrounded on all sides by stands. Handfuls of tourists and villagers turned up every day to watch training from a playground by the side of the pitch, and several newspapers sent reporters to try to blend in with them so they could monitor what was happening. On the Thursday before the Japan game, their initiative was rewarded when they saw Gerrard fall to the floor in pain a few minutes into a session.

Gerrard had strained the calf muscle in his right leg and took no further part in training that day. He didn't complete the training session the following day either, and when Capello announced his team to play Japan on Sunday, Gerrard was not in it. The FA insisted the injury was not serious, and his absence was explained away as a precaution, but the worries lingered. There were already nagging concerns about Rooney's fitness. He had played for 90 minutes against Mexico, but had asked to be substituted near the end because of a sore neck.

Rooney was included in the starting line-up to play Japan, but Capello sprang surprises elsewhere in the side. He picked Darren Bent to play in attack with Rooney in preference to Emile Heskey. Many interpreted that as a sign that Heskey, who had had a mediocre season at Aston Villa, was fast falling from favour. It had long been assumed he would be one of Capello's untouchables when it came to naming the final 23. Much was made of the fact that Rooney loved playing alongside him because of the openings Heskey's physical strength and unselfish hold-up play created for him, and it had been thought that that alone was Heskey's guarantee of a place on the plane, and probably in the starting line-up against the USA. Heskey's lack of goals had been tolerated because he was making opportunities for others, but now doubts about Capello's faith in him began to creep in.

Capello also chose to start the Japan game with both Lennon and Walcott on the flanks, the first time he had picked both fliers. Huddlestone was preferred to Parker as Lampard's central midfield partner, even though Parker had been impressive all week in training. David James was given his chance in goal. It meant that seven players – Parker, Matthew Upson, Michael Dawson, Stephen Warnock, Shaun Wright-Phillips, Joe Cole and Heskey – would watch the start of the game in Graz having not kicked a ball since being selected in the 30-man squad. Some thought that suggested they would be the unlucky seven to miss out on the final 23. Others argued that Capello did not need to give time to players like Heskey and Upson because he already knew and trusted them. The guessing game turned frantic.

11 THE BREAK CLAUSE

ENGLAND came down from the mountains the evening before the match against Japan and stayed the night in a hotel in Graz. Fans from both countries began to roll in. Before the game, they sat in gentle sunshine at the small cafés that ringed what was now known as the UPC Arena. It had once been called the Arnold Schwarzenegger Stadium, in honour of the area's most famous son, but the name was changed when Schwarzenegger, as Governor of California, refused to block the execution of a murderer called Stanley Tookie at the end of 2005. However, the stadium still had a branch of Hooters, the American chain of bar-restaurants noted for the fact that its waitresses wear skimpy outfits. The English supped from great tankards of lager and sang. The Japanese took pictures.

There was optimism in the air. There always was in the weeks leading up to a World Cup. Whatever misfortunes had befallen England, however poor their recent form had been, no matter how many key players were missing through injury and how well the other leading contenders were playing, all of England usually convinced itself it was going to win the tournament in the weeks leading up to it.

Brian Woolnough, one of the great tabloid journalists of his generation, and the presenter of Sky's *Sunday Supplement* programme, used to have a mantra before every World Cup or European Championship. 'Always back England,' he said. It stemmed from a mixture of patriotism and hope that our under-achievement in major finals might at last be cast off. Most England supporters abandoned the worries and fears they might have begun to harbour, and followed his example.

In that context, what unfolded in Graz that afternoon at the end of May presented something of a challenge. The sunshine disappeared and rain blew in from the Alps in nasty squalls. England played like dogs in the first half. It was not just that they were playing badly. This was a warm-up match and nobody was expecting a display of breathtaking football. But England were worse than bad. And this was not a leading nation they were playing. Japan were a shadow of the team that had done so well at the 2002 World Cup. They were an ordinary side now.

At half time, England were 1–0 down, trailing to a seventh-minute strike from Tulio that was the product of bad marking at a Japan corner. England supporters tried to recall the last time the team had played quite so poorly. Most settled on the 1–0 defeat to Northern Ireland in Belfast in September 2005. Against Japan, the players who thought they were sure of their place in Fabio Capello's final squad played as if they were nervous about getting injured, and some of those who suspected they were borderline picks looked paralysed with fear.

Darren Bent, England's centre-forward, was damned even before the kick-off. When England's starting 11 was flashed up on the digital scoreboard behind one of the goals, the names of most England players were instantly recognisable. But opposite the number 9, a slip of a typist's finger had led to a mistake – D. Brent, it read, and the jokes began immediately. It was going to be a bad day at *The Office*, some said. Others chose to adapt a different line from Ricky Gervais's comedy: Darren Bent is not going to the World Cup – Fact.

There was plenty of sniggering. People laughed because somehow D. Brent seemed to fit. Bent remained a misfit at international level, someone to peep at through your fingers when he wore an England shirt. He had scored 24 Premier League goals for mid-table

Sunderland the previous season, a total exceeded only by Didier Drogba and Wayne Rooney, who played for the best two clubs in the country, Chelsea and Manchester United. And yet long before England got to Austria, people had written Bent off as a credible contender for Capello's final 23.

Despite his superb season in the northeast, Bent still suffered in the public mind from his experiences at his previous club, Spurs, where he had not been a success. After one glaring miss in a Premier League match against Portsmouth in January 2009, his manager, Harry Redknapp, had been so exasperated that he could not stop himself from poking fun at Bent. 'You will never get a better chance to win a match than that,' Redknapp said. 'My missus could have scored that one.'

Even though Bent had excelled for Sunderland, he found it hard to shake off those comments. The day Capello announced his provisional squad of 30, Bent's father Mervyn said that he and his son could hardly stand the tension of waiting to see whether Darren had made it. Mervyn was a former professional footballer himself, but he had never played at international level. Darren making it to the World Cup was a dream for them. When his name was included among the 30, they were both jubilant. At least now he had nearly a fortnight with the squad, an opportunity to prove himself to Capello and his coaches.

But things didn't go well. Bent suffered a minor hamstring injury in the run-up to the Mexico game, which ruled him out of it. That left just Japan. He had won five caps for England, but being selected for his previous appearance, against Brazil, in Doha, in November 2009, was international football's equivalent of a hospital pass. England had struggled to get a foothold in the game against a very good, defensively strong Brazil team, and Bent had sunk into anonymity.

Against Japan, Bent knew he needed to have an outstanding game to have any chance of making the final 23, but he was marooned in the midst of England's ineptitude, starved of service. He missed two half-chances, headers that he might have done better with. He worked hard and won a few flick-ons. He chased and he harried. But he did nothing to alter the conviction that he was going to miss out on South Africa. At half-time Capello substituted him, bringing on Joe Cole in his place. Debate might have raged about the other 29 players in the provisional squad of 30. Opinion was divided on which of them Capello would cull. But no one was in any doubt about Bent's fate. They knew that, short of an injury to Rooney, Peter Crouch, Jermain Defoe or Emile Heskey, Bent was not going to make the plane.

Nobody played well for England in the first 45 minutes in Graz. Tom Huddlestone, who might have had a chance of edging out Michael Carrick in the final 23 if he had shone, looked slow and lumbering against a Japan team who pressed hard and were eager in the tackle. He misplaced pass after pass. He came off at half-time too. It was obvious he hadn't done enough. There were five substitutions in all at the interval. Theo Walcott was another. The experiment of playing him and Aaron Lennon together had not worked, and Walcott was the one Capello withdrew. Walcott had not played well, but his replacement, Shaun Wright-Phillips, made little impact in the second half. Walcott was struggling for form, but he was one of Capello's favourites, and many analysts still believed that when England lined up against the USA for their opening game in Rustenburg, Walcott would be standing on the right wing before kick-off.

The changes Capello enforced at half-time made a difference. And for the first time in either of England's warm-up games, one man came on to the pitch and played in a way that demanded the England manager take him to South Africa. Joe Cole's season with Chelsea had been disrupted by injury and dogged by whispers that his club boss, Carlo Ancelotti, did not rate him. Ancelotti often confirmed that idea by preferring either Deco or Salomon Kalou to Cole in the Chelsea starting line-up. As Cole was pushed to the margins for his club, Capello lost faith in him too.

Cole had squeezed into the provisional squad of 30, probably at number 30. Some sources close to the England management were briefing the night before the squad announcement that Cole had been left out, but Capello's retreat from including Owen Hargreaves reprieved Cole. Many assumed the reprieve would be temporary, particularly when Cole did not play against Mexico or start against Japan. But from the moment the second half began in Graz, Cole played with such irresistible verve and creativity that it soon became clear it would be impossible for Capello to ignore him any longer.

It helped that Cole played in what many consider to be his best position in Graz, behind the main striker. In his time at Chelsea, Cole had gradually been converted into a hard-working left midfielder by Jose Mourinho, and even though he had still matured into a fine player, he had not been allowed to develop into the playmaking number 10, England's next Paul Gascoigne, that many had believed he would become when he was a child prodigy rising through the ranks at West Ham.

Even when he was 15 and playing in the West Ham youth team, the legend of his talent was already well known in English football. Redknapp, who was then in charge at Upton Park, told a story about how, whenever they met, Sir Alex Ferguson would always ask the same question first: 'How's Joe Cole?' Cole was a brilliant ball-player with great vision and a low centre of gravity that allowed him to wriggle away from challenges that might unsettle others.

But the demands of the modern game, the emphasis on work-rate, the ProZone culture that lionised a footballer purely for the distance he covered during a match, and the reclassification of creative talents like Cole as 'luxury players' arrested his development and pushed him into a more prosaic role. He still showed flashes of the things that made him special, but most of them were aggressively discouraged, by Mourinho in particular. However, Cole responded well to Mourinho's demands and became the player his boss wanted him to be. He played a leading part in Chelsea's back-to-back title victories in 2004–05 and 2005–06 as a left-sided midfielder, and scored England's best goal of the 2006 World Cup finals, a superb volley from the edge of the box against Sweden.

Cole was in an invidious position. Such great things had been predicted for him in his youth that unless he dominated the world game, there were still those who would label his career a disappointment. The reality was that Cole had become a very successful footballer, one of the elite. He had avoided the pitfalls that snag so many lavishly talented kids and stop them even making it to the professional game. When Cole was rising through the ranks, another young player called Leon Knight, a Chelsea trainee, was bracketed with him as one to watch. But Knight's career withered. He sank into the lower leagues with Brighton & Hove Albion, Rushden & Diamonds and others. In the summer of 2010, as Cole was fighting to regain his England place, Knight was being released by Scottish first division club Queen of the South.

Cole was a title winner, an England international, a man who had played in a World Cup on an equal footing with the heroes of the game, and it was a joy to see him playing as a free spirit against Japan. Capello did not shoehorn him into left midfield and order him to cover the runs of the Japan right-back. He asked him to operate behind Rooney, in the space between the Japan midfield and defence, and Cole responded by playing like he was a lad in the West Ham youth team again. Five minutes into the second half he had already changed the complexion of the game in England's favour. Suddenly, Japan were faced with someone who not only matched their energy, but who was running at them without fear.

After the aridity of the first half, it was a relief to see Cole controlling the ball with his back to goal in the centre circle, turning away from his marker and then slipping a simple pass out to Lennon who was in space on the right wing. It felt as if it had just needed one piece of spontaneity, one expression of confidence, to open the game up, and Cole was providing it. In the first half, England had possessed no guile, no unpredictability, no spark. Cole gave them all three. It was his run and cross that brought the equaliser. Tanaka, who was to find notoriety a week later against Ivory Coast with a high tackle that threatened to put Didier Drogba out of the World Cup, tried to clear it, but headed the ball past his own goalkeeper. England got a winner later on, courtesy of another own goal. Cole, to the great relief of all those who felt he should be an automatic pick for the national team, appeared to have forced his way into the final 23 at the last gasp.

If Cole had transformed the game, another England half-time substitute had made an impact too. Steven Gerrard was hardly fighting for his place in the 23, but he did suddenly glimpse the opportunity of playing in the World Cup in his favourite position. Capello had always been suspicious of playing Gerrard in central midfield, but with Barry injured and Huddlestone apparently overawed, the England manager moved the Liverpool skipper into place alongside Frank Lampard. And, against Japan at least, it worked. Gerrard played superbly at the heart of the team. His understanding with Rooney, their telepathic awareness of each other's runs and intentions, helped to make England a different team, and in the dying minutes he curled in a delicious cross that Emile Heskey, a late substitute, somehow contrived to head wide from two yards.

The Gerrard–Lampard conundrum dominated Capello's post-match press conferences. It was obvious he was still reluctant to endorse the idea of the two men playing together in central midfield, but it was equally obvious he was beginning to realise he might have no choice. Barry was improving all the time, but the most optimistic estimates of when he might be ready to return suggested that it would not be until after the opening game against the USA. Instead of dismissing the idea of a Gerrard–Lampard axis, as he had after the Mexico game, Capello's attitude shifted. Now he was not shaking his head quite so much. Now he was saying 'maybe'.

There were reasons why the dilemma was such a favourite of the English press. It was because Gerrard and Lampard were both such good players. It was because they both dominated midfield at their clubs. It was because it would have been such a potent weapon for the team if they had been able to find a way to combine effectively. They were both intelligent men with sharp football brains. It should not have been beyond them and a clever manager to work out the problem and fix it.

Every match they had played together in the centre in the past, everyone crossed their fingers and hoped that this would be the time it would finally click. But it never clicked. Not really. Capello felt it was because they both liked to get forward so much. Others felt it was because they were both such responsible team players that they both played too deep when they were together because they were so concerned about leaving the defence exposed if they got too far forward. But that was just as damaging as being caught out of position because it meant they left the forwards isolated and without support.

Capello did not attempt to disguise his irritation with the English fixation about the partnership that day, but that was partly because he was also preoccupied by another matter that had come to the fore in the week leading up to the Japan game. The Italian had been given a four and a half year contract when he became England manager in December 2007, but there was a break clause in it that allowed him to speak to potential suitors in a stipulated period after the 2010 World Cup. The clause worked both ways. It also allowed the FA to end its association with Capello after the tournament without having to pay him the remaining two years of his salary.

When Lord Triesman was still FA chairman, Capello had offered to remove the clause. News of his proposal was greeted as another example of his commitment to England. The idea was welcomed because it would prevent any speculation about a move back to club football disrupting England's build-up. Lord Triesman and Capello had shaken hands on the deal, but when Triesman was forced to resign in mid-May, the amendment to the contract was still being finalised by the FA lawyers. It had not yet been signed.

Several weeks earlier, Capello had turned down the chance to manage Juventus, but now, as England prepared to fly home from Graz, there was another, more serious, issue. Mourinho, who had just led Inter Milan to victory over Bayern Munich in the Champions League final, had left San Siro to become boss at Real Madrid. Inter were looking for a new coach to take over, and Massimo Moratti, the Inter president, who had tried to recruit Capello several times before, said he was encouraged by the revelation of the existence of the break clause and the suggestion that the England manager would be free to negotiate a possible move after the World Cup.

Capello had enhanced his popularity in England with his swift dismissal of the interest from Juventus. It made a welcome change from the incorrigible flirtatiousness of Eriksson. But when Capello held a press conference with journalists from the Sunday newspapers in Irdning the day before the Japan game, there was a change in his tone. He refused to commit himself to England and was coy about the interest from Inter. 'I signed with one chairman, who changed to another chairman and I haven't met the new chairman, so now I don't know what will happen,' Capello said. Suddenly, the FA's worst nightmare, losing their manager on the eve of the World Cup, seemed to be edging closer. 'Fabioff' was the back-page headline in the *News of the World* the next day.

After the sketchy victory over Japan, Capello was pressed again about his future, and again he was evasive and ambiguous when asked to commit himself to England. This was all happening two days before he was due to name his final World Cup squad. Those who had always pointed to his love of London life and his happiness in his job as reasons why he would never walk out on the FA began to remember that he had done it in other jobs. He walked out of Roma in 2004 to join Juventus, a club with whom he had previously been locked in some of his most bitter battles. And when Juventus was brought to its knees by the Calciopoli scandal two years later, Capello headed to Real Madrid.

Sitting next to Capello on the dais in the press room, Adrian Bevington, who was in his first day as managing director of a new FA body called Club England, which had been given responsibility for all England's representative football sides, tried to calm the atmosphere. Bevington said Capello merely wanted reassurance that the agreement he had reached with Lord Triesman still stood and that the organisation still had faith in him.

At the very least, Capello's manoeuvrings now seemed undignified with the World Cup so close. The chaos at the FA did not affect him, and there had never been any suggestion that there was any faction within the organisation who wanted to be rid of Capello after the tournament. His desire for reassurance felt specious. It added to the sense that, in the most important month of his England reign, he had lost his sure touch. After the farce of the Capello Index and his panicky attempt to bounce Paul Scholes into coming out of international retirement, now there was this mess.

After he and Bevington had spoken from the dais, Capello then went into a separate huddle with the football correspondents of the daily newspapers who were often granted extra access to the manager. Capello denied he had had any contact with Inter, but hinted at his frustration with the blizzard of changes occurring at the FA and the power vacuum it seemed to have created. 'I spoke with the first chairman,' Capello said, alluding to Brian Barwick, chief executive before Ian Watmore, 'I spoke with Lord Triesman, now I need to speak with the other one.'

His reference to 'the other one' caused great amusement. The other one was Sir Dave Richards, who was the new chairman of Club England, a man with a keen sense of his own importance. Sir Dave would speak to Capello the next day, Bevington said. Bevington was confident that everything could be quickly resolved. Capello was making a quick trip back to Italy to visit his mother, but Sir Dave would speak with him on the phone. Not everyone was confident that entrusting Sir Dave with the future of the England manager was such a good idea, but he got the job done. He spoke to Capello as planned. He reassured him as planned, and on the day England flew from Heathrow to Johannesburg, the FA announced Capello had signed the amendment to his contract. The release clause had been deleted.

Most hailed the deal as an unreservedly positive development, and in terms of allowing Capello, the players and the media to concentrate solely on the World Cup, it was. Some thought that the anarchy at the FA helped to drive the deal through. So far, the majority of comment had concentrated on the fact that England had secured a fine manager for another two years. A minority pointed out that if things went wrong at the World Cup and Capello's sheen dulled, it would now cost the FA £12 million to get rid of him. Avoiding that liability was the whole point of the break clause, and now it was gone. But it was too negative to dwell on that side of the bargain for long. Capello had orchestrated a masterful qualifying campaign, and his recent mis-steps were surely merely glitches. All anyone really cared about was that, finally, the Inter Milan story was dead.

The day before he signed the amendment to his contract, Capello had seven other telephone calls to make. To seven men who were going to hear bad news.

12 | SUITED AND BOOTED

THEO Walcott was on the golf course at Brocket Hall in Hertfordshire when his mobile phone rang. He took it out of his pocket and saw Fabio Capello's name on his screen. His heartbeat quickened, but it was with excitement rather than dread. He knew that Capello had told his Arsenal manager, Arsène Wenger, some time ago that as long as he was fit, he would go to the World Cup. He knew he had had an uneven season, disrupted by injury and by often being restricted to a substitute's role at his club, but he felt that he was finally fully fit and beginning to hit form at just the right time. Walcott is one of the most modest, unaffected and down-to-earth of Premier League players, and he had not taken his place in the final 23 for granted, but he was convinced he could make a big impact in South Africa.

Playing a proper part in the tournament meant more to him than most. Four years earlier, Sven-Goran Eriksson had caused astonishment when he picked Walcott in his squad for the Germany World Cup. Walcott was only 17 then. He found out he had been selected when he turned his phone on after he had taken the theory exam for his driving test. He had been signed by Arsenal from Southampton a few months earlier and had not appeared in a Premier League game. There was great excitement about his potential, but also considerable consternation that he had been chosen ahead of proven top-flight goalscorers, such as Darren Bent and Jermain Defoe. Eriksson had not even seen him play in a proper match. The only time he had watched him was in a practice game on a small-sided pitch at Arsenal's London Colney training ground.

Initially, Walcott had felt intimidated by being in the company of established Premier League stars in the England squad, and struggled with homesickness. He rattled around the team hotel on top of a mountain outside Baden-Baden, filming some of his experiences on a camcorder he had been given by the FA. In an interview he gave to the *Guardian* in the spring of 2010, he recalled watching a game of snooker between John Terry and Wayne Rooney a couple of days before England's first game. Rooney was so angry when he lost that he snapped his cue in half. The young Walcott was startled by Rooney's intensity and competitive hunger. But he adapted to his new situation as the tournament went on, and was desperate to be given a chance to play and prove that he could be of worth. Eriksson never gave him the opportunity.

Walcott came home without having kicked a ball, and in the post-World Cup disillusionment that followed England's lacklustre displays and quarter-final exit to Portugal, he found that he had been cast as one of Eriksson's follies, one of the symbols of a flawed campaign and a discredited regime. Liverpool captain Steven Gerrard was scathing about Walcott's inclusion in the squad in his autobiography, which was one of several released after the tournament. 'He had no right to be in Germany,' Gerrard wrote. 'None at all. I was gobsmacked to find him on the plane. My faith in Sven has always been strong but to select a kid who hasn't played any part in a Premiership game, or a competitive international, was clearly a massive gamble. Could Sven throw him into a World Cup game? No chance. Theo was still a baby.'

Walcott was a shadow player in Germany. When Eriksson took him and then overlooked him, he condemned him to four weeks of being treated as England's World Cup curiosity. His call-up and subsequent failure to make an appearance loaded intense pressure on

Walcott when he returned to Arsenal. Other young players might have folded under the strain and never been heard of again, but Walcott was a confident young man with strong, loving parents and a secure, nurturing club environment, and he refused to fade away. Instead, he came out fighting. He starred in Arsenal's first game of the new season, their opening game at their new stadium, The Emirates, and even though Eriksson's successor, Steve McClaren, left him out of the England senior squad, Walcott played regularly for the England Under-21s.

He also did more than any other England player to get England to South Africa. When Capello picked his starting 11 for his first competitive match in charge, the World Cup qualifier away to Andorra in Barcelona in September 2008, he sprang a surprise by choosing Walcott ahead of his mentor, David Beckham. Many assumed that Capello was resting Beckham in preparation for the crucial match against Croatia in Zagreb the following Wednesday, but Capello picked Walcott in the starting line-up again. Walcott responded by scoring three superb goals in an emphatic 4–1 victory. It was the first England hat-trick in a competitive match since Michael Owen did it in the 5–1 destruction of Germany in Munich in 2001. Walcott was England's new hero, the great hope of a generation.

England's crushing victory in Croatia launched Capello's England reign in style. Until then, no one had been quite sure what to make of his headmasterly manner, but triumph over the nation that had tormented England in the European Championship qualifying campaign seemed to vindicate the autocratic rule Capello exercised over his players. The contrast between McClaren's struggles against Croatia and Capello's jaunty victory at the Maksimir Stadium – the first time the Croats had ever suffered a competitive home defeat – put the maximum possible distance between the new regime and the old one, and established Walcott as one of Capello's favourite and most trusted players.

Then, two months after his heroics in Zagreb, Walcott suffered a fractured dislocation of his shoulder as England trained at the Olympic Stadium in Berlin the night before a friendly against Germany. He returned to the Arsenal team later that season, but then, as summer approached, he found himself at the centre of a tug of war between the England senior team, the Under-21s and Arsenal. Capello picked him for the qualifiers away to Kazakhstan and at home to Andorra at the beginning of June, and then Stuart Pearce insisted on taking him to Sweden for the European Under-21 Championships. Walcott did not complain, but Wenger and many others felt that he should have played either for the Under-21s or for the senior side, but not both. Some reports said that Walcott had defied Wenger by insisting on playing for the Under-21s, but those reports were not true. Walcott was stuck in the middle of the horse-trading for his services. He was conscious of the dangers of playing too much football before the start of what was going to be a long season with a World Cup at the end of it. But he did not want to refuse to play for the Under-21s. He had seen what had happened to people like David Bentley, who turned their back on their country. He felt, correctly, that the decision was not his to make. Many of those close to Walcott hoped Capello might step in and prevent him from playing in Sweden, but Capello seemed happy for him to be playing football the entire summer.

That is exactly what Walcott did. He played for the senior team in Kazakhstan on 6 June, complete with a nine-hour flight to Almaty and a nine-hour flight back. He played 90 minutes against Andorra at Wembley on 10 June. Five days later he was lining up for the England Under-21s against Finland at Halmstad in the opening game of the European Championships. He played five games in a fortnight in Sweden, including the final against Germany on 29 June that England lost 4–0. A couple of weeks later he was reporting for pre-season training with Arsenal. England's laissez-faire policy towards Walcott was utter madness. It was a shameful abrogation of responsibility towards a young player who needed protection. Walcott might have missed much of the previous season through injury, but that did not change the fact that England needed him to be fresh and rested for the start of an important season that everyone hoped would end in him starring at the 2010 World Cup.

By forcing him to play for the senior team and the Under-21s, the complete opposite happened. Walcott had a brief holiday after the Under-21 final, but because he missed the beginning of pre-season training with Arsenal, he was rushed back into action for his club more quickly than normal. Capello reaped what he had sown when Walcott was drafted straight into the Arsenal side for a high-profile friendly against Valencia at the Mestalla and promptly suffered a side strain that kept him out for several weeks and set the tone for another season disrupted by injury. Walcott's treatment that summer, and Capello's refusal to exercise any duty of care towards him, was one small example of the mismanagement of England's players in the build-up to the World Cup. Four of the Germany Under-21 team who played against England in the final in Sweden – Manuel Neuer, Sami Khedira, Jerome Boateng and Mesut Özil – were involved in the World Cup match against England in Bloemfontein a year later, but none of them had been asked to play for the senior team in the summer of 2009 as well. That was partly because the German football association, the DFB, had made sure their senior team did not have a fixture that clashed with the Under-21 tournament, and partly because they did not want to exhaust the best of their young talent by flogging them the summer before the World Cup.

Even though Walcott's various muscle and ligament injuries made it impossible for him to string a run of games together for most of the 2009–10 season, they did not protect him from criticism from those who felt that he had failed to mature into the player they had expected him to become. Chris Waddle, the former England winger, launched a particularly vitriolic attack on Walcott. He said the Arsenal star did not understand the game. 'I just don't think he's got a football brain and he's going to have problems,' Waddle said after Walcott had struggled to impress in England's friendly against Egypt in March. Walcott took more criticism from Sky football anchor Richard Keys, who aimed withering comments at him when he thought his microphone was switched off during Arsenal's Champions League quarter-final second-leg defeat to Barcelona. 'You've been shite, son, in your daft pink boots,' Keys blurted out.

But the criticism took little account of the injury problems he had been fighting. People quickly forgot about his schedule the previous summer. It was still assumed, though, that Walcott was guaranteed a place in Capello's final 23. Wenger spoke to reporters in South Africa during the tournament and confirmed that Capello had told him Walcott would definitely go to the World Cup as long as he was fit. And Walcott was fit. He had started the last three league games of Arsenal's season and had made a dramatic impact when he came off the bench in the second half of the first leg of the tie against Barcelona at The Emirates at the end of March. Arsenal were 2–0 down and had been mesmerised by the brilliance of the Catalans, but Walcott broke the spell. His pace startled Barcelona left-back Maxwell, and Walcott darted on to a through ball and slotted it past Victor Valdes. Then another Walcott run and cross caused havoc in the Barcelona box, Arsenal won a penalty and Cesc Fabregas equalised from the spot. Arsenal were overwhelmed in the second leg at the Nou Camp, but it was Walcott who set up Arsenal's only goal for Robin van Persie.

Some thought that Aaron Lennon, who was also sidelined with injury for much of the second half of the season, might have crept ahead of Walcott in the competition to start on the right of England's midfield because he had excelled at Spurs before Christmas. But most still favoured Walcott. And when Lennon, Walcott and Shaun Wright-Phillips were all named in Capello's initial 30-man squad, the assumption was that Wright-Phillips would miss out when the party was whittled down to 23. Walcott started the first World Cup warm-up game against Mexico and played until 13 minutes from the end, when he was replaced by Lennon. Wright-Phillips did not get off the bench. He started the final pre-World Cup international against Japan in Graz too, but was anonymous in a poor England first-half performance. He was one of five players Capello substituted at half-time in Austria. Wright-Phillips replaced him and was part of the improved second-half England display.

Later it was reported that when Capello watched a DVD of the Mexico game with his players, he tore into Walcott in front of them. Capello was frustrated, it was said, because Walcott kept cutting in from his position wide on the right touchline rather than trying to beat his man on the outside, which was what Capello wanted him to do. Capello felt Walcott was running into trouble more and more, and he was exasperated by his lapses in control and technique, and his inability to follow instructions. Walcott's first-half performance in Graz had done nothing to ease his concerns. Ever since his hat-trick in Croatia, Walcott had been an automatic first-team selection if he was fit, but now, just a couple of days before England flew to Johannesburg, Capello was starting to harbour serious doubts about whether to take him to the World Cup at all.

As late as the evening of 31 May, 24 hours before the final squad [illegible]d to be submitted to Fifa, Capello was toying with the idea of [illegible]g all three of Lennon, Wright-Phillips and Walcott, and sacri[illegible]g the second-string left-back to accommodate them. Leighton [illegible]ines, the Everton defender, had been the favourite to make the plane as Ashley Cole's understudy, but he had frozen in the spotlight when he played against Mexico, and had then given an interview where he admitted he had missed his family badly while he had been away in Austria. As Baines pointed out later, he was hardly alone in that respect among the England players, but the juxtaposition of his remarks and his performance was unfortunate. Stephen Warnock, the Aston Villa left-back, had impressed Capello in training and moved ahead of Baines in the struggle to make the final 23. Walcott's situation had also been made more precarious by the fact that Joe Cole's dazzling display against Japan had pushed him into the squad, probably alongside James Milner in one of the two left-sided midfield places. Capello distrusted Cole as a player and was looking for an excuse to leave him out, but Cole would not give him one. Cole's late push had further restricted Capello's room for manoeuvre. It looked like a straight choice between Walcott and Warnock.

The provisional squad of 30 players had disbanded after the game against Japan to have a couple of days with their families before those selected in the final squad flew to Johannesburg on the evening of 2 June. There was no question of Capello telling seven unlucky players face to face that they were going to miss out. He was still in Italy and his players had scattered. There was no easy way of breaking that kind of news anyway. Inflicting the biggest professional disappointment of their lives on a group of footballers was one of the grotesque rituals of each World Cup year. Different England managers had tried different methods of minimising the pain. The former Arsenal forward Alan Smith, who had become a respected writer on the *Daily Telegraph*, remembered discovering he had been left out of Sir Bobby Robson's final squad for the 1990 World Cup when Sir Bobby assembled his players in a room and turned over a page on a flip-chart to reveal a list of names. Smith's was not on it.

In 1998 Glenn Hoddle had taken his provisional squad of 29 players for a pre-World Cup training camp at La Manga in Spain, and when the deadline for submitting the final party grew close, he

David Beckham (*left*) and Sven-Goran Eriksson feel the pain of England's exit from the 2006 World Cup after a quarter-final penalty shoot-out defeat by Portugal.

Left England manager Steve McClaren was derided as 'The Wally with the Brolly' after he sheltered under an umbrella during England's Wembley defeat by Croatia in a crucial Euro 2008 qualifying tie.

Below Fabio Capello was welcomed as the authoritarian manager England's players needed when he was appointed by the FA in December 2007.

Above Theo Walcott completes a stunning hat-trick against Croatia in Zagreb in a 4-1 victory that got England's World Cup 2010 qualifying campaign off to a flying start.

Right Wayne Bridge ignores John Terry's outstretched hand in the final act of a football soap opera that had convulsed the nation.

Joe Cole seized his place in England's World Cup squad with a stand-out performance against Japan in a dire World Cup warm-up game in Graz.

South African football fans blow their vuvuzelas at a World Cup match after calls from European television viewers to have the instruments banned from grounds had failed.

The tension is written all over the faces of the England players as they line up to face the USA in their opening match of the World Cup. *Front row, left to right:* Glen Johnson, Steven Gerrard, Wayne Rooney, Aaron Lennon, Ashley Cole. *Back row, left to right:* Emile Heskey, John Terry, Robert Green, Ledley King, James Milner, Frank Lampard.

England skipper Steven Gerrard gets England's tournament off to a dream start with this fourth-minute strike against the Americans.

Robert Green tries desperately to recover the ball after Clint Dempsey's speculative shot had squirmed out of his grasp and trickled over the line to give the USA an equaliser.

Right Fabio Capello barks orders at his players as his assistant, Stuart Pearce, looks on. Capello's temper grew worse and worse the longer the tournament wore on.

Below Jermain Defoe scores the winner against Slovenia to ensure England make it through to the second round but it did not herald the rebirth England fans hoped for.

John Terry hurls himself head-first into the path of a shot as England defend their lead against Slovenia. Terry's bravery did not spare him from criticism during the tournament.

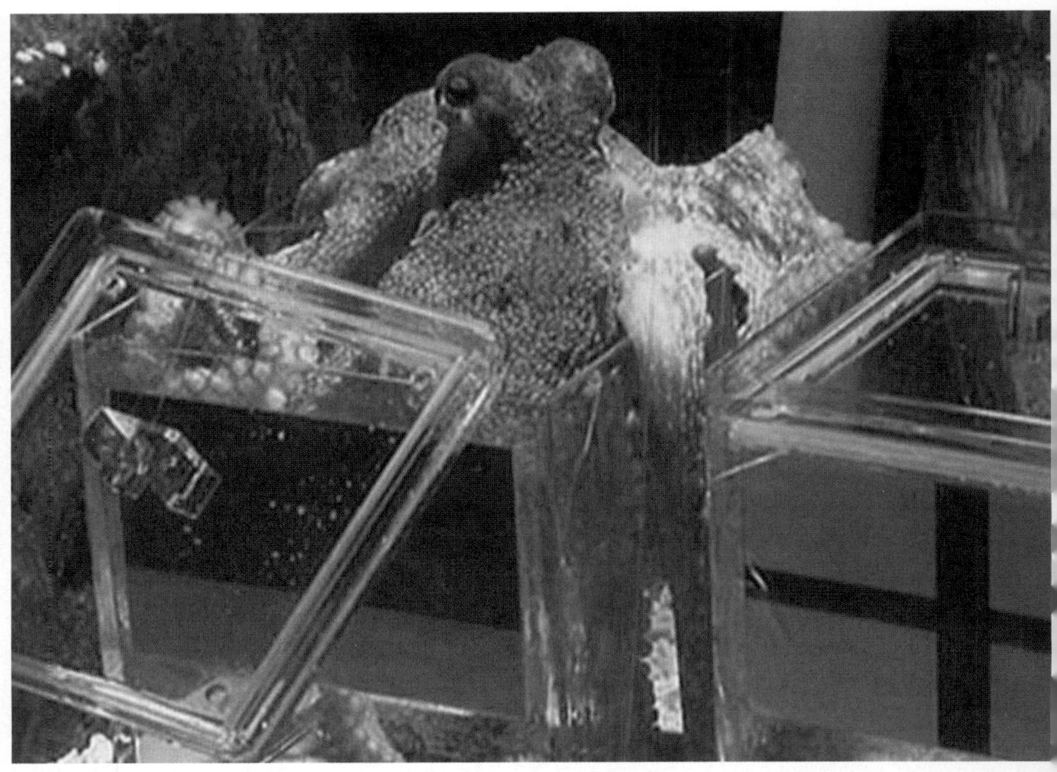

Paul the Psychic Octopus became a celebrity when he correctly predicted the results of all Germany's World Cup matches and the outcome of the World Cup final.

Right Germany striker Miroslav Klose celebrates after embarrassing Matthew Upson and David James to score the opening goal against England.

Below Germany goalkeeper Manuel Neuer twists in the air and sees Frank Lampard's chip bounce down off the crossbar and land a foot over the goal-line. The Uruguayan linesman ruled the ball had not crossed the line and play continued.

Left Gareth Barry tries to take out Germany play-maker Mesut Özil but cannot get close enough to him even to do that. Özil ran on to set up Germany's fourth goal for Thomas Muller.

Below Capello screams instructions as the England bench looks on forlornly but England are already 4-1 down against Germany and heading out of the World Cup. *Left to right:* Peter Crouch, Ledley King, Aaron Lennon, Michael Carrick, Jamie Carragher, James Milner, Joe Hart, Robert Green, Fabio Capello and David Beckham.

issued each of them with a time to visit him in his room so that he could tell them their fate. The players said later that it had been like being given an appointment card for a doctor's surgery. The system turned into a cruel farce. Some appointments overran, so players soon found themselves sitting outside Hoddle's room in a queue, watching teammates emerging either crestfallen or elated. The tension became too much for Paul Gascoigne, who had sensed Hoddle was going to leave him out. He burst into Hoddle's room while the manager was telling Phil Neville that he would not be going to France. Hoddle told Gascoigne he was not going either, and Gascoigne responded by kicking a hole in Hoddle's wardrobe, overturning a table and smashing a vase, cutting his leg in the process. Neville, Ian Walker, Dion Dublin, Nicky Butt and Andy Hinchcliffe joined him on a private plane back to England that evening. It is remembered as the most brutal, chaotic, traumatic, badly handled culling of all.

Eriksson did things differently in 2002 and 2006. He did not bother with a provisional, larger squad, and named his group of 23 straight away, putting one or two players on standby in case any of the original choices were injured before the final deadline for the submission of names. That system avoided Hoddle's doomsday scenario of last-minute omissions, but it created awkwardness instead. In 2002 Danny Murphy was named as the first reserve and was drafted into the squad when Steven Gerrard had to pull out of the tournament with a groin injury. But then Murphy himself was injured, so Trevor Sinclair was called up in his place. Eriksson was out of reserves by that point, so he had to find some more and put David Dunn and Leeds United's Alan Smith on standby as well. They were not needed. The system worked more efficiently in 2006, although it probably did not seem that way to Defoe. Defoe missed out on the original squad when Eriksson picked Walcott ahead of him, but was taken to Germany anyway in case Rooney did not recover from his broken metatarsal. Defoe shone in training in the build-up to the tournament, but when Rooney was declared fit, he was sent back to England. The rest of the squad assembled in the lobby of the Schlosshotel Bühlerhöhe to bid Defoe a regretful farewell.

Capello's method fell somewhere in between Hoddle's and Eriksson's. On the morning of Tuesday, 1 June, he picked up his phone and started making calls. Walcott was midway through his round at Brocket Hall when his mobile rang. He was playing with a group that included Jake Thomson, an old friend from the days when they were scholars, or apprentices, together at Southampton. Walcott took the phone out of his pocket, saw Capello's name and answered. The reception was poor. He thought he heard Capello say something about being sorry. His heart began to beat faster and then the line went dead. Walcott still thought everything might be all right. The reception had been so bad that he could not be sure what Capello had been saying. He phoned Capello back. This time the line was better and the message was clear. Walcott was out. Walcott wanted to ask him why he had been omitted, but did not get the chance. Capello told him he would be a big part of his plans for the qualifying competition for the European Championships in 2012, and then he brought the conversation to a close.

Walcott was devastated. 'At the last World Cup I was in the squad but I didn't get the chance to appear at all,' he said. 'This time I thought I'd play a proper part. I thought I deserved my place, but there's no point me sulking about it. I've just got to get on with it.' The reaction was typical of Walcott, honest but always respectful. A statement was also released on Walcott's behalf. 'I am very disappointed not to be included in the squad going out to South Africa,' it read, 'but completely respect Mr Capello's decision. I would like to wish the team the best of luck and hope they have a really successful tournament.' Everyone felt tremendous sympathy for

Walcott, but many also believed Capello had made the right decision and that Walcott's form had not been good enough to warrant a place in the squad.

He had been the big story four years earlier when he was selected. Now he was the big story again because he had been left out. Ironies were everywhere. Walcott knew when Eriksson included him that he was not ready to play in a World Cup. This time, when Capello overlooked him, Walcott knew that he was ready. Whenever he had been fit, Capello had always picked him, not just in the squad but in the first team. Now, when it mattered most, the England manager, a man Walcott loved playing for, had discarded him. Walcott's chance of banishing all the frustration he had felt over his experiences at the 2006 World Cup, of showing how much he had matured, of proving once and for all that he was not a kid who had never grown up, had been ripped away from him. The front page of the *Sun* the next morning carried a picture of Walcott wearing England's Marks & Spencer World Cup suit. It was part of a planned FA advertising campaign that would now have to be scrapped. 'Suited and Booted' the headline read.

Others suffered too. Darren Bent had gone to his mother's house in Cambridgeshire to wait for the news. Part of him feared the worst and he did not want to be by himself when the phone rang. He was sitting in the same chair he had been sitting in four years earlier when Eriksson called him, and now the phone was ringing again. Bent's mother was standing by the door, saying, 'Answer it, answer it.' Bent picked it up. It was Capello. 'He just told me that I wasn't going to South Africa,' Bent said in a superb interview written by George Caulkin in *The Times*, 'that I had to keep working and that was it. It was short, brief, no explanation. Afterwards, I sat there for a few minutes and soaked it up. I just wanted to get on with things. I phoned my friend, went for a drive, got a haircut – funny little things. It has to be like that. There's no point throwing myself to the ground and whining about life because that's no good to anyone. I'll pick myself up and start again.' From the English, Spanish, Italian, French and German leagues, Bent was the only man to score 20 goals or more that season who was not going to the World Cup. 'People say that if you do well for your club, the rewards will follow,' Bent told Caulkin, 'but it doesn't feel like that's happened.'

Omitting Walcott and Bent was highly controversial. Even if Walcott had been inconsistent, it was hard to imagine that Shaun Wright-Phillips would make any meaningful contribution to the World Cup. He was more inconsistent than Walcott. Walcott had also proved at Arsenal that he could make a dramatic impact coming off the bench against high-quality opposition such as Barcelona. Leaving him at home was a mistake. As for Bent, he had missed out because the belief remained that Emile Heskey was one of the keys to unlocking the talent of Rooney at international level. That was his only purpose. Everybody had given up on the idea that Heskey might actually score a few goals himself. Rooney was Heskey's ticket to South Africa, but if Heskey failed to help Rooney ignite, he was a waste of a place. It was hard to know which was more cruel for Bent: losing out to a kid who had never played a Premier League game in 2006, or being rejected in favour of a non-goalscoring centre-forward in 2010.

Adam Johnson, the only naturally left-sided player in the 30, was left out too. That decision deprived the squad of balance and one of the few players carrying any forward momentum and playing without fear. But Capello's version of 4–4–2 used Gerrard on the left of midfield. Milner and Joe Cole were also named in the final 23, so there was no room left for Johnson. Scott Parker did not make it either, even though the other England players felt he had excelled in training in Austria. Gareth Barry had passed a fitness test on his damaged ankle, so he was included, and neither Parker nor Tom Huddlestone, who also missed out, could dislodge Michael Carrick, even though Carrick had had a mediocre season for Manchester United and appeared to be low on confidence. Carrick made the plane, but it was a hollow achievement; he did not kick a ball in South Africa.

Baines was left out too. He complained later that he had never said he'd been worried about homesickness, but it did not really matter. It was probably his performance against Mexico that raised concerns about his ability to cope with the pressure of the World Cup rather than any worries about how badly he would miss his family. The last of the seven was Michael Dawson. He was probably in the best form of all the central defenders in Capello's initial 30-man squad, but the England manager was bound to take Jamie Carragher now that he had tempted him out of international retirement, and he also retained an unfathomable attachment to Matthew Upson, who had had a poor season at West Ham and had made too many errors on England duty to make him a safe selection. Still, it was Dawson who got the short, sharp call of rejection, and Upson who was told he would be taking his seat on the Virgin flight leaving Heathrow for Johannesburg the next evening. The die was cast.

13 CAPTAIN'S CURSE

ENGLAND opened their training camp to the media the day after they arrived. Capello had chosen the Royal Marang Hotel on the Bafokeng Sports Campus, two hours northwest of Johannesburg by road, as the team base. When the news first emerged in the autumn of 2009, it had seemed a baffling decision. The village of Phokeng, which was the closest settlement to the hotel, was a long way from any of South Africa's urban centres, the landscape was dominated by the pit-head buildings and slag-heaps associated with the area's platinum-mining industry, and the only local restaurant was a fast food Chicken Licken in a small shopping mall, which was about a mile away. Its sole advantage seemed to be that it was on the Highveld Plateau, 1500 metres above sea level, and offered England training at altitude.

There was no Garibaldi's, no Brenner's Park, no karaoke joints, nowhere to buy a bottle of Cristal champagne, nowhere to dance on tables, nowhere to parade for paparazzi, no place for mini-excursions, nowhere that the industry that had grown up around the England team could set up as an alternative camp that the players could escape to. Sun City, with its casino and hotels, was half an hour away, but it was out of season and some of the swimming pools were closed. It was a poor man's Las Vegas, nowhere near glitzy enough to tempt England's usual coterie of hangers-on, and even if some of them did turn up, there was no chance of the players being allowed to Sun City to see them regularly.

England's camp was isolated. The World Cup literature said

England were based in Rustenburg, but that was inaccurate. Rustenburg was ten miles away, and anyway, even Rustenburg was a small town with little to recommend it. The Royal Marang Hotel was set a mile or so back from a dusty country road on the outskirts of Phokeng. Most of the traffic that passed by was either carrying miners to and from work or heading west towards the border with Botswana. The closest thing to designer shops were the roadside stalls selling fruit and vegetables. Instead of gazing out at the Black Forest from their rooms, the England players had an uninterrupted view of a giant slag-heap. In other words, it was about as far removed from Baden-Baden as almost anywhere on Earth could possibly be, which was exactly what Capello wanted.

There had been concerns about the state of the pitches in the complex, and worries about whether the hotel, which was being built for the World Cup, would be ready, but all those doubts had disappeared by the time England arrived. It was obvious to everybody who saw it that Friday morning a week before the tournament kicked off that England had actually secured one of the best training camps in the country. The players had been dubious about the venue, but they were impressed too. They also knew that because of both the security situation and the attitude of their manager they would not have had any more freedom to roam wherever they had stayed in South Africa.

Security surrounding all the teams was tight. The build-up to the tournament had been dominated by stories about soaring crime figures in South Africa, and dire warnings that football fans travelling to the tournament were in grave danger. The host country was infuriated by what it saw as a smear campaign, and insisted that visitors to South Africa would be safe, but the bad publicity had an effect. Hotels in Johannesburg, where there were two World Cup venues, Soccer City and Ellis Park, were running at full occupancy for the duration of the tournament, but elsewhere, there were signs that tourists were staying away because they were worried about violent crime.

The fear had spread. Most of the English media covering the tournament had been sent on security courses to try to prepare them for all eventualities. Many found themselves in classrooms alongside contractors who were about to leave for Iraq and Afghanistan and being told how to apply a tourniquet if one of their arms was blown off. It began to feel to many journalists as though they were heading into a war zone rather than covering a football tournament. When the main body of journalists covering England arrived in South Africa, they found the coach they were travelling in was escorted by a car containing armed guards and paramedics. The more mischievous among them asked whether there was any provision for air support.

The majority of teams were staying in Gauteng province in the area around Johannesburg because it also offered them training at high altitude and was close to the country's biggest airport, O.R. Tambo, on the eastern edge of the city. The Dutch were based at a Hilton in the northern suburb of Sandton; the South Africans were at a Southern Sun hotel a few hundred metres away; Brazil were a little further out in Randburg; the Ivory Coast were in Sharpeville, on the southern outskirts of Johannesburg; the Americans were between Johannesburg and Pretoria; and Diego Maradona's Argentina were staying on the campus of Pretoria University. Their press conferences were crowded with journalists from the start, but because England were another two hours' drive away, there was a more relaxed air about their first day of training.

The English journalists were in good spirits too. Most of the newspaper chief football writers and their sidekicks, the leading sports reporters, were staying in Sun City in shared apartments, and they were full of their first encounters with the local wildlife. A monkey had stolen the sugar off the table of the *Daily Mirror*'s John Cross, and Matt Lawton, who was training for a triathlon, had been startled by a wild boar while he was jogging on the running track around the golf course. Giancarlo Galavotti, the laconic London correspondent of *Gazzetta dello Sport*, was amused. 'Wild boar meets English bore,' he said.

Around 10.30 a.m. the journalists were escorted from the media centre near the heavily guarded entrance to the complex, past the hotel buildings towards the main training pitch. The hotel was a handsome building that looked like a terrace of smart red-brick houses with balconies and big windows. Even though many of the television journalists had visited the hotel before the team arrived and been shown around it, they were told they were not allowed to film the buildings now. The team coach was parked outside the front entrance. 'Playing with Pride and Glory' said the slogan etched on the side of it. Mounted police patrolled the perimeter. Soon after the journalists had taken up position on the sidelines, the players began to file out.

Fifa rules state that the majority of training sessions must be open to the media for a minimum of 15 minutes. Each team was also obliged to stage one training session that was open to the public and, in return, was allowed to hold one session that was totally closed. So on England's first day, the media stayed for its regulation quarter of an hour and watched the players do some stretching exercises before they were ushered away. The focus, though, was not on the players, who were wearing navy England tops, but on a man in one of the bright red sweatshirts worn by the coaches: David Beckham.

Beckham's presence at the England camp had been a subject of fierce debate. Soon after he had ruptured his Achilles tendon in March and been ruled out of the World Cup as a player, Capello had let it be known that he would still like Beckham to accompany the squad to South Africa. Some thought it was a smart move and that Beckham, who was respected and admired by many players in the squad, would be a valuable member of the backroom staff. He was a sympathetic character, always happy to offer advice if he was asked. Some of the younger players were as awed by Beckham's celebrity as his 115 caps. No one could doubt his World Cup experience either.

In his three World Cups he had been subjected to a whole range of pressure and emotions. He had been vilified, lionised, mobbed, shunned, sent off, dropped, recalled and canonised, in no particular order. In the 1998 World Cup in France he had been criticised by the England manager, Glenn Hoddle, for not being focused when the tournament began. Then he had been sent off in the second-round tie with Argentina, which ended in England losing a penalty shoot-out. He was pilloried in England for his immaturity and irresponsibility in kicking out at Diego Simeone, the action that earned him his red card. He was hung in effigy from a gibbet outside a pub in south London. Many said his actions had vindicated Hoddle's reservations about him. Others argued that Hoddle's treatment of Beckham had piled so much pressure on him and built up so much frustration inside him that his dismissal in St Etienne could be traced directly to appalling man-management.

In the 2002 tournament in Japan and South Korea, Beckham's fame was at its height. He was the pop star of the tournament. His participation had been a source of frenzied speculation after he broke a metatarsal a few months before, and Sven-Goran Eriksson was heavily criticised for including him in the squad when it was clear he was not fully fit. But drama still found him. England played Argentina in their second group game in Sapporo, and Beckham and Simeone faced each other again. Argentina were strong favourites, but England played superbly, and when they won a penalty, Beckham stepped up to take it.

The pressure on him was enormous. Miss it and he would be

castigated anew. He would be the scapegoat again, the preening dilettante who lost the World Cup. Score and this would be a redemption tale, a moment of sweet revenge that would help to banish the demons that had chased him since his dismissal four years earlier. Simeone, an Iago of a footballer, tried to whisper in Beckham's ear as he prepared to take his run-up, but Beckham ignored him. He drove his penalty straight and true, hitting it so cleanly that the Argentina goalkeeper, Pablo Cavallero, could not stop it even though it was perilously close to his left foot. The ball nearly burst the back of the net. England won 1–0.

For a few days, Beckham was the hero. But when England lost to Brazil in the quarter-finals, he jumped out of a tackle in the build-up to Brazil's equaliser. Even though David Seaman, the England goalkeeper, was at fault for Brazil's winner – a 42-yard free kick from Ronaldinho that sailed over his head – many blamed Beckham for the defeat. They said that only his vanity and Eriksson's indulgence had taken him to the tournament in the first place.

In Germany, four years later, some accused him of creating the celebrity culture around the England team and persuading Eriksson to allow the Wags to accompany the squad to Baden-Baden. When England lost in the quarter-final penalty shoot-out to Portugal, Beckham was sitting on the sidelines and wiping away tears after sustaining a knee injury that would have ruled him out of the rest of the tournament if England had progressed.

So Capello's decision to ask Beckham to stay with the squad in South Africa was not based on emotion. He was not bowing to Beckham's celebrity or to the FA's desire that Beckham should be a visible presence during the tournament to help with the English bid to stage the 2018 World Cup. Capello distrusted the celebrity element in footballers' lives almost as much as Sir Alex Ferguson did. But he had also seen Beckham's strength of character at first hand when he banished him from the Real Madrid squad after Beckham announced his move to LA Galaxy in 2007. Beckham did not sulk or criticise Capello. Instead, he forced his way back into the team and helped Madrid win La Liga. Capello had also been impressed when he had left Beckham as an unused substitute during an England game and Beckham, once again, had reacted not by sulking, but by seeking out younger players and offering them advice.

There were still those who harboured conspiracy theories about Beckham's presence. He had always inspired plenty of those. Some said he was only with the squad because the sportswear giant, Adidas, wanted him to be there and Capello had links with Adidas dating back to his days at AC Milan. Quite what value there was for Adidas in having Beckham pictured day after day in England's Umbro training gear was never explained. Others were convinced Beckham was only in Phokeng because Capello had bowed to FA pressure.

Most of the theories were also based on an assumption that Beckham was desperate to be involved with the England squad because he was addicted to the limelight. Being in South Africa was a vanity project, people said. The truth was rather different. Beckham had been unsure about Capello's offer, partly because it had initially been couched in vague terms and did not define a role for him. He also knew he would be accused of being a publicity whore and of undermining the authority of the captain, Rio Ferdinand. Critics of the move suggested Beckham's presence would be a distraction because of the media attention it would create. Beckham was so concerned that he telephoned Ferdinand, Frank Lampard and Steven Gerrard and told them that if they had any misgivings about him travelling with the squad, he would turn down Capello's offer.

Each of the three senior players told Beckham that they thought his presence would be valuable, so he decided to commit himself to the South Africa trip. Capello still struggled to identify exactly what it was he was doing in Phokeng. 'He is important because he is one of the symbols of England,' Capello said. It was easier to say what he wasn't doing. Even though Beckham wore a red top like the rest of the coaches, and sat with the coaches rather than the players at mealtimes, Capello was adamant that he would not be doing any coaching. He could still barely kick a ball, so he certainly wasn't going to have any input as a player. The closest the England manager came to identifying a role for Beckham was after that first day of training when he said he would provide 'liaison' between the players and the coaching staff. He would be a sympathetic ear for players who developed concerns or resentments during the long weeks ahead.

The move made sense. Capello was not big on pastoral care. He was not an approachable man. After Michael Dawson and Tom Huddlestone had been left out of the final 23 following the trip to Austria, their Spurs manager, Harry Redknapp, said Capello had ignored them to such an extent that they had been made to feel like ghosts. Beckham was in South Africa to be a bridge between the players and Capello at a tournament when the usual stresses and strains of travelling with England would be exacerbated by the length of the trip.

When the 15 minutes were up, the journalists left the players behind and wandered back to the media centre to wait for Capello. The England manager had not made any public statements since his final squad had been announced, so he had agreed to discuss his selections and, more pertinently, his omissions after the training session. It looked as though it was going to be a slow news day. So the tweeters tweeted, the bloggers blogged, and the idle played table football. Somebody pointed out that there were three goalkeepers on each team, which seemed like a good solution to Capello's indecision about which of Joe Hart, David James and Robert Green he should select. Individually, none of them inspired confidence, but if he played all three, maybe they would have a chance of getting the job done.

Capello arrived just before one o'clock and marched into the TV press conference. (Radio journalists and the print media had separate press conferences with him later.) Capello answered a couple of questions about England's training facilities and a few more about his squad selection. Then he said he had some bad news. Ferdinand had injured his knee in the last minute of training and had been taken to hospital for a scan. Capello did not know yet how serious the injury was, but when he spoke to the press a few minutes afterwards, it was clear he feared that Ferdinand was out of the World Cup. 'It is the virus of the captain,' Capello said with a wry smile. Adrian Bevington, who was sitting beside him, blanched. 'Virus' was a loaded term in a country ravaged by HIV. Capello sensed his unease. 'OK, OK,' he said, 'the curse of the captain'.

If Ferdinand was out, it meant Capello had lost two captains in four months. For the next 15 minutes he spoke in a way that suggested he was already resigned to losing Ferdinand. Gerrard, the vice-captain, would be the new skipper, he said. A phone call had already been placed to Dawson to find out whether he was available to fly out as a replacement or whether he had gone on holiday. Capello was stoical about the news. He said it was part of what every coach had to prepare for. It was unfortunate, but the loss would be absorbed. As he was speaking, a group of photographers was driving to the hospital in Rustenburg where Ferdinand was having his scan. By mid-afternoon it was confirmed: Ferdinand had sustained medial ligament damage. He would be out for four to six weeks. His World Cup was over before it had begun.

The slow news day just got fast. Reporters phoned their offices. Tweeters tweeted. A row broke out because Neil Ashton, the *News of the World*'s excellent chief football writer, had tweeted that Ferdinand's injury had been caused by a collision with Emile Heskey. Capello had mentioned Heskey's involvement in his press briefing with the daily newspaper journalists, which the Sunday journalists, including Ashton, had listened in to on the basis that they would not disseminate any of the information until after the daily newspapers had gone to press. Ashton, who has superb contacts, insisted he had not heard Capello mention Heskey, and had gleaned the details from another source. The daily journalists were still livid. It was another indication of some of the issues that new technology and the proliferation of media were forcing journalists to confront.

Despite Capello's stoicism, the loss of Ferdinand was a crushing blow. To lose him on the first day of training in South Africa felt like outlandishly bad luck. His long-standing back injury had been causing concern and appeared to have limited his mobility and affected his pace. But Ferdinand had insisted he was close to regaining full fitness, and his central defensive partnership with Terry had always been one of England's strongest features. Both of them were fine players individually, but they complemented each other so well that they were even better together. It did not help that the obvious replacement for Ferdinand in the first 11 was Ledley King, who was physically fragile. Next in line was Jamie Carragher, just back from international exile. Ferdinand was inconsolable. The rest of the squad were stunned. England's campaign had been born under a bad sign.

14 PLATINUM STARS

ENGLAND'S base in Phokeng was at the heart of an area that provided 70 per cent of the world's platinum. Rustenburg boasted the two largest platinum mines in the world. In the afternoon sun, platinum ash shone white on the giant slag heaps that rose up from the veldt. The signs outside Rustenburg welcomed visitors to the Platinum City. The motorway running from Pretoria to Rustenburg, the N4, was called the Platinum Highway. So it seemed to make sense that England's final warm-up game before the World Cup started was against a side called the Platinum Stars.

The game had been arranged for the Monday after England arrived. It was to be played at a stadium on the outskirts of a small town called Moruleng, about an hour north of Sun City, and would double as the obligatory open training session that Fifa demanded from every nation. The FA had to hold an emergency meeting with police officials on the eve of the game after concerns grew about crowd safety. Eight supporters had been injured earlier that Sunday in a stampede as fans tried to get into a game between Nigeria and North Korea in Tembisa township on the outskirts of Johannesburg. There were also chaotic scenes at Argentina's open training session at Pretoria University, where thousands of fans were locked out. Some journalists were taken into the university grounds in the back of police prison vans because there were fears of another stampede if the crowd saw them being led in.

But there were no crowd problems in Moruleng. The FA had organised the game well. The Moruleng Stadium might have been in a semi-rural location, but it was a smart arena with a 20,000 capacity. There was no danger of it being a sell-out. It was not in the midst of a conurbation, as both Tembisa and Pretoria were. It was a three-hour drive from Johannesburg, far enough to discourage all but the most committed fan. The FA had handed out tickets to local schools and police stations, and even if supporters turned up without tickets, there were FA officials outside some of the turnstiles to supply them. Before the game, the England team posed with a banner that said 'Happy to Be Here with You' in Setswana, the local language. They were met with cheers and the blare of thousands of vuvuzelas.

Vuvuzelas were already becoming a hot topic in England. A type of plastic horn popular with South African football supporters since the early 1990s, the vuvuzela emitted a deafening monotonal sound that resembled the buzzing of a million angry bees when they were blown in unison. At matches in South Africa, the noise of the vuvuzelas was unremitting from the first whistle to the last. In fact, they were ubiquitous during the World Cup. Supporters blew them on the streets day and night. They blew them on buses and trains going to and from matches. People went to sleep hearing them and woke up hearing them.

Their crazed blare infuriated many English fans watching at home. When the World Cup started, many television viewers preferred to watch with the sound turned right down rather than put up with the background noise. The BBC and other broadcast organisations explored ways of tuning the vuvuzelas out of their commentaries. There was also a feeling that the instruments stifled the spontaneity that so many England supporters love about crowd noise. There was no singing at the World Cup in South Africa because the noise of the vuvuzelas was so dominant. Sometimes they seemed even to affect the action at matches. The constant flat noise appeared to dampen some of the momentum swings that can happen when a side is in the ascendancy and is being roared on by its supporters.

In England a movement to ban the vuvuzelas gathered pace soon after the World Cup began. A Facebook campaign claimed hundreds of thousands of backers. There were worries that the vuvuzelas were a health risk because they could damage the hearing of supporters in the stadia. But an English campaign to ban vuvuzelas was about as legitimate as a South African effort to ban communal singing at English football grounds would have been. In a small way it was another indication that many in the developed world were still finding it hard to accept the idea that the World Cup was being held in Africa for the first time and that some different rules applied. There was a presumptive arrogance about the idea that it was within the power of English television viewers to ban an instrument that was germane to the football experience for South African supporters.

Part of the problem was that vuvuzelas were embraced by European supporters at the World Cup too. When they blew them, it was in a tuneless drone. It was an amusement to them. For the black South Africans who made up the vast majority of football supporters in the country, they were a more sophisticated form of entertainment. In the mouths of European fans, a vuvuzela was a mournful thing. But when the South Africa supporters at the tournament went to work with them, they were part of choreographed collective dance moves, large groups of fans turning their heads one way then another as they blew their vuvuzelas like a hundred Dizzy Gillespies in a big band. The supporters of the South African Premiership side, Bloemfontein Celtic, were famous for the exuberance of their routines. The shame was that very few black South Africans could afford to buy tickets for the World Cup, so the true potential of the vuvuzela was glimpsed only rarely.

The average wage of a man living in a township such as Tembisa was about 1000 rand (just less than £100) a month. The average price for a seat at a World Cup match in Soccer City or Ellis Park was about half that. The vast majority of residents in the townships simply could not afford to go. One journalist took two youths from Tembisa to watch the Holland–Denmark group game at Soccer City. They told him that they did not know anyone who had been to a match, nor did they know anyone who was planning to go. They could not afford tickets, but many were also frightened off by superstitions and concerns about crowd safety. 'They think they will die if they go to a game,' one of the lads told the journalist. 'They think there will be a crush at the stadium.' There was great enthusiasm for the tournament in the community, and the streets emptied when games were on, but it did not occur to people to try to see a game live. In Tembisa, everyone watched on the giant screen that had been set up on a patch of open land in an area called Ivory Park.

The match against the Platinum Stars was the first time the England players had heard the vuvuzelas. The din was soon the least of their worries. For the third successive warm-up game they struggled to find any sort of fluency. The Stars were hardly exalted opposition. They had finished 14th out of 16 clubs in the South African Premiership the previous season, and were under no illusions about their role that afternoon. They were there to help England prepare for the World Cup, not throw themselves into tackles that might cause more injuries. Their ambitions were strictly limited, and when Jermain Defoe scored after three minutes, it looked as if England might amass a cricket score.

Defoe had started in attack alongside Peter Crouch, with Steven Gerrard and Frank Lampard paired together in the centre of midfield. Joe Hart was in goal, behind what looked as though it was the new first-choice back four, with Ledley King partnering John Terry in central defence. The blend didn't work. After the early goal, England struggled. In fact, they were outplayed for large parts of the first half. The Stars played neat, passing football and England chased shadows. If there had been an African tradition, during long periods of possession for one team, of cheering every time a player touched the ball, the crowd in Moruleng would have been busy cheering the Stars. The home team were not without flair either. A fast right-winger called Joseph Molongoane gave Ashley Cole a difficult 45 minutes. He even nutmegged him.

The game began to turn into a very English farce. The Stars were awarded a penalty when Glen Johnson lost concentration, failed to clear a long, hopeful pass, and brought down Mzikayise Mashaba. The referee awarded a penalty, but Bradley Grobler missed his chance of 15 minutes of fame when he lifted his spot-kick high over the bar. England did not seem to appreciate the reprieve, though. They did not improve and, on the touchline, Capello became increasingly angry. He screamed at the players, his face contorted in rage, and when the female fourth official, Amelia Masiu, wandered over to him and told him to calm down, Capello yelled at her too. 'His behaviour was pretty bad,' Masiu said later. When she told him off a second time, Capello grew apoplectic. A man in a suit walked out of the tunnel and whispered something in Masiu's ear. She stopped rebuking Capello after that.

At half-time Capello substituted the entire team, with the exception of Joe Cole, who remained at left midfield. The England manager made obvious his displeasure with the first-half display. He disappeared into the dressing room briefly at half-time, then stalked back onto the pitch, sitting on the bench with his arms folded stiffly. It transpired he had lambasted the players and told them exactly what he thought of their efforts. He was so angry that he had thrown a glass tray while he was berating them and smashed it to smithereens. 'I hope you are enjoying your holiday,' he screamed at them. England's football improved in the second half, but elements of farce were still there. This time, instead of Capello losing his cool, it was Wayne Rooney.

There were still lingering concerns about Rooney. Mostly, they centred on nagging doubts about his fitness. He never seemed to have fully recovered from the ankle ligament injury he sustained against Bayern Munich in March. Manchester United had rushed him back the following week, but then he missed a week, played a couple of games and missed a fortnight. He was never quite the same after the injury at the Allianz Arena. He had scored 34 goals that season, but after the game in Munich he did not score again. The form that he had shown for United earlier in the season, when he had been unstoppably brilliant, had not returned either. And when Capello talked to the press after that first day of England training when Ferdinand had been injured, he made a throw-away remark about Rooney that went almost unnoticed.

When Capello was asked whether he would rest Rooney for the match against the Platinum Stars, he smiled and said that Rooney had been begging to let him play. 'He says he needs to play to get his form again,' Capello said. It was a small glimpse into Rooney's state of mind. He was becoming increasingly frustrated that the brilliance that had been his trademark all season and that had carried United to within an ace of the title had deserted him since his injury. The fear was that because he was so important for both club and country, because he was such an impetuous, impatient man, that he had not been given the rest and recuperation he needed. The truth gradually began to dawn on England supporters that for the second World Cup in succession, Rooney was going into the tournament short of full fitness.

It made the burden that he had to bear even heavier. So much expectation rested on his shoulders. He was the player all England was pinning its hopes on. All the team's other weaknesses – the lack of a world-class goalkeeper, the loss of Ferdinand and Beckham, and the injury to Gareth Barry – were almost disregarded. As long as England had Rooney, the argument went, anything was possible.

Everybody knew how vital he was to England's hopes of success, and nobody hid it. Not even Capello. Earlier in the season the England manager had given an interview to Italian television in which he said he grabbed his own testicles with his hand – a Roman superstition to ward off bad luck, the English equivalent being perhaps touching wood or crossing the fingers – every time Rooney played because he was so afraid of him getting injured.

In Moruleng, Rooney's frustration boiled over. He flung himself into a couple of reckless challenges on Stars midfielder Kagiso Senamela, the kind of scything, clumsy tackles that were always a sign Rooney had lost his composure. There was some barging too, and the referee, Jeff Selogilwe, lectured him about his behaviour. Rooney responded by swearing at him, so Selogilwe booked him for dissent. Selogilwe spoke to English reporters by the touchline afterwards and told them what Rooney had said. He also pointed out that if Rooney did that in the World Cup, he would probably be sent off. England improved in the second half and Rooney was the best player, making a goal for Joe Cole and scoring a late volley himself to complete a 3–0 win. But the back-page headlines the next morning were all about his loss of control.

England supporters still remembered how Rooney's indiscipline had cost England dearly at the last World Cup, when he was sent off after stamping on Ricardo Carvalho. If he was acting like this against the Platinum Stars, how would he cope when the pressure was on against the USA? To underline that he would be under scrutiny, it was announced that the Brazilian referee and his assistants for England's opening match had been given a list of 20 English swear words to study in preparation for the game in Rustenburg. 'We can't do this in 11 different languages,' linesman Roberto Braatz said, 'but at least we have to know the swear words in English.' Rooney had been warned.

Events in Moruleng posed wider questions about England's

prospects in South Africa too. As with their performances in the other warm-up games against Mexico and Japan, England had been disappointing against the Platinum Stars. Their confidence appeared to have deserted them. There were only so many times you could say performances were meaningless just because they happened in non-competitive matches. The reality was that England were struggling. In fact, they appeared to have entered a decline. The consolation was that they had been drawn in Group C with Slovenia and Algeria as well as the USA. It was probably the weakest group of the eight in the first round. As soon as the draw had been made in Cape Town in December 2009, England supporters had begun to speculate about who Capello's side would face in the second round. Being eliminated before then was not a prospect that occurred to anyone.

On the eve of the World Cup's opening game between South Africa and Mexico at Soccer City, England were still one of the favourites to win the tournament. Only Spain, Brazil and Argentina were shorter priced in the bookmakers' odds. The hyperbole about Capello redoubled too. He was hailed as the greatest England manager since Sir Alf Ramsey, and Frank Lampard gave an interview praising Capello's tough management style and saying it had been exactly what England's players needed after the way they had been indulged under Sven-Goran Eriksson and Steve McClaren. 'He brought us into line straight away,' Lampard said.

The USA were regarded as a decent side, probably England's greatest threat in the group, but nothing Capello's team couldn't handle. Landon Donovan, the right-sided midfielder who had enjoyed a successful loan-spell at Everton earlier in the year and had played with David Beckham at the LA Galaxy, was probably their best player. Michael Bradley, son of the US coach Bob Bradley, was an accomplished central midfielder who did simple things very well, and Clint Dempsey, who played on the opposite flank to

Donovan, had had a fine season with Fulham and appeared in the Europa League final defeat to Atletico Madrid in Hamburg. It was also worth remembering that the Americans were the only team who had beaten Spain in the last four years.

England had sent Beckham and Franco Baldini to scout the Americans' final warm-up game against Australia at the Ruimsig Stadium on the outskirts of Johannesburg the Saturday before the tournament began. The US had played well, particularly Bradley and his central midfield partner Ricardo Clark, but they appeared vulnerable when they were defending set-pieces, even against a mediocre Australia side. Beckham chatted to a few English reporters at half-time, but stressed that he couldn't say anything on the record. When he was asked whether it was him or Baldini who would compile the scouting report for Capello, Beckham used it as an opportunity to poke fun at himself. 'It won't be me,' he said. 'I can't write.'

When the English writers spoke to Donovan after the game, his expression tightened slightly when he was told Beckham had been watching him. A year earlier, Donovan had cooperated with a book written by the *Sports Illustrated* journalist Grant Wahl about Beckham's first year with the Galaxy. It was called *The Beckham Experiment* and in it Donovan was fiercely critical of Beckham. The book caused a furore when it was published, and Donovan quickly made a grovelling apology to Beckham and said he regretted all the things he had said to Wahl. He did not emerge well from the episode.

The day before the USA game, Capello appeared at the pre-match press conference at the Royal Bafokeng Stadium where the match was taking place. It was less than two miles from England's base, and if England won the group, they would also play their second round match there. Capello told the media he was confident England could reach the final. 'I exist to win,' he said. Steven Gerrard spoke too. The England captain said it was time for the players to deliver. The doubts that had crept in after England's poor performances in their warm-up matches were swept away on a tide of optimism. 'Yes We Can' said the *Daily Mirror*'s front-page headline on the day of the game.

The previous afternoon, the World Cup had begun at Soccer City, a spectacular stadium near Soweto designed to evoke a calabash, an African cooking pot. Johannesburg was gripped by World Cup fever. Two days earlier, more than 200,000 fans had spilled on to the streets of Sandton to cheer the South African players as they rode in an open-topped bus. Now the streets were choked again as the world turned its eyes to Soccer City. The gridlock meant that it took some reporters more than four hours to make a 15-mile journey to the stadium. South Africa and Mexico fought out an entertaining 1–1 draw, and later that Friday, in Cape Town, France and Uruguay drew 0–0.

England were up next, waiting at the end of the Platinum Highway, ready to begin their journey.

15 THE HAND OF CLOD

IF there were going to be a terrorist attack at the World Cup, logic suggested a match between England and the USA would be high on any hit list. But the security at the Royal Bafokeng Stadium on the Saturday of the game was disconcertingly slack. Taxi drivers were able to get their vehicles into the grounds of the stadium without any of the required parking passes, journalists were waved through scanners without their bags being checked, and four hours before the game, people without any accreditation were wandering around the dressing room area underneath the main stand. In some ways, it made a refreshing change from the pass-dominated culture that ruled at sporting events in the West. In others, it raised concerns that the tournament might be a soft target.

Things were not quite as relaxed among the England squad. There was speculation about several starting positions in the team right up until two hours before the kick-off. There were suggestions that Joe Cole might have stolen ahead of James Milner, who had been suffering from a stomach bug, to claim the place on the left of midfield, but most of the guesswork revolved around who would start in goal. Robert Green, the West Ham United goalkeeper, was a narrow favourite, partly because he had played so well in the warm-up match against Mexico and partly because he had come closer than either of his rivals to establishing himself as Capello's first choice in the recent past. But despite what Capello had said about Joe Hart at Munich airport back in March, he had let it be known that he had become increasingly impressed with the young goalkeeper who had been promoted from the Under-21 side. Many thought Hart would start against the USA.

David James, who was the most naturally talented of England's three World Cup keepers, appeared to have been discounted. He had been plagued by injury throughout the previous Premier League season, and there were suggestions that he was not fully fit. There were also rumours that he had fallen out with Franco Baldini, and it was said that Capello and his backroom staff were disappointed with James's attitude. James was a football eccentric, and Capello and Baldini felt he sometimes appeared too casual. James was adamant that was not the case, but whatever the truth, there appeared to be a rift. James, who was eight weeks short of his 40th birthday and the oldest player in the tournament, was seen as the third choice even though there were rumours that some of the senior players wanted him to start because he was a better communicator than Green.

Capello did not tell the players his starting 11 until two hours before the game. That was the way he worked. When he first took over as coach at AC Milan in 1991, he told his players the team the night before the game, but on a couple of occasions, when players got injured on the day of the match, changed his mind. He felt that the players he had to draft in at the last minute had switched off mentally when they had been told the night before that they were not playing and were not in the right frame of mind to play. Naming the team two hours before kick-off kept everyone alert and on edge, Capello argued. It also stopped the line-up being leaked to the press the night before the match.

Nobody complained too much about this particular part of Capello's man-management, but most players said privately that they would prefer to know the night before if they were in the side because it would help them psychologically. Their argument was that even though, in theory, every member of the squad should prepare for the match as if they were playing, knowing that you were in the team added extra intensity to a player's build-up to kick-off, both mentally and physically. In particular, it was felt that goalkeepers benefited from being told the night before whether they were in the side because of the more solitary nature of their job and the pressure they were under.

But Capello would not change his ways, and two hours before the USA game he got the squad together in the England changing room at the Royal Bafokeng Stadium and told them the side. Milner would start on the left of midfield, Emile Heskey had won the battle with Peter Crouch to be Wayne Rooney's strike partner, Ledley King would partner John Terry in central defence, Glen Johnson and Ashley Cole would be the full-backs, Frank Lampard and Steven Gerrard would be given another chance to prove they could play together in the heart of midfield, and Aaron Lennon would line up on the right. Green would be the goalkeeper.

Green looked desperately nervous as he lined up behind Gerrard in the tunnel before kick-off. His eyes staring straight ahead, it seemed as if he could hardly breathe. He knew that many people lacked faith in him and viewed him merely as the best of a bad bunch. The days when English goalkeepers had been a byword for reliability and brilliance had long gone. The country's proud lineage of fine goalkeeping talent had boasted some of the best in the world. Gordon Banks, England's 1966 World Cup-winning goalkeeper, was usually rated second only to the USSR goalkeeper Lev Yashin in lists of the best there have ever been. Banks's famous save from Pelé at the 1970 World Cup was an astonishing piece of athleticism that immortalised him as one of the greats of the game. Peter Shilton and Ray Clemence were so good that England manager Ron Greenwood could not choose between them at first, and alternated them from match to match. Despite that, Shilton still earned 125 caps in an international career that lasted from 1970 to 1990. David Seaman was not quite in their league, but he was still viewed as one of the team's strengths rather than one of its weaknesses.

But Seaman had gone on too long (at the 2002 World Cup a German newspaper described him as 'a piece of meat with eyes'), and after he retired, England's goalkeepers had come to be defined by their mistakes rather than their saves. James laboured under the nickname 'Calamity' after a series of errors, eccentricities and lapses in concentration. Paul Robinson was haunted by a moment in a European Championship qualifying tie against Croatia in Zagreb in 2006 when he tried to clear a backpass by Gary Neville, only for the ball to bobble over his foot and trickle into the net. Robinson always insisted that it was not a mistake and that the pitch was to blame, but his England career never recovered from it. In November of the following year, when England needed to avoid defeat against the Croats at Wembley to qualify for Euro 2008, Steve McClaren handed a competitive debut to Scott Carson, who promptly allowed an eighth-minute long-range effort from Nico Kranjcar to squirm from his grasp and roll into the net. England lost 3–2 and Carson has not played for England since.

England fans tried to banish thoughts of that tainted heritage from their minds as Capello's side walked on to the pitch at the Royal Bafokeng Stadium for the national anthems. Maybe the World Cup would be the making of Green. Maybe the pessimism about England's goalkeepers would prove to be unfounded. And nobody was thinking about the goalkeeping situation when England got off to the best possible start. Only four minutes had gone when Lampard controlled a throw-in from Johnson about 30 yards out and worked the ball to Heskey. Heskey laid the ball off and Gerrard burst through the heart of the USA defence and clipped the ball past Tim Howard with the outside of his right foot. As Gerrard sprinted over to the touchline to celebrate in front of the England fans, it felt as if all the travails of the warm-up games and all Capello's missteps had been meaningless after all. Now that England's tournament had begun and begun so well, maybe the England that had qualified so effortlessly for the World Cup would return and replace the impostor that had appeared in recent months. In the stands, English journalists began plotting their travel arrangements for the knock-out phase.

But England did not build on Gerrard's goal. In fact, the USA, inspired by Landon Donovan, forced their way back into the game. They should have equalised when Donovan curled an inviting cross on to the head of Jozy Altidore, the striker who had played much of the previous season at Hull City, but Altidore glanced his header wide. On the bench, Capello became increasingly animated and frustrated. His notorious hair-trigger temper had only rarely exploded in his time as England manager, but now that the stakes were raised, it was back immediately. He had been involved in an altercation with photographers at the England training ground a couple of days earlier because they had been pointing their cameras at the medical room. 'No excuses,' he had yelled at them when they had tried to explain that the photographer taking the pictures had been unaware of the rules.

Capello's outburst had been interpreted as a sign that the pressure of the build-up was getting to him, and now he was up and down on the England bench all the time, his face contorted with rage, his hands outstretched in angry pleading. The FA had been running adverts for its Respect campaign featuring the actor Ray Winstone playing an angry dad on the touchline bullying his little boy. Capello was not on message. He seemed particularly annoyed with Milner, who was struggling to cope with the forward runs of USA right-back Steve Cherundolo. When Milner was booked for persistent fouling after another in a series of illegal challenges on Cherundolo, Capello snapped. He told Shaun Wright-Phillips to warm up and brought Milner off. There were still 15 minutes to half-time.

It was a humiliating moment for Milner. It also suggested Capello was acting out of a mixture of impatience and panic. Later that night, some English reporters spoke to a Premier League manager who had been at the match. He said he was astounded by Capello's decision. He pointed out that there were any number of ways Capello could have dealt with the problem to save Milner the ignominy of being hauled off before half-time. If Capello was so worried about Cherundolo, he could have switched Lennon to the left for 15 minutes and moved Milner to the right. Or he could have asked Rooney to drop back into left midfield, where he had often played for Manchester United, and moved Milner into a central midfield three with Lampard and Gerrard. Milner had excelled in that position for Aston Villa. But Capello acted immediately, substituted Milner and moved Wright-Phillips to left midfield. It worked. The threat from Cherundolo was snuffed out.

England hung on to their lead until five minutes before half-time. Then disaster struck. Clint Dempsey picked up a loose ball midway inside England's half and ran towards goal. Gerrard challenged him, but Dempsey span around, turned in a circle and shook him off. Gerrard challenged him again. This time Dempsey span around the opposite way and shook him off again. He was 25 yards out now and he swung his left boot at the ball. It was a speculative shot. It was hit with pace but it was close to Green, and even though it left the ground briefly, it did not bounce awkardly. For a goalkeeper of Green's quality, it should have been a routine save.

It was so close to him that Green did not even have to dive. He was right in the middle of the goal and the shot was straight at him. As it came in, Green sank to one knee in the manner of an outfielder in a cricket match who kneels to use his leg as a safety net in case he misfields the ball. But as Green tried to gather it, the ball squirmed out of his grasp and bounced down and behind him to his right. Green took a split second to react and then flung himself backwards in a desperate effort to try to stop it crossing the line. He span around and reached out his left hand, but it was too late. The horror of what had happened hit him. Green bowed his head and let it rest on the goal-line for a second. Then he jumped up and retrieved the ball from where it had nestled in the back of the net. He threw it back towards the centre circle and held up his hand in acknowledgement of his mistake.

The television screens in the press box at the stadium showed the moment over and over again. It was like watching reel-by-reel footage of a crime. The ball going into Green's hands, then bouncing off them and spinning back and to the right, back and to the right. His desperate attempt to recover and the realisation that he could not. His head sinking slowly to the floor and resting there. It was compelling viewing. It was misery voyeurism. It was probably the most spectacular mistake an England goalkeeper had ever made at a World Cup. Seaman's error in Japan in 2002, when he had allowed a speculative free-kick from Ronaldinho to fly over him from 45 yards during England's quarter-final with Brazil in Shizuoka, was more costly because it led to England's exit from the tournament. The same could be said of Peter Bonetti's mistakes in the quarter-final against Germany at the 1970 World Cup, when he dived over a shot from Franz Beckenbauer and was stranded by a looping header from Uwe Seeler. Those errors wiped out England's 2–0 lead, and when Gerd Müller scored Germany's winner in extra time, England's defence of the World Cup was over. Green's mistake did not cost England a place in the tournament, but it was a worse error. And in the age of YouTube and highlight reels, it was bound to be given more exposure.

Some attempted to blame the Jabulani ball, which had already caused controversy at the World Cup. Manufactured by Adidas, with fewer seams than previous balls, it was smoother and supposedly rounder than its predecessors. The Bundesliga and the

Japanese J-League had used it throughout the previous season, and Germany and Japan both seemed more confident with it than most of the other teams at the tournament. But it was an annoying novelty to most players. Goalkeepers hated it. Tim Howard had said before the tournament that a player could strike it the same way five times and it would move in a different way each time. Others said it reminded them of the cheap plastic balls bought at the seaside for a kick-around on the beach. 'There will be goals scored from 45 yards at this World Cup,' US reserve keeper Marcus Hahnemann said. 'They will be called great goals, but they won't be great goals. It's just the ball.' Adidas tried to claim the criticism was a Nike conspiracy. It wasn't. The ball bounced too high and acted too erratically in the air. It transformed crossfield balls that should have been brilliant passes into kicks for touch. Strikers didn't like the Jabulani either because it made it harder to anticipate the flight of a pass or a cross as they tried to get on the end of it. The Jabulani turned the ball from the player's friend into his enemy. It made some of the world's best strikers of the ball look like novices at a time when the game was supposed to be showcasing their talents. But the Jabulani wasn't to blame this time. It was pure human error.

The other England players looked stunned. Gerrard held his head in his hands. So did some of his teammates. Lampard had the presence of mind to try to offer Green some encouragement, but all the confidence England had gleaned from their early goal drained away. Fear took over. They made it through to half-time without conceding again, but when they emerged after the interval, it was without King. King's knees had always been the worry, but this time it was a groin strain that prevented him playing any further part in the match. He did not play again in the World Cup. Jamie Carragher came on in his place. His appearance vindicated his decision to make himself available for the World Cup, but his performance and the way King had immediately succumbed to injury raised more questions about the wisdom of Capello's selection policy.

England should have taken the lead again seven minutes after half-time when Lennon played Heskey through on goal. Heskey, though, had scored only seven times in his 60 international appearances and was hardly a clinical finisher. Unusually for a centre forward, his main role was not to score goals but to create space and opportunities for Rooney. He was probably England's best player against the USA, but the chance fell to the wrong man. Heskey advanced on Howard but hit his shot straight at him and without any conviction. Howard saved it easily. Ten minutes later the USA nearly made England pay for their profligacy. Altidore turned away from Carragher, who could not cope with his pace, and burst past him into the box. Altidore miscued his shot and Green achieved a small measure of redemption by pushing it on to the post.

England never looked like scoring again after Heskey's miss. They did not play badly, but they were still in recovery from Green's error. Rooney, who had already gone five games without scoring for England, was subdued. He did not look fully fit. Capello brought Crouch on for Heskey for the last ten minutes, but he could not break the deadlock either and the game dwindled to a draw. The US players celebrated and walked around the ground to thank the pockets of their supporters. England stalked straight off without even acknowledging the tens of thousands of supporters who had filled the stadium with their flags and their noise. It felt as though England had lost.

It felt, in fact, as if England had been here before. Sven-Goran Eriksson, with a new lady on his arm, had waltzed back into the World Cup as manager of the Ivory Coast, but that night in Rustenburg it felt as if he was at England's helm again. England were besieged by the same doubts and the same exasperation that had haunted Eriksson's reign. They had been matched and sometimes outplayed by a team they should have beaten. Individually, not one of the US players would have forced their way into England's side. England were back to the days when Michael Owen was observing, a couple of days after England had been humbled by Croatia at Wembley in 2007, that not a single Croat would have got into the England team. The reputations of the USA players were not nearly as elevated as those of the England players. None of them made the short-lists for Fifa World Player of the Year. None of them had played in Champions League finals. None of them were counted among the elite of the world game. Yet collectively they had been England's equal. All the old questions about why England could not muster the same kind of team spirit as other nations began to be asked again but, of course, the aftermath was dominated by the reaction to Green's mistake.

The result felt worse than it was because it had been such a shocking error. It felt like such a careless, frivolous way to throw away a victory. It coloured the evening in funereal black when actually drawing with the USA was not such a bad result. Many had predicted before the finals that it would be a stalemate and that both teams would go on to use it as a springboard to qualify for the second round. But it did not feel that way now. Green's error sapped England of the momentum they desperately needed. A victory in Rustenburg would have soothed some of the tensions that were building within the England camp about the suffocating nature of the regime the players had been subjected to since they left for pre-World Cup training in Austria. Nothing quelled resentments and dissent as efficiently as winning football matches. Nothing prevented media criticism more completely than victory after victory, but that happy cycle had been broken.

Even if the draw with the USA was far from a disgrace, the abiding memory from it was bound to be Green's error and the picture of English incompetence it painted. It made England a World Cup laughing-stock in their first match, and the confidence of some of the players never recovered. Because they were the kings of the Premier League, legends in their own land, secure in their own environment, no one had thought of these men with their gilded lives as being susceptible to bouts of self-doubt or introspection. That was where the USA game represented a crushing setback for England. Its aftermath showed that even though many of the England players might have had giant egos, they were fragile egos too.

Some of them found it hard to cope with adversity. And they were scared of the criticism they were going to face in the press and among the fans at home. They knew that Green would be singled out because this kind of incident shone a light on one of the reasons why some of the England players sometimes felt an ambivalence about playing for their country. Only Carragher had really had the courage to talk about it, but if players did not perform for England, they were subjected to a level of opprobrium that was out of all proportion to anything that was thrown at them if they had a bad game for their club. They knew defeat to the USA would spawn a virus of bad headlines and stinging remarks. Their heads went down. The mood plummeted.

And for the first time, serious questions were asked about Capello's stewardship of the team. Not winning in Rustenburg made him vulnerable. The secret doubts and concerns many had harboured about Capello as they watched England labour through their warm-up matches came bubbling to the surface. Suddenly, England had been found wanting in a game of real importance, and it was legitimate to ask Capello awkward questions. Why had he spread uncertainty among the defence and the goalkeepers in particular by taking so long to decide on who would be his first choice between the posts? Why had he taken such a big risk on selecting King when every instinct should have been telling him King's body would not be able to stand up to the demands of a World Cup? Why had he risked shattering Milner's confidence by substituting him after half an hour of his first World Cup game? Why had his demeanour on the touchline changed so dramatically that he now looked like a raging madman incapable of making cool, calm decisions? Had the pressure got to him already? Could he handle it? Green's error stripped England of the momentum they needed, and it stripped Capello of his invincibility too. He had had a two-and-a-half-year honeymoon as England manager. Now it was over.

Green did the best he could after the game. He was besieged by reporters when he walked into the mixed zone, but he answered every question fully and honestly. When Seaman had come into the interview area in Shizuoka after his error, he had dissolved into tears when the questions began, but Green set his jaw and did his best to rationalise what had happened. He did not blame the Jabulani. He apologised to all the fans back in England and at the ground. 'I would have loved to have stopped it,' he said. 'I do it time and again in training. It's just a genuine, horrible mistake. The important thing is that you have to be willing to work on it mentally. I'm 30 years old and I've learned to deal with these things. That's what football's all about. It's got a wonderful habit of coming round and kicking you in the balls. It's how you bounce back from that.'

Bouncing back would not be easy. Green was pilloried and mocked in England's Sunday newspapers. The *News of the World* and the *Sunday Mirror* came up with the same headline. 'Hand of Clod' their front pages screamed. Former England captain Terry Butcher said it was the worst error an English goalkeeper had ever made. Things had calmed down a little by the next day, but Green still made the front page of the *Daily Mirror*. It printed a picture of Green's former girlfriend, Elizabeth Minett, wearing a tiny bikini decorated in the colours of the Cross of St George. Above the picture was one of the best headlines of the World Cup: 'Here's One He Dropped Earlier'. The mood in American papers was buoyant.

The *New York Post* captured the mood in England and the USA with its front-page headline: 'USA Wins 1–1'.

Some analysts offered only cold comfort. They found it hard to understand the disappointment about England's performance in Rustenburg because they thought the performance was entirely predictable. They said it was an accurate reflection of how good, or bad, the side was and that it was merely the first sign of what was to come. After the game, Steve Howard had stood outside the media centre at the Royal Bafokeng Stadium, dragging on a cigarette and talking to colleagues. The *Sun*'s chief sportswriter was one of the few who had predicted this would be a miserable World Cup for Capello's team, and he listened with increasing exasperation as other writers debated the laboured performance against the States. In the end, Howard could stand it no longer.

'What did you expect from England?' Howard blurted out. '*Swan Lake*?'

16 A MESSAGE FOR FLOYD

IT was good that Algeria were next up. That was what everybody thought anyway. The match was set for the Friday after the USA game, in Cape Town. Beating them was a gimme, a given, a cinch. They were a 90-minute open goal. Just what England needed to get back on track. So England's World Cup dreaming was not disturbed for long by the draw with the States. Among the fans and the media at least, the superiority complex kicked back in straight away. Other results helped too. Italy drew with Paraguay; Spain lost to Switzerland; France drew with Uruguay. Suddenly, England's result in Rustenburg did not look so bad. And now Algeria were here to help take the pain away completely. Everyone had always maintained that England had been handed an easy group, and Algeria's presence in it was part of the reason. Algeria had only qualified for the World Cup after a play-off with Egypt, they had been beaten 3–0 by the Republic of Ireland in one of their warm-up matches, and they had not scored a goal in the World Cup finals since 1986.

The fact that their team contained hardly any Premier League players was widely seen, in England at least, as another indication of their mediocrity. The tournament in South Africa would change the view that the Premier League was the best domestic football competition in the world, but that opinion began to crystallise only later in the tournament. When the World Cup began, the Premier League was still seen as the gold standard, and the fact that Algeria could point to only Nadir Belhadj, Hassan Yebda and Adlene

Guedioura as players who plied their trade in it was interpreted as a sign of weakness. When it was also taken into account that Belhadj and Yebda, who was on loan from Benfica, had played for relegated Portsmouth, while Guedioura was a midfielder for humble Wolves, the idea took hold that England needed only to turn up to secure their first victory of the competition. It was expected that Fabio Capello's side would win – and win in some style. When Prince William, who was in Cape Town helping to promote England's bid to host the 2018 World Cup, was asked to predict the score, he showed that he had caught the mood. 'Ten–nil would be quite nice,' he said, 'but I'm not sure that's realistic, so three–nil or something like that.'

A couple of days after the USA game, the presumption that England would be resuscitated in Cape Town was challenged by an old enemy, Franz Beckenbauer, the former Germany captain and manager, and one of only two men to win the World Cup as player and boss. Beckenbauer had not been impressed by what he had seen in Rustenburg, and did not attempt to hide his disdain in a newspaper column he wrote for the South African paper called *The Times*. 'It looked to me as if the English have gone backwards into the bad old days of kick and rush,' said Beckenbauer, whose nickname as a player was Der Kaiser. 'I am not sure if Fabio Capello can still change much there. The English are being punished for the fact that there are very few English players in the Premier League as clubs use better foreign players from all over the world.'

Beckenbauer's views unleashed a wave of righteous indignation in English newspapers. 'Kaiser Sticks Das Boot In' said the headline on the back page of the *Sun*. In the *Mail on Sunday* Piers Morgan condemned the 'sheer, breathtaking arrogance of the man' and asked, 'Who the hell does he think he is?' Beckenbauer's comments were also put to Wayne Rooney when he spoke to the media at England's base on the Wednesday after the draw with the USA. Rooney said that Beckenbauer was entitled to his opinion, but no one in the England squad was listening to him. And when a German journalist asked him if he was hoping England would play Germany in the second round, Rooney nodded. 'Of course,' he said, 'because it would be nice to beat them.'

England flew to Cape Town on Thursday and trained at the Green Point Stadium at dusk, ahead of the match against Algeria the following night. It was a beautiful evening. As the players trained, the setting sun turned slivers of cloud into red shards above the stadium, and the rocky majesty of Table Mountain faded with the light until it was just an outline, a looming presence in the darkness. It was the first time England had ventured more than an hour away from their compound in Phokeng, and the first time that most of the English journalists who were shadowing them had left their base in Sun City. There was a feeling of liberation about being in Cape Town, a feeling of spirits lifting. Even Capello seemed a little more relaxed.

It was his 64th birthday on the day of the game against Algeria, so when Gabby Logan interviewed Capello as part of a BBC preview, she asked him if he knew the Beatles song 'When I'm Sixty-Four'. Capello looked baffled. Logan sang a small part of it. Now Capello looked at her like she was completely mad. Maybe he thought it was going to turn into one of those stunts he had been caught up in on Italian television, where the presenter started to undress. Logan pressed on and mentioned the lyric in the first verse that goes 'birthday greetings bottle of wine'. She presented Capello with a bottle of red wine and his face burst into a smile. He said he had not had an alcoholic drink for a long time. If Logan was tempted to say everyone had guessed that already, she resisted. Instead she laboured her Beatles theme and mixed up her lyrics. 'The next line is "will you still please me",' she said, which it isn't. But Capello wasn't to know and she continued. 'So will you still be pleasing us, pleasing

England, by Friday?' Capello smiled again. 'I would like a good result after the game, yes,' he said.

Capello still seemed in a good humour when he took the stage for his press conference at the stadium on the eve of the match. There was a light-hearted air about the place. An Australian radio journalist dressed as an Algerian pirate called Barbarossa, who had terrorised British merchant ships in the 17th century, had been sitting in the room and was planning to ask a couple of flippant questions about the history of Anglo-Algerian conflicts, but the FA objected to his presence and he was forced to discard his eye-patch, his false beard and his cape. He had looked like a flamboyant and happily unpredictable corsair when he had been dressed in his finery, but when he returned to his seat, he was revealed as a rather timid, balding and unremarkable fellow, cowed by his own unmasking.

Capello produced standard answers in halting English at the press conference. It was the first time he had spoken since the day of the USA game. 'It was only the result I was not happy about against the USA,' Capello said. 'Only this. But all the teams who played the first game found that it was not easy. The pressure of the first game is higher than in other games.' A journalist from Sky Italia asked a fawning question about whether Capello had been surprised by the level of criticism directed at him and England by the English media. The journalist said that in Italy the reaction to the country's draw with Paraguay had been more temperate. Capello dismissed the question. He knew that most of the criticism in England had been personalised towards Robert Green. He also knew it was disingenuous to suggest that the Italian press was more balanced than its English counterpart. A week or so later, when Italy were knocked out of the World Cup in the group stage, no one was talking about the reserve of the Italian media any more. *Corriere della Sera* called it 'the ugliest Italy team ever'. *La Stampa*'s headline read: 'The aircraft called Shame is ready to leave'.

After the main press conference, Capello was ushered into a side-room at the Green Point Stadium so that he and Steven Gerrard could speak in more depth to the football correspondents from the English newspapers, and without the presence of television cameras and journalists from agencies such as Associated Press, Reuters and Agence France-Presse, whose job it was to file their reports immediately. It was supposed to be a more intimate forum too, with only one writer from each paper allowed so that it was easier to ask questions. The idea was that it would also be a more relaxed setting for Capello to answer them in. In Cape Town, he rewarded those who had squeezed into the room with something approaching a cabaret.

Capello did not like the separate press conferences that were convened especially for the English; he viewed them as a drain on his time that he could do without. He was not compelled by Fifa to do them, but Adrian Bevington had convinced him that observing this particular ritual would help things run a lot more smoothly. It worked on two levels: the human one that dictated the more contact the journalists had with the manager the better disposed they felt towards him, and the pragmatic one, where the more information the press was given, the more the journalists tended to reflect what Capello was saying rather than concentrating on the opinions of critics among the ranks of ex-England players or managers.

Capello radiated a mixture of boredom and impatience as he listened to the questions. He did not look like a man cracking under pressure, but he did look taut and tense. Everyone stood in a big, messy circle: Capello, Gerrard and about 20 newspaper journalists. Capello listened as Gerrard spoke. He started gyrating his hips as if he was limbering up for some sort of exercise routine. Or a fight. Soon the questions were directed at Capello and the vexed topic of his habit of telling the players the starting line-up only two hours before kick-off. Matt Dickinson, the chief sports correspondent of

The Times, and a man Capello knew and respected, asked him whether the goalkeepers in particular would benefit from having more time to prepare for the game. Capello's eyes danced. He asked Dickinson whether he thought it was better to tell the goalkeeper the night before. Dickinson said he did.

'Then you'd better take my place,' he said. 'I've always used this way, this method. It's my way. I'd prefer not to change.'

Gerrard caught the eye of one of the journalists standing behind Capello and grinned. It was obvious it was not the first time he had seen Capello engaged in this type of exchange.

When Capello was pressed again on the issue, he turned away and smiled. 'Another manager,' he muttered.

Capello went back to gyrating his hips as Gerrard answered a final question. Then he was reminded by Giancarlo Galavotti from *Gazzetta dello Sport* that the next day was his birthday. Maybe it was a good omen, Galavotti said, because Capello had won the Italian title with Roma in 2001 on the day before his birthday. Capello reached down and grabbed his testicles with his fingers, an Italian superstition for warding off bad luck, the equivalent of the English touching wood. It was the gesture he had mentioned earlier in the season when he said he observed the same superstition every time Wayne Rooney played because he was so worried he was going to get injured. 'Bye-bye,' he said as he did it, then marched off.

One selection issue had dominated the build-up to the game. All week the debate had raged about whether Green should keep his place after his error in Rustenburg or be dropped in favour of David James or Joe Hart. The argument came down to this: should a player be left out because of one mistake? Capello had procrastinated over his choice of goalkeeper until the very eve of the tournament, and weighed the merits and weaknesses of his three candidates exhaustively before making his decision, so it was felt by many that it would be illogical to drop Green because he had made one freakish error.

It was not as if he had fallen apart in the second half against the USA. In fact, he had kept England in the game by pushing Jozy Altidore's second-half shot on to the post. That showed a certain amount of strength of character.

Then again, Green's mistake had not been just any mistake. It was spectacular. From now on it would be in every DVD of goal-keeping bloopers ever made. It would have pride of place in any misery montage of South Africa 2010. It was the kind of mistake that makes a goalkeeper wince if he ever has the misfortune to see it again. So the issue was whether Green had been able to banish it from his mind in the long days that had elapsed between the game in Rustenburg and the start of the match against Algeria. Capello knew he had to be sure that Green had recovered mentally from what had happened. This was tournament football. Everything accelerated. Decisions had to be taken more quickly. Mistakes had to be rectified immediately. The World Cup was not big on second chances. England could not afford another goalkeeping error against Algeria.

If Capello was still unsure about what to do, watching training in the Green Point Stadium made his mind up. Green was all over the place. His handling, particularly when he fielded crosses curled in from the wings, was poor. His confidence had been shattered. Capello knew he had to be ruthless. He dropped Green, who did not appear in the tournament again. Capello was tempted to replace him with Hart, who had impressed him in training with his ability and his attitude. But he realised it was too big a game to entrust to a goalkeeper who had won only three caps for his country, all in friendlies. It was another failure of planning on Capello's part. He had backed the wrong horse earlier in his reign by identifying Ben Foster as the best young goalkeeper coming through the ranks, and had given him the opportunities he should have given Hart. When Foster began to struggle with form and confidence and fell out of contention, Capello was still slow to give Hart the experience he needed, and by the time England got to South Africa, it was too late. Scott Carson's performance against Croatia had shown what can go wrong when an untried goalkeeper is thrown into a crucial international match, and Capello did not want to repeat that misjudgement. He picked David James.

The other selection issues were simpler. Gareth Barry came back into the holding role after recovering from his ankle injury, which meant that the England midfield regained the shape it had had in qualifying. James Milner was left out, Gerrard moved to a nominal position on the left, and Jamie Carragher was preferred to Matthew Upson alongside John Terry in central defence. There had been suggestions during the week that Jermain Defoe had looked so sharp in training that Capello might start him alongside Wayne Rooney, but when the teamsheets were released at the stadium, they showed that Emile Heskey had kept his place. It looked like a solid team. With an average age of 29 years and 322 days, it was also England's oldest starting line-up at a World Cup since 1954. At his press conference a couple of days earlier, Rooney had said that England could beat Algeria without playing at their best. What he didn't say was whether they could beat Algeria playing at their worst.

That is what they tried to do. England were shocking in Cape Town. Right from the first whistle, Capello's side looked lethargic, listless and out of sorts. There was no eagerness or enthusiasm in their body language. There was no hunger, no invention, no zip, no determination, no energy, no imagination, no control, no creativity, no spontaneity, no originality, no defiance, no pride, no skill, no accuracy, no ambition, no confidence, no teamwork, no pace, no courage, no responsibility, no fun, no athleticism, no coordination, no desire, no anger, no fortitude, no intelligence, no embarrassment, no method, no technique, no competence, no flair, no care, no pain and no shame.

Within the first quarter of an hour, the mood of optimism among the tens of thousands of England fans who had packed the stadium had turned to disbelief. There was a void where their football team used to be. The first-half performance against Japan in Graz had been lacklustre, but this was something else. The way England played against Algeria made it clear that something had gone badly wrong in the England camp. The players looked exhausted. They were unrecognisable from the stars who had made the headlines in the Premier League each week. Players such as Rooney, Gerrard, Lampard and Lennon were fans' favourites at their clubs because the way they played elevated them above their illustrious foreign teammates. But at the Green Point Stadium they looked like impostors. It was as if Karl Power, the confidence trickster who had inveigled his way into arenas at several major sporting events and had even knocked up on Centre Court during Wimbledon, and ten of his mates had locked the real England team in the dressing room, donned England shirts and were taking on Algeria by themselves.

No one could quite grasp what they were seeing. It was not just that England were being outplayed by Algeria. It was not just that the Algerians mocked their underdog status by passing the ball in and around England. It was more that England looked utterly lost. There was a terrible bleakness about them. They did not look terrified so much as drained of all emotion. Barry was the closest to being excused criticism, but he only just reached mediocre. As for the rest of them, no one was innocent. 'Playing with Pride and Glory' said the slogan on the side of the England team bus. They should have doused that bus with paint stripper during the game because there was no pride in England's performance, and there was certainly no glory.

Amid the general sense of bewilderment about the events that were unfolding in front of them, it was the performance of Rooney that perplexed England supporters and journalists the most. Many of those watching quickly concluded that his ankle injury must be far worse than England had revealed. His technique was as good as anyone's in the England squad, yet he could barely control the ball. His passing was abysmal, his movement was poor, his face was a mask of surly misery. He was playing so badly and with such an absence of passion that journalists speculated over whether the FA would announce that the Manchester United forward's injury meant that he would play no further part in the tournament and that he was flying home.

There had been indications earlier in the week that Rooney was becoming increasingly frustrated. When he and some of the other England players were pictured on a rare outing to Sun City, where they were playing golf, the photographers noticed that Rooney had scrawled something in capital letters on each of his golf shoes. On the left shoe he had scrawled the message: FCUK U. On the right shoe was a name: FLOYD. Just to make sure the photographers did not miss the shot, Rooney had opened up his body so that his left foot was side-on to the camera and the letters were visible. It bore some of the hallmarks of a jape that the rest of the squad had put Rooney up to, the kind of in-house joke that sometimes flourishes at tournaments.

At the 1998 World Cup, for instance, it had gradually become apparent that the players were having a competition predicated around who could insert the titles of hit records from designated bands into television interviews. Early in the tournament, Gareth Southgate drew George Michael and Wham before an interview with ITV's Bob Wilson. Asked what he thought of England's training camp, Southgate told Wilson: 'It's hardly "Club Tropicana".' When Wilson quizzed him about who would feature in the team for England's opening game against Tunisia, Southgate scored again. 'You won't be getting any "Careless Whispers" from me,' he said.

The bet also explained why Alan Shearer punched the air unexpectedly during a different interview. He had been challenged to slip titles of Phil Collins songs into the conversation, and when he told the interviewer he thought some of the less favoured team would do well 'against all odds', he realised he had scored without intending to.

So perhaps this was an England squad joke updated for the 21st century. A little cruder than the 1998 version, but maybe that was another sign of the times. Nobody was quite sure who Floyd was either. One of the photographers who had annoyed the players by chasing them round the Pilanesberg game reserve before the tournament perhaps? Another suggestion was that it was a sports journalist who shared certain character traits with the late TV chef Keith Floyd, but that theory was unproven too. Whoever it was, the message on his golf shoes suggested resentment was starting to boil up inside Rooney again.

There were other theories about what might be eating at him. One was that he had come to detest Capello for the dismissive way in which he treated the players. Rooney was used to working with an autocratic manager at United, but he viewed Sir Alex Ferguson as a benign dictator. Ferguson had always been renowned as among the best man-managers in football, but many of the England players felt Capello was sorely lacking in that area. On one occasion at England's base, Rooney stayed out on the pitch after training had finished for extra shooting practice. He wanted to try everything he could to coax his game back into form, but when Capello saw what he was doing, he ushered him back inside and told him he had to rest. When Rooney objected, Capello dismissed his protests curtly and ordered him to his room.

Rooney's discontent was fuelled by the system England were playing. At Old Trafford he had thrived as the lone central striker in a 4–3–3 system that allowed him to feed on the service provided by wide players such as Nani, Ryan Giggs and especially Luis Antonio Valencia. United's system was more fluid and flexible than the 4–4–2 formation that Capello had favoured throughout his career, and it had been the foundation for Rooney's most successful goal-scoring season in the Premier League. Even if Capello refused to switch from 4–4–2, many thought that playing Gerrard in the hole behind Rooney would get the best out of both men and fix the problem of Gerrard neglecting his role on the left side of midfield, a situation that left Ashley Cole increasingly exposed and outnumbered against Algeria. Even during qualifying, Capello had played a system closer to 4–2–3–1 than 4–4–2, which Rooney also preferred. But Capello would not countenance a change in his World Cup tactics.

It was also clear that Rooney was under immense pressure. He had arrived at the World Cup not only bearing the main burden of English expectation, but also loaded with predictions that he would be competing with Lionel Messi, Cristiano Ronaldo, Kaka and Fernando Torres for all the major individual honours at the tournament, such as the Golden Ball and the Golden Boot. Even after the opening round of games, observers were pointing to Messi's scintillating performance for Argentina against Nigeria and asking what had happened to Rooney against the USA. So the pressure was already higher for Rooney going into the game against Algeria than it had been when he arrived in South Africa. He had always seemed impervious to pressure before, but not any more. As the game went on and his performance got worse and worse, he looked as though this stadium, this city, this country, this World Cup was the last place on Earth he wanted to be.

As the match dragged on and on like slow torture, the England fans were trapped in their dismay. It had been an appalling spectacle right from the start. England had given possession away at will in the opening minutes, another old failing that crept back into their game right on cue for the World Cup. Gerrard had a shot after a quarter of an hour, but it went high, high over the bar. England were floundering. Former England manager Graham Taylor, commentating from the stadium for the BBC, told radio listeners that if Algeria had a decent centre forward, England would be in trouble. Algeria worked harder and were technically superior. By half-time the match had already become an ordeal for England.

On the touchline Capello had, once again, lost his composure completely and was screaming furiously at his players. His antics were so extreme, his anger so untrammelled, that footage of his behaviour became a huge hit on YouTube. It showed the England manager sitting in the dug-out between a grim Stuart Pearce and an even grimmer Gary Lewin, the England physio. Every so often, Capello exploded in rage, elbowing both men in the ribs in his involuntary fits of disgust. On one occasion, he manhandled Pearce out of his seat and told him to go and stand on the touchline. Pearce looked shocked. 'Pass the ball,' Capello kept screaming at his players. 'Pass the f***ing ball.' His players did not seem to be listening, but at least Capello's annoyance provided some entertainment. There was precious little of it on the pitch.

There were a couple of other highlights. Henry Winter, the *Daily Telegraph*'s football correspondent, noticed that even the local wildlife sensed England's ineptitude: 'A grey bird alighted on the Algerian goal, appreciating it to be a place of sanctuary, having clearly checked on Rooney's recent form and being familiar with Heskey's work. The ultimate ignominy for England was that the bird actually changed ends at half-time.' A few minutes after the interval, Heskey nearly fell as he tried to do a step-over near the Algeria byline, and then hit his attempted cross behind for a goal-kick. Carragher was booked for a foul on Yebda, which meant he would be suspended for the final group game against Slovenia. James had to race off his line to clear a back pass that Terry had left short. And two minutes from the end, Lampard, so consistently dangerous with his free-kicks when he wore a Chelsea shirt, sliced a dead ball opportunity wildly wide. That was it: finally, the England fans in the stadium had had enough.

England's supporters had often been criticised for booing the team or individual players in the past, but their support in Cape Town that day had been magnificent. When Lampard's free-kick sailed wide, though, they vented their anger with a chorus of boos. And when the final whistle blew, they booed again as the players trudged off. It was louder booing this time, louder even than the wail of the vuvuzelas, and as Rooney stomped towards the tunnel, a television cameramen ran alongside him and filmed his exit. As he neared the touchline, Rooney stared into the lens. 'Nice to see your own fans booing you,' Rooney said, pressing his face right into the camera and seething with aggression. 'That's what loyal support is.'

It was heat of the moment stuff, born of crushing disappointment and intense frustration, but it was a foolish remark. England supporters had been a credit to their country in South Africa, better ambassadors than the team. They had not caused any trouble either inside or outside the stadia, they had mingled well with the locals, many of them had visited the townships, and some groups of fans had made the trip to the Hector Pieterson Museum in Soweto to learn more about the 1976 Soweto Uprising and the life of Pieterson, a schoolboy who was shot dead by police during a protest. They had paid thousands of pounds for long-haul flights to South Africa and accommodation once they were there, and they had given England the best support possible both at the Royal Bafokeng Stadium and in Cape Town, outnumbering opposition fans by about ten to one in each venue. There were 40,000 of them inside the Green Point Stadium. Their passion and dedication were things to be proud of.

They had been patient with the team too. Their reaction to England's performance against Algeria was not comparable with the way England fans had jeered Ashley Cole during a Wembley qualifying tie against Kazakhstan in October 2008, nor with the manner in which they had baited Frank Lampard before that. Booing your own team may be pointless and may only damage confidence and spread fear in the very players that the supporters want to play well. But the catcalls at the Green Point Stadium only started two minutes from the end of the match. It was too late for it to have any negative effect on the players. It was a visceral expression of the dismay the fans felt at the performance. It was worse than anything most of them had seen before, worse than the performance away to Andorra under Steve McClaren, worse than the defeat to Northern Ireland in Belfast under Sven-Goran Eriksson. Worse than anything because it was so lifeless. The dreams of the fans that England might be credible contenders to win the World Cup had just collapsed in front of them.

And now they were being upbraided by the player upon whom they had pinned all their hopes. If Rooney had played superbly, if he had got even close to the level of which he was capable, if he had been let down by those around him, it might have been a little easier to accept his criticism. But his performance against Algeria was one of the worst of his career in both club and international football. The fans were disillusioned with him, and it looked as if Rooney was disillusioned with himself. He knew this was the big stage, and he knew he was blowing his chance to shine. People who had been expecting a talent on a par with Messi and Ronaldo were watching Rooney play and wondering why so much hoopla had surrounded him. When Rooney spoke into the camera as he left the pitch there was not just anger towards the fans in his voice – there was self-loathing too.

One of the England fans let the players know how he felt in person.

Pavlos Joseph, a 32-year-old mortgage adviser from Crystal Palace in south London, was looking for a toilet after the game when he was directed down a corridor beneath the stadium. Mr Joseph turned a corner, walked through a door and found himself in the England dressing room. He was confronted by David Beckham.

'Whoa,' Beckham said to him. 'Who are you?'

'I'm Pavlos and I actually need the toilet,' Mr Joseph said to him. Then he decided to say what he thought of the side.

He told Beckham the performance had been a disgrace, then he rounded on the rest of the players, who were sitting on benches with towels around their waists. 'That was woeful,' he told them. The players sat in silence, their chins on their chests. Mr Joseph said they looked ashamed.

Mr Joseph's story appeared in the *Sunday Mirror* that weekend. He was later arrested and accused of trespass. He was released after paying a £65 fine. The *Sunday Mirror* journalist who interviewed Mr Joseph, Simon Wright, was also arrested and charged with defeating the ends of justice. He too was released after paying a fine.

By the time England got back to their hotel, Capello's 64th birthday was nearly over.

17 | TRAVIS BICKLE STANDS UP

ENGLAND sought sanctuary at The Vineyard, an elegant hotel with beautiful views of Table Mountain on the affluent edge of Cape Town. The England cricket team often stayed there when they played Test matches at Newlands. There was a terrace at the back of the hotel that was packed with tables and diners in the summer and overlooked extensive gardens that led down to the gurgling Liesbeeck River. It was a serene place, the kind of environment ideal for soothing troubled minds and calming frayed nerves. The bar, which was set back from the garden terrace and was an occasional haunt of Sir Ian Botham when he was in town, was usually open late.

When the team bus arrived back at The Vineyard after the Algeria match and pulled into the small forecourt, John Terry asked Franco Baldini if he could have a word. Terry told Baldini that the players were emotionally drained. He said they needed some sort of release from the straitjackets that Fabio Capello had fitted them with at the training camp. The players had not been permitted an alcoholic drink since they arrived in South Africa, so Terry asked Baldini if the squad could have a beer each and a chat so they could try to relax, talk things through and kick a few opinions around. It was a modest enough request, hardly the stuff that rebellions were made of. Terry had not demanded anything of Baldini and Capello. His conversation with Baldini was closer to a plea.

Baldini relayed the request to Capello. Capello said it was fine. Capello went to the bar to have a glass of red wine with some of his staff. Some of the players went to bed. A small group of them took up Capello's offer and decided to have a drink. Frank Lampard, Wayne Rooney, Aaron Lennon, David James, Peter Crouch, Glen Johnson, Jamie Carragher and Steven Gerrard joined Terry in the bar. They sat at a table not far away from Capello, ordered a bottle each of Castle beer and tried to get to the bottom of why things had been going so badly on the pitch. It felt good being able to talk openly and honestly after such a disappointing night. It was an overdue catharsis.

The players were given the next day off to explore Cape Town. It was a rare chance for those whose families had flown to South Africa to spend time with them. Some took the cable car up Table Mountain. Others played golf. Terry visited a township and watched a local football game there. Some strolled around the gardens at The Vineyard and tried to put their performance against Algeria behind them. They knew now that they had to beat Slovenia in Port Elizabeth the following Wednesday to be sure of going through to the last 16. If they drew, Slovenia would go through, and unless it was a high-scoring draw, either the USA or Algeria would go through with them. Many now believed England were only a few days from going home.

England flew back to Rustenburg on Saturday evening. To say they were refreshed would be an exaggeration. They still felt burdened with disappointment about the way they had performed. But they knew that all was not lost. They had also been reminded that in 1986 England had lost their first group game to Portugal and drawn their second with Morocco, yet still made the quarter-finals. In 1990 they had drawn their first two group games against the Republic of Ireland and Holland, and made the semi-finals. It was obvious to everyone, though, that there was no more room for error. Some of the players felt they needed to have a clear-the-air meeting that was a larger version of the conversation at The Vineyard.

There was particular resentment among the players about the restrictions that were being placed on them at their camp. It was not just that they were cooped up in the Royal Marang Hotel for hours on end. They knew there were not a lot of leisure opportunities in the Rustenburg area and that, for security reasons, their movements were bound to be limited. But Capello had taken things too far at the camp. The food was desperately bland and boring, and some felt there was not enough of it. Many of the players were hungry most of the time. Some of the FA media staff, who were on the same meagre rations, were allowed to supplement their supplies with occasional trips to the local supermarket. Now and then a player would wander into their office at the hotel and beg them for one of the profiteroles sitting in a plastic tray on their desk. There was a bar at the Royal Marang Hotel, but the grille was drawn down over it for the entire length of England's stay. Journalists noticed with amusement that when the media staff joined them for a night out in Sun City late in the tournament, they eschewed any of the healthier options on the menu. They ordered plates and plates of chips and devoured them as if it was the first food they'd had for weeks.

There were also restrictions on the players' movements, even within the hotel. More than the food, it was the claustrophobia that Capello's private nanny state induced in the England squad that was the most damaging thing of all to morale. When Rooney was asked before the Algeria game to describe his daily routine in Phokeng, his answer went like this: 'Breakfast. Train. Lunch. Bed. Dinner. Bed.' He made it sound like something from *The Gulag Archipelago*. Other players complained that they were forced to spend so much time lying on their beds watching Sky Sports News or DVDs that they were worried they were going to stiffen up and start getting muscular problems. The regime was so severe that they were afraid to venture outside their rooms in the long afternoon hours when they had been ordered to rest in case they incurred the wrath of the manager or one of his henchmen. Capello had become farcically despotic. 'On the training pitch he was one of the best managers I have ever worked with,' said one player. 'Off it, he was one of the worst.'

Capello made no attempt to dilute the intensity of the regime for the England players in South Africa. If anything, he seemed to want to increase it. Several of the players pointed out that the lifestyle they were being asked to endure was so radically different from the pre-match preparations they experienced in their club careers that it was bound to be unsettling. The Manchester United, Chelsea and Liverpool players in the squad had all enjoyed periods of considerable success with their clubs doing things a certain way, so it was natural that when they were asked to submit to a regime that was as far removed from the culture at their clubs as it was possible to be, they should feel uncomfortable about it.

One player pointed out that two days before a Premier League match he was at home with his kids, taking them to the playground, pushing them on the swings, catching them at the bottom of the slide. In Phokeng, he said, it felt as if he would be court-martialled if he walked down the stairs too quickly two days before a game. Many of the players found the level of these restrictions absurd and infantilising. They felt as though Capello was behaving like a headmaster determined to bend a bunch of seven-year-olds to his will. He behaved as if he wanted to crush their spirit. It was working. England had begun to play like a group of broken men.

Capello's defenders argued passionately that it should not be beyond a group of young men to dedicate themselves totally to trying to win the World Cup for a short period of time. It was six weeks out of their cosseted existences, six weeks to forget everything except football, six weeks to try and achieve moments of glory that would be with them for the rest of their lives. On the *Guardian* website, its deputy sports editor, Barry Glendenning, spoke for a strand of opinion when he mocked the sympathy for the squad by alluding to 'the assorted human rights abuses visited upon the England players in their Rustenburg HQ'. The players were accused of being pathetic for complaining about boredom. Even players from other nations joined in the criticism and argued that it should have been impossible to be bored at the World Cup. It should have been the highlight of every player's career, something he committed himself to absolutely and without qualification, something that should have dominated his every waking thought.

Part of the issue was that when England's players were away from their homes and their clubs for only a short period – during the World Cup qualifying campaign, for instance – they could deal with the bleak austerity that Capello imposed on them. They could laugh together at their prison conditions and have some harmless fun trying to bend the rules. They could get by on gallows humour. It also helped that they were winning matches under Capello in qualifying. Everything went smoothly. Capello's methods went unchallenged because the most Spartan regime seemed acceptable when everything was going well and the public and the media had acclaimed them as heroes.

But by the time England returned from Cape Town, they had been subjected to the regime for close to five weeks, including the time spent training in Austria, and it had become obvious that the conditions in the camp were gnawing at their spirit. The critics could say what they wanted about how the England players ought to feel. They could argue that they should be grateful to be in South Africa and that it was a sign of their psychological weakness that they could not cope with Capello's regime. But those arguments missed the point. It was up to Capello to get the best out of his players, and after the first two games of the tournament, it was clear that he was not doing that. He was not even getting close.

Maybe the players were mentally weak, maybe they should have been deliriously happy in the asceticism they were being asked to embrace, but it was not Capello's job to try to break them and turn them into snivelling wrecks. It was his job to try to get them to play like World Cup winners. If his players were revealing themselves to be spoilt millionaire brats, then it was his job to get the best out of those brats. If that meant compromises in his methods, then he had to attempt to make them. After Algeria, it had got to the point where he had nothing to lose. If that meant relaxing his regime so that the players were allowed out of their rooms for a couple of hours in the afternoon rather than being imprisoned inside them, then now was the time to do it. This was not a case of a player rebellion. This was a group of players sliding miserably towards the oblivion of early elimination. Something had to be done. Something had to change.

Capello seemed paralysed. His lack of experience in managing a side at a major tournament had found him out. He had misjudged the effect that five weeks of isolation would have on his players. He had turned the World Cup into a joyless ordeal rather than something to be savoured and relished. He had not got the balance right. No one wanted a repeat of the Baden-Baden experience, but Capello had taken things in South Africa to the opposite extreme, and it became apparent in Cape Town that the players had reached breaking point. Capello's unblinking, unsmiling, unbending regime gave the players no release, no variety, no respite from boredom and isolation. The England players had developed advanced cases of cabin fever.

On Sunday morning, back in Phokeng, they woke up to news that there was a fresh round of unfavourable headlines in the English newspapers about the atmosphere in the camp. In the *News of the World* a front-page story, researched and written by Neil Ashton, alleged that Rooney had become an unpopular figure with many of his teammates. Usually fêted as being down-to-earth, he was now said to be regarded by some of his teammates as a 'preening prima donna' because he expected the side to be built around him and blamed everyone else when things went wrong. Rooney's representatives angrily denied that the story was true, but it added to the sense of crisis in the camp.

The English football writers staying in Sun City agreed that, in the light of the performance against Algeria and the fact that they were now facing elimination, they should request that the captain, Steven Gerrard, appear at that day's scheduled press conference. A text was sent to the FA to that effect. But the FA sent a message back saying that Terry, not Gerrard, had been designated as the man to face the flak. Baldini, who was assuming more and more responsibility for the team's media duties, had apparently drawn lots to decide which player would speak to the media. It was another sign of a regime in stasis, unable to make decisions. The journalists were surprised that Gerrard was not speaking for the rest of the team, but they were not disappointed that Terry was taking his place. Both men were articulate speakers who were not afraid of unsparing self-analysis. The writers knew Terry would provide more than clichés.

If there was added expectation, it was because Terry had not appeared alone on a stage at one of these press conferences since he had been stripped of the captaincy by Capello in February. There was speculation that he still felt resentful towards Capello for the way he had been treated, and some wondered whether that resentment might betray itself during the press conference, especially as the squad's unhappiness with the conditions at the camp was an open secret. Many also felt that England's slide towards mediocrity had coincided with Capello's decision to take the armband away from Terry. For all the many qualities of Gerrard, who was a decent, approachable man and a fine player, Terry remained the team's natural leader.

Terry walked into the England press centre with the FA's media officer, Mark Whittle. He spoke to the broadcasters first, and even though some of the questioners invited him to pour scorn on Capello's man-management abilities, Terry demurred. 'We are all fully behind the manager,' Terry said. 'He has had his ways and his philosophies and his ideas that he has brought to the side, and that has worked during the qualifying campaign. We are here supporting him. All we can do as players is stay unified and get the win against Slovenia.' So far, so diplomatic, but it was what he said next that grabbed the attention of the football writers waiting to speak to him in the next room.

Terry mentioned that there was a meeting scheduled for that evening when the Algeria game would be discussed and analysed. To Capello it was a chance to watch footage of the game in Cape Town and tell the players what they had done wrong and the improvements they needed to make. It was not his intention to turn it into an open forum where the players could air grievances or put forward their own opinions. That was not his style. Capello did not listen. He did not do consensus. But Terry, who had been used to a more democratic atmosphere at Chelsea, where the players' opinions were valued, told the media he expected the meeting to provide a valuable and necessary opportunity for the players to thrash out exactly what was going wrong before it was too late.

'We need to think "Sod it",' Terry said. 'We have got one game where we can make or break our tournament. As a group of players we owe it to ourselves and the country back home, if we feel as though there is a problem, there is no point keeping it in. Whether we have an argument with the manager or us expressing our opinions upsets him, everyone needs to get off their chest exactly how they are feeling, and if we feel that, we need to go to him.' It was hardly the stuff of revolution, but it was the first hint there had ever been of a willingness to challenge Capello's diktats, and, in the febrile atmosphere of an England team in disarray, his words carried the whiff of cordite.

Terry spoke to the broadcasters for ten minutes, then moved into the room where the press were waiting. He began by talking about how he had been briefed by the FA over what to say on his way from the hotel to the media centre. He gave the impression that he was about to ignore much of what the diplomats had told him. He repeated some of the things he had said to the broadcasters, but he went into more detail and spoke more strongly to the newspaper journalists, many of whom he knew well. A couple of times during the press conference he half-turned to Whittle and prefaced a remark by admitting, 'I don't know if I am going to get myself in trouble here but . . .'

Terry mentioned the plea he had made to Baldini to let the players have a beer and a chat at The Vineyard after the Algeria game. He was asked which players had joined him for a drink. He looked unsure about whether to continue. He said he might get into trouble for saying it. And then he named the eight others who had sat in the bar with him that night. He also mentioned that Capello had been on the next table. He then talked about that night's meeting again, emphasising that he saw it as a chance for the players to get things off their chest and then move on. He was asked if that signified a challenge to Capello's authority. He shook his head. 'If it upsets him, then I'm on the verge of just saying: "You know what? So what? I'm here to win it for England." He's feeling the same, the players are feeling the same, and if we can't be honest with each other, then there's no point being here.'

Terry had spoken to other players about how they were feeling. He knew how much discontent there was about the Spartan regime. Many of them told him they were desperate for some of the restrictions to be relaxed. Terry said several times during the press conferences that he was there representing all the players. Later that was interpreted as an attempt to undermine Gerrard's captaincy and re-establish himself as the leader of the team, but the reality was that Terry had never stopped being the leader. That was what Capello wanted him to be. He had said as much openly in the immediate aftermath of sacking him.

Gerrard did not feel comfortable with the tub-thumping, rabble-rousing, motivational side of the captaincy. Terry did. He was similar to Tony Adams like that. 'Since I have lost the armband, nothing has ever changed for me,' he told the newspaper journalists. 'I will still be the same. I was born to do stuff like that and I will continue to do that in the dressing room and on the training field. If I feel something needs changing, that's a discussion I'll have with the manager tonight in the meeting. If we feel things need to be changed, whether he needs to change personnel or change his ways, we'll say so. Everyone needs to voice their opinion and we hope he then takes it on board. But it's the manager who has the final decision.'

Terry was also asked about Joe Cole, his friend and teammate at Chelsea. Capello's failure to select Cole in his starting line-up had been fiercely criticised by fans. Pressing for his inclusion had become a cause célèbre. Terry was sympathetic. He said he thought Cole and Rooney were the only two players in the England squad who could unlock a defence with a piece of skill. But he stressed that team selection was none of his business and that he would never seek to try to influence Capello's choice of personnel in any way.

When the journalists emerged from the press conference most of them were energised by what they had heard, partly because they knew they had a story, partly because they felt someone had finally had the courage to stop hiding behind platitudes and say what needed to be said. Paul Hayward, the *Observer*'s much-acclaimed chief sports writer, drew a comparison between Terry and Travis Bickle, the anti-hero of Martin Scorsese's movie *Taxi Driver*. 'He looked like a man who would not take it any more,' Hayward said. 'It was a real tour de force, probably the best

England press conference for 20 years. We came out of there with a sense of euphoria about what he had said.'

Terry had struck a chord with the public too. He had only said what needed to be said. It was obvious it was a desperately unhappy camp. It was common sense that Capello needed to change something. He needed to let the tensions dissipate. He needed to listen to the players' observations and then decide whether to act on any of them. Terry had not advocated anything more radical than that. He had not questioned Capello's ability to manage the side or take England further in the competition. Far from it. He had offered him support several times in both press conferences and said unequivocally that he believed Capello could lead England into the later stages of the tournament.

But the problem for Terry was that what he had done was so terribly un-English. English footballers did not question authority. Not even in the mild, almost consensual, way that Terry had done. Terry was not openly challenging Capello. He was pleading with him to talk to the players. He was just asking him to engage. The England players had a basic respect for Capello, but they were longing for him to show a little respect back. They did not want to take him on. They did not want to topple him or oust him. They just wanted to talk to him and to see if he would listen. But the English were so conservative, so conditioned to respecting the establishment, so scared of authority that Terry's words sounded to them like apostasy.

If Terry had been part of the Dutch camp, what he had said at the press conference would not even have broken the waves. It was the Dutch way to question authority. In his seminal book about Dutch football, *Brilliant Orange*, David Winner spoke to former Dutch international Wim van Hanegem about Dutch querulousness. 'If things around the national team are quiet,' Van Hanegem said, 'everyone thinks everyone is sick. If we don't have a problem, we have to create a problem.'

In this England squad it was the opposite. Everyone knew there was a problem, but nobody apart from Terry wanted to talk about it. They told Terry they did, but when it came to the crunch, they disappeared. It was typically English behaviour. Lots of national traits were there. English reserve, English unwillingness to acknowledge emotions, English denial, English stiff upper lip, English respect for authority. And so, as the afternoon wore on, Terry's colleagues backed away from him until he stood isolated and facing a fresh onslaught of criticism and character assassination. His only consolation was that he was used to it by now.

It was not just that Terry had been stripped of the England captaincy back in February. Further back in his career he had been accused of playing a part in the departure of Jose Mourinho from Chelsea, an accusation that Terry fiercely denied. Terry was a strong captain and he exerted considerable influence at Chelsea, but he was not a schemer. The same thing applied with England. His remarks at his press conference were straightforward expressions of concern about a situation that was in freefall. They were meant to provoke debate and quicken a solution, not to bring about the downfall of the manager.

Now, though, he was portrayed as being as devious as Lord Haw-Haw, as mutinous as Fletcher Christian and as manipulative as Rasputin. Given the amount of plotting he was supposed to have done, the only surprise was that he had not already been flown home and chained to Traitor's Gate. The invective that was aimed at him was actually an indictment of the regime he was playing under, a regime that stifled individuality and responsibility, a regime that was scared of discussion. And some of it was fuelled by briefings against Terry from within the England camp.

One story that appeared in the aftermath of Terry's press conference alleged that the Chelsea captain had caused trouble the day after the USA game by refusing to finish a training session at the team base in Phokeng and sneering at the coaching staff. The truth was that on that particular Sunday, Terry and Frank Lampard were the only players who had been involved in the game who were doing any running at all. The rest of the side were doing light exercises and swimming, and Terry only stopped running and went inside to the treatment room when he felt his hamstring tighten. Similar smears were also aimed at David James. The snitch in the camp was targeting the strongest characters.

Some journalists felt that Terry was being misrepresented after his press conference. Henry Winter wrote in the *Daily Telegraph* that it was 'one of the most dramatic days in England's history'. He described Terry as 'a rebel with a cause' and acknowledged that 'home truths need to be aired'. Many of those who covered England from match to match and sat through the tedium of evasion, banality and cliché that made up many player interviews craved honesty and candour in their subjects. Yet now that Terry had provided a stream of honesty, some did not know how to deal with it. As a result, meanings and motivations were attributed to him that he had simply not intended. The drink in the bar at The Vineyard became 'The Cape Town Coup'. It is a funny kind of coup that features plotters plotting at the table next to the object of their supposed putsch, but nevertheless, by later that afternoon, that was how Terry's plea to Baldini to allow the players to have a beer was being interpreted.

By the time the journalists got back to their rooms in Sun City after Terry's press conference, some of them were getting calls from other players' agents insisting that Terry had spoken out of turn and that he did not represent the views of the rest of the squad. The fear was kicking in. The English reserve was taking hold. Players suddenly forgot about the bigger picture and the desire to try to improve the spirit in the camp, and watched their own backs. Their agents span the line that Terry was driven by a desire for revenge over Capello. It was also said that some of the players who had been for a drink in the bar at The Vineyard were furious that their identities had been revealed.

It was not as if Terry had divulged a terrible secret when he mentioned the players who had had a drink at The Vineyard. It was not as if he was saying that the group had met behind Capello's back or that they had gone on some clandestine all-night bender to defy his strictures. Terry had mentioned they had had one bottle of beer each in the hotel bar with the permission of the England manager who was sitting at the next table. What had things come to if a group of men were petrified about the repercussions of revelations as tame as that? Why did they think there was any stigma attached to what they had done? No wonder some of them looked scared of their own shadows on the football pitch.

It was never revealed which players were upset with Terry. None of them ever came forward. Certain players in the England squad were very adept at hiding when they needed to – on and off the pitch. When Terry heard the reports claiming that he had alienated members of the squad with what he had said at the press conference, he confronted Gerrard and Crouch to ask them if they felt he had let them down. Both men said nothing could be further from the truth. Terry and Gerrard had always got on well. Terry had even been involved in the efforts to persuade Gerrard to move from Liverpool to Chelsea when Jose Mourinho was in charge at Stamford Bridge. Gerrard said that if he had a problem with what Terry had said, he would have knocked on his hotel room door and told him. Terry took him at his word.

Capello was told about what Terry had said too. He pulled his former captain aside at the hotel later in the afternoon and told him that another journalist had phoned him to tell him what had gone on. Capello said the journalist had told him that Terry had tried to undermine him. Terry said that was not true, but Capello told him he had been a fool for talking about the squad's problems in public.

And he ridiculed the idea that the players would be allowed to express their opinions at the meeting that evening. Later he gave an interview to ITV where he accused Terry of making 'a big mistake'. He went on: 'When you speak, you have to speak privately.' So a few hours after admonishing Terry for talking about the squad's problems in public, Capello was talking about the squad's problems in public. It was a strange way of trying to motivate his best defender a couple of days before the biggest match of his reign as England manager. None of Terry's teammates, none of the players who had spoken so eloquently to him about their despair, backed him up now. Some of them ran for the cover of their rooms so fast that they might have tweaked a hamstring. Terry was left to take the criticism by himself.

He got plenty. Matt Lawton wrote the hardest piece about him in the *Daily Mail*. It was a superbly written and well-sourced piece of polemic that included fierce criticism of Terry, but that did not spare Capello either. Lawton accused Terry of effectively attempting to become England player-manager and drew a comparison with the 1990 World Cup in Italy, when senior England players responded to their two opening draws in the tournament by lobbying Robson for a switch to a 3–5–2 formation. Lawton agreed that Terry's press conference performance had been impressive, but only because it had been 'so wonderfully Machiavellian'. He said Terry had backed the manager while undermining him in the same breath, and that he had tried to lead a move to 'rip up the Capello rule-book and have a beer when they fancied one'. He pointed out that Terry had claimed to have the support of the rest of the squad, but had been sorely mistaken. He said his comments merely amounted to the latest in a long list of serious misjudgements by the former England skipper.

The squad meeting came and went exactly as Capello said it would. He began it by barking out orders to the players. 'Nobody speak,' he said, 'nobody speak.' It was unequivocal. There was to be no discussion. There was to be no clear-the-air session. There was to be no attempt to discuss why the team had been under-achieving so spectacularly. There was to be no exchange of views. The players sat in silence as they watched the footage of their miserable performance against Algeria. Capello made a few points about their individual and collective failings.

Then they went to dinner.

Then they went to bed.

18 THIS ROUND'S ON FABIO

FABIO Capello sat on a table in a small room at the Nelson Mandela Bay Stadium in Port Elizabeth. The sign on the door said Medical Officer. It was Tuesday, the eve of the game against Slovenia, England's last chance to salvage some pride. Capello's legs dangled above the floor. Behind him there was a sign on the wall: Help Desk, it said. There was a number to call. Capello must have been tempted to ring it, but instead he sat and listened to a mournful question from the *Sun*'s Steve Howard. Howard reminded him how, when he was manager of AC Milan, he had once had mighty players like Marco van Basten, Paolo Maldini, Alessandro Costacurta and Franco Baresi at his disposal. The question trailed off, but Howard's meaning was clear: once he had had great players, now he had just the dregs of a team.

Steven Gerrard was perched on the table next to Capello. He had been staring at the floor while the question was asked, but now he looked up and his eyes flashed briefly with defiance. He had heard the question about the great players. He knew it was directed at Capello, but he also knew that it concerned him and some of the others in England's rusting Golden Generation. So he whispered his own answer, almost as if he were talking to himself. Only the journalists standing closest to him heard it. 'You still have them,' Gerrard breathed. Capello turned towards him and smiled sympathetically, as if he felt embarrassed for him. Then he nudged him on the shoulder and grinned. He looked pleased that Gerrard had spoken up.

Things had improved since Sunday. The mood had lightened a little after the drama of John Terry's press conference, the rebuke he received from Capello, and the draconian instructions at the silent team meeting. Terry had telephoned Matt Lawton to talk to him about his piece and had offered an apology to anyone he might have upset. The players had taken part in a relaxed training session in Phokeng and had been allowed to play touch rugby. Pictures were released of them laughing and fooling around, which was a first, and now that they had arrived on the shores of the Indian Ocean ready for a game that was effectively sudden death, some of the tension had gone. It was all or nothing now.

Slovenia were no pushovers. They were not a free pass into the next round. They had beaten Guus Hiddink's Russia in a two-legged play-off to qualify for South Africa, and they were going into the game against England clear at the top of Group C with four points after a victory over Algeria and a 2–2 draw with the USA. They had outplayed the USA for much of their clash too, leading them 2–0 at half-time and clinging on to a one-goal lead until eight minutes from the end. A draw against England would be enough to take them through to the next round.

Capello was trying to be upbeat. Even he appeared to have realised at last that something needed to change. He praised the players as best he could. He said that they bore comparison with the AC Milan legends that Howard had mentioned. 'This is strong, no?' he said, pointing at Gerrard as they sat in the medical room. 'I think the English players are strong, the same. This group is really good. I'm not crazy when I said my target is the final of the World Cup. If . . . not if . . . when we win against Slovenia, then all the teams have to fight against us. We are not in a good moment, but against Slovenia we will be fit. My reputation is not important, but the group and the team are important.'

It also emerged that Terry's decision to highlight the tensions in the squad caused by the suffocating nature of Capello's regime had not been in vain. When England arrived at the stadium on the day of the game they were wearing their tracksuits, not the official suit and tie that had been their uniform on match day up until then. It was a small sign of softening from Capello. And on the plane journey to Port Elizabeth the previous day, Baldini had sat next to Gerrard and told him that if the players wanted to have a beer with their meal the night before the match, Capello would have no objections. None of the players wanted a drink because it was the eve of the match, but they appreciated the offer. It was another sign that Capello was beginning to grasp the fact that the management of players at a tournament required subtle touches as well as the continual thumping of an iron fist.

Terry was not given any credit for the shift in attitude, but it was he who had brought it about. It was he who had had the courage to make a stand and point out that something was wrong. No one else did it, but after Terry had been slapped down and humiliated, the rest of the squad reaped the rewards. That included Capello, who turned the episode to his advantage. It was a classic piece of strong management. He had faced down the ringleader of the opposition to his methods and stripped him of his support. Then, when he re-established his authority, he had chosen to make concessions on his own terms and at a time of his choosing. The bigger picture was that it did not matter how the concessions had come about. If they were improving England's chances of escaping elimination in the group stage, that was enough.

By the time the England teamsheet was handed in an hour before the game, the news had seeped out that Capello had dropped Emile Heskey and Aaron Lennon and replaced them with Jermain Defoe and James Milner. 'This selection has the smell of the players being involved in it,' former England boss Graham Taylor told radio listeners. To many, though, it seemed like a conservative line-up. There was no Joe Cole and, most significantly, there was no sign of a reshaping of the team that might have moved Steven Gerrard inside from his exile on the left. Rumours that Ledley King had recovered from injury proved unfounded, and Matthew Upson was picked to play alongside Terry. The England fans packed inside the stadium were nervous. Most still believed England could win, but they had been scarred by the performance against Algeria and some were angry and disillusioned. One banner draped over the second-tier balcony spoke for the unforgiving: '6,000 Miles For What?' it read.

Once again, England did not begin well. Hearts sank. Glen Johnson committed a couple of silly fouls and was lucky to avoid a booking when he brought down Andraz Kirm. Gareth Barry made a rash lunging tackle on Aleksandar Radosavljevic, and Milner looked bereft of ideas wide on the right flank. But gradually, England steadied themselves and began to look more assured. Rooney was getting more involved than he had in the previous two games, and one cross intended for Gerrard was intercepted only at the last moment. When Johnson attacked, he forced Slovenia goalkeeper Samir Handanovic into a good save from an awkward bouncing shot.

Then, midway through the first half, the great moment of relief and joy that England players and fans had been longing for finally arrived. When the ball was worked to Milner on the right, there was little sense of anticipation. Milner had been looking overawed, and even though Lennon had been disappointing in the opening two games, it was beginning to look as though Capello had made a mistake by dropping him. But what Milner did next was sweet vindication for the England manager. Barry played a short, simple pass to him on the right, and Milner took one touch to control it and another to push it a couple of yards closer to the byline before bending a beautiful cross around his marker and behind the Slovenia defence. Defoe had gained half a yard of space on Marko Suler and got to the ball first as it flew across the edge of the six-yard box.

The ball cannoned off Defoe's right shin, and even though Handanovic got a hand to it, it flicked off his head and ricocheted into the roof of the net.

England were euphoric. Maybe this was the moment that would free them from their locked-in syndrome. For the rest of the first half it seemed that way. Four minutes after the goal, Milner sent over another perfect cross from an almost identical position on the right. Again, it created havoc in the Slovenia defence. Handanovic dived full length to try to gather it, but could only push it into Lampard's path. Lampard, sensing his own moment of redemption, tried to lash the ball back past the goalkeeper with his left foot but he could not keep it down and it flew wildly high.

Suddenly, England were cutting loose, ridding themselves of all the frustration and disappointment that had been building up inside since well before they arrived in South Africa. Gerrard played Defoe in, and when his snap-shot was beaten into the ground by Handanovic, Gerrard headed it down to Rooney. Rooney teased a couple of Slovenia defenders on the edge of the box, then, when Gerrard made a dart to his right, Rooney slipped a brilliant pass inside the Slovenians to put Gerrard in on goal. Gerrard tried to curl his shot around Handanovic, but the goalkeeper flung out his left hand and blocked the shot. The ball squirmed underneath his body and looked as if it might trickle over the goal-line, but Handanovic grabbed it just in time.

That moment lifted the spirits of the England players and fans more than anything. It held out the promise that the real Rooney had reappeared at last and that he and Gerrard had rekindled the on-field relationship that so many felt was the key to England achieving anything of worth in the World Cup. Rooney and Gerrard were England's two most potent attacking talents, and analyst after analyst had all but begged Capello to free Gerrard from his role on the left so that he could support Rooney more closely. That one moment of glorious vision from Rooney as the first half drew to a close in Port Elizabeth was a glimpse of what might have been and what could yet be.

Rooney started the second half brightly too. There was more urgency about him. He took a quick corner that Handanovic could only punch out to Barry. Barry nodded the ball back into the box where Defoe was waiting unmarked, but instead of grabbing his second goal of the game, he hooked the ball just wide. Minutes later, England put another good move together. Lampard played a clever reverse pass through to Rooney, who let the ball run and squared it for Defoe, who prodded it into the empty net. A linesman's flag against Rooney ruled that effort out, but still the chances kept coming. A towering header from Terry was saved superbly, and then, when Rooney ran on to a lofted-through ball from Lampard and found himself with only the goalkeeper to beat, it seemed as though another landmark in England's escape from their padded cell was about to be reached.

A goal then for Rooney would have lifted some of the pressure off his shoulders and sent his confidence soaring. A goal then would have rid him of the stigma of having played in two World Cups without scoring in either of them. Rooney did everything right too. Lampard's pass was a difficult ball to control, especially with the Jabulani, but Rooney executed the skill perfectly, killing it with his left foot. Then he swivelled and hit his shot with his right foot so that it went across Handanovic towards the bottom right-hand corner of the Slovenia net. But Handanovic got his fingertips to the ball, and even though it barely brushed them on the way past, the slight deflection was enough to divert it on to the post. As it hit the face of the upright and bounced out to safety, Rooney stood with his head in his hands, then looked to the heavens in despair. He had started limping by then, so Capello substituted him with Joe Cole. Both men were given big ovations by the England fans. Rooney's outburst in Cape Town seemed to have been forgotten.

England were almost in the second round, but as the game entered its final quarter, Slovenia came desperately close to an equaliser. The ball was knocked down to Milivoje Novakovic on the edge of the England area, and as Terry tried to block him, Novakovic made space by pushing the ball to his left and lashing a shot at goal. He hit the ball sweetly, but Terry flung himself at it and got in the way. The ball stuck underneath his legs and he flicked it away. But now it broke to Zlatko Dedic in an even more dangerous position. In what seemed like slow motion, Terry scrambled back to his feet and as Dedic pulled the trigger, Terry tried to hurl himself head-first into the path of the ball in the manner of a bodyguard ready to take a bullet. It missed Terry and hit Johnson instead, but Terry's kamikaze dive was still one of the images of the game. An hour or so after the match had finished, a couple of England fans sneaked on to the pitch and larked about trying to re-enact it. Before Vanessa Perroncel, before Wayne Bridge refused to shake his hand, before he was accused of plotting a coup d'état, it was the kind of absurdly brave, comic-strip defending that England fans loved Terry for.

One other England defender deserved an honourable mention too. Upson had travelled to South Africa lower down the hierarchy in central defence than Rio Ferdinand, Terry, Ledley King and Jamie Carragher, but a mixture of injuries and suspension had given him his chance against Slovenia. He had looked unsure for much of the game, as he always did when he stepped up to international class, but right at the last he made a critical interception that justified his place in the squad. Tim Matavz, a 79th-minute substitute, burst into the England box, sensing his moment of glory, but as he drew back his right boot to shoot, Upson slid in and nicked the ball away from him with a tackle that could not have been timed any better. When the final whistle went soon afterwards, Upson raised his hands in the air like the rest of the England team.

England breathed again. 'We're not going home,' the England fans sang happily as they streamed out of the stadium towards the bars on the beachfront. England had not set the tournament alight at the Nelson Mandela Bay Stadium. They had not made a statement. They had not played well enough to make Spain, Brazil or Argentina take a second look. But they had taken a leap forward from their performance against Algeria. They had at least shown hints of recovering their fluency. There were glimpses of interaction between Gerrard and Rooney, there were tentative signs that Lampard was starting to find his form, David James had looked solid in goal and Defoe had been dangerous in attack.

No wonder Capello was all smiles afterwards. The result was a triumph for him too. It was not just that he had avoided the ignominy of leading one of the tournament favourites to their only World Cup first-round exit since 1958, a failure that would have been a nasty black blotch on a fine curriculum vitae. It was also that he had resisted the calls for change and won the match his way. He had stuck with 4–4–2, and each of the changes he had made from the Algeria game – Defoe for Heskey, Milner for Lennon, Upson for Carragher – had paid off handsomely. It would mean little if England fell at the next hurdle, but nobody was thinking like that any more.

Capello wrote the next morning's back pages when he said the players had had a beer on the eve of the game. Maybe he did not know none of them had taken advantage of his offer. 'Yes,' Capello said. 'It's true. I changed something. I used my imagination.' Capello said it like it was the first time it had ever happened. As if he had surprised even himself with such a revolutionary gesture. Capello's tone was conciliatory and magnanimous. He praised Terry warmly. 'He is a leader,' Capello said. 'I have no problem with the players. I respect the players and they respect me. It was a very important performance from Terry. But all the players played really well. I'm sure we will start to play more with confidence. We have found the spirit, the quality of the play was really good and we improved a lot physically. We ran a lot. I spoke with the players when we saw the first half against Algeria. We understood it was not a good way to go forward, and during training it was very good, focused and fast. We found the physicality that we know usually. The players were the same that we see in the Premier League.'

Amid the celebrations, though, some shook their heads and urged caution. At almost the very moment the referee put the whistle to his lips to signal England's victory in Port Elizabeth, the television screens in the press box, which had been tuned to a new channel for the closing minutes of the other Group C match between the USA and Algeria, showed a 92nd-minute scramble in the Algeria box and Landon Donovan running on to a loose ball and smashing it into the net. That goal changed everything. It meant that the USA, not England, had finished top of Group C on goals scored. It meant that the USA, not England, would play the runner-up in Group D. England would face the group winner the following Sunday in Bloemfontein.

It was still unclear who their opponent would be. Going into the final round of matches in Group D, Serbia, Ghana and Germany all had a chance of winning the group and facing England. The matches began a couple of hours after England's game against Slovenia had finished. Germany played Ghana at Soccer City, and Serbia played Australia in Nelspruit. Serbia blew it by losing to Australia, but at Soccer City Mesut Özil, Germany's gifted young playmaker, scored a stunning left-foot shot from the edge of the area early in the second half to win Germany the game and the group. It was inevitable, really. England would play Germany. Rooney had got his wish and another chapter would be added to a rich World Cup rivalry that fans in both countries identified just by saying the year. After 1966, 1970 and 1990, now we had 2010.

'With his last-minute, group-winning goal against Algeria,' Marina

Hyde wrote in the *Guardian*, 'the USA's Landon Donovan effectively assassinated Archduke Franz Ferdinand and invaded Poland. England now face the old enemy – the old enemy being the one within, namely some people's pathological inability to view football games with Germany through any other prism than war.' What was more, if England beat Germany in Bloemfontein, they would likely face Argentina in a quarter-final in Cape Town a week later. All our 'Achtung, Surrenders', all our 'Gotchas', had come together. Some sought to calm the delirium with reminders that England had not beaten a major footballing power in the knock-out stages of a World Cup since 1966.

But they were like voices in the wilderness. No one heard them.

19 GERMANY CALLING

IT was an hour's drive from Johannesburg to the Velmore Hotel west of Pretoria, where the Germany squad was staying. The road took travellers past the huge faux-Italian shopping and entertainment complex called Montecasino, on past the Fourways junction and the miserable roadside shanty town of Diepsloot, with its corrugated-iron shacks, open sewers and teeming market, and further out into open countryside. Fires burnt in the fields, flames dancing and crackling through the dry grass to prepare the ground for a spring crop. Now and again football matches appeared out of the smoke. Each time the pattern was the same. Ten or 15 kids had levelled a patch of scrub as best they could and erected goalposts and a crossbar with long sticks, tree branches or thin planks of wood.

The Velmore Hotel was a handsome building, used as a conference centre and a wedding venue when it wasn't occupied by a World Cup squad. The DFB, Germany's equivalent of the FA, had set up a media centre in its grounds and, on the Friday before the match with England, held interviews there with the coach, Joachim Löw, and the captain, Philipp Lahm. Some of the English media too had travelled there the day before to hear the confident young Germany goalkeeper, Manuel Neuer, say that if the match went to penalties, the shoot-out would hold no fears for him. There was laughter among the German reporters when the subject was raised. They knew penalties had become an English obsession.

Löw looked like Iggy Pop without the wear and tear. He was 50, but dressed like a preppy student. Some of the German media had nicknamed him the School Prefect. At the Velmore Hotel press conference he wore a grey V-necked sweater underneath a black jacket. The contrast with the stiff deportment of Capello could hardly have been starker. He was scrupulously respectful towards England and dismissed the idea that he might have been encouraged either by the mediocrity of their performances so far or by the reports of unrest from within the camp. Löw said it was normal that ambitious men like Capello and John Terry should engage in debate. He said England had been 'reaffirmed' by their victory over Slovenia. 'This match is about our youthful lightness against their international class,' Löw said. 'England remain England. They can fight, they can run, they are mentally strong and incredibly experienced. Give Rooney and Lampard lots of space and they cannot be stopped.'

Löw pointed out that the Germany side England were to face in Bloemfontein was still a developing team that had been built around a new philosophy. Germany seemed to have been dealt a blow before the finals when their captain, Michael Ballack, was ruled out of the tournament with an ankle injury after he fell victim to a brutal late tackle from Portsmouth's Kevin-Prince Boateng in the FA Cup Final, but even though the country was stunned by Ballack's misfortune, there was also a feeling that his absence might liberate some of the younger German players, such as Thomas Müller, and allow Germany to play with more fluidity and pace on the counter-attack.

It was a young team that featured four of the Germany Under-21 side that had thrashed England in the final of the European Championships in Sweden the previous summer, and it played with a flair and creativity that previous German teams had lacked. Löw, who had taken over from Jürgen Klinsmann after the 2006 World Cup, set great store by attractive, attacking football, and his Germany played with verve and enthusiasm. One of the questioners at the Velmore Hotel said that at this World Cup the Germans played like the Dutch used to and the Dutch played like the Germans used to. Löw did not disagree. He took it as a compliment.

Löw also talked about the racial make-up of his squad. Nine years earlier, Gerald Asamoah had become the first black football player to represent Germany when he appeared for the national team in a friendly international against Slovakia in Bremen. A couple of months before that, in March 2001, the determined and resourceful striker Miroslav Klose, who had been born in Poland to Polish parents but had moved to Germany when he was eight, had made his Germany debut too. Klose had been bullied at school because he could not speak German, but now he was one of his adopted country's most famous and successful players.

Helped by a reform to nationality law passed by the Bundestag in 1999, which made it easier for resident foreigners, and especially their German-born children, to acquire German citizenship, this Germany squad was taken from diverse ethnic backgrounds. Eleven of its 23 players were either born abroad, had at least one foreign parent, or had links to another country in a previous generation. Klose, Lukas Podolski and Piotr Trochowski were born in Poland; Marko Marin was Bosnian; Serdar Tasci had Turkish parents; the fathers of Mario Gomez, Jerome Boateng, Dennis Aogo and Sami Khedira were from Spain, Ghana, Nigeria and Tunisia respectively; Mesut Özil, Germany's superb creative midfielder and the man seen as the main threat to England, was a third-generation Turkish immigrant and the son of a *Gastarbeiter* (guest worker) who sometimes recited passages from the Koran during the national anthem. Cacau had left Brazil when he was only 19.

The stereotype of a racially pure Germany side packed with blond-haired, blue-eyed men had been redundant for a long time (Mehmet Scholl, whose father was Turkish, made his debut for the national team in 1995), but Germany had an immigrant population of more than 15 million and the pace of change in its football team was accelerating. 'We have been working for two years to add nice things to the traditional German values of strength, power and running,' Löw said. 'I strongly favour attractive football. Sometimes it is natural to do the safe pass, the no-frills pass, to hit it backwards or to the goalkeeper. I have told my players that I want them to do the daring thing.'

Wolfgang Niersbach, the general secretary of the DFB, spoke to the *Observer*'s award-winning columnist Paul Hayward during the tournament and told him more about the organisation's encouragement of integration. 'Situated in the very centre of Europe, there is no doubt that Germany has certain melting-pot features, with people from many nationalities and of different ethnic backgrounds living together,' Niersbach said. 'The DFB has made integration a key item on its sports-political agenda, and quite a lot of young players are beginning to reward those efforts by declaring their preference for Germany, just like Özil, Khedira, Boateng and many others.'

The team was a window on the modern Germany in a way that England's side was not. That was partly because a large proportion of immigrants to England came from India and Pakistan. While Indian and Pakistani immigrants made considerable contributions to their new homeland in many sports, especially cricket, football had never been as popular on the subcontinent, and even when Asian players did try to participate, they quickly came up against casual and active racism. In 2001, when the Leeds United players Lee Bowyer and Jonathan Woodgate were tried on charges relating to an assault on an Asian student called Sarfraz Najeib that had happened when he was chased through Leeds city centre and then savagely beaten, it symbolised the estrangement between Asian youth and football in England. Bowyer was found not guilty of all charges, while Woodgate was sentenced to 100 hours of community service after being found guilty of affray. But the incident highlighted the fact that Britain's Asian population was not being integrated into the football community. In 2008, only five British Asians had professional contracts with English football clubs.

At the World Cup the only ethnic diversity in the England side came from the presence of players with Afro-Caribbean roots. In the England team that started the World Cup against the USA, Glen Johnson, Ledley King, Ashley Cole, Aaron Lennon and Emile Heskey all had links to the Caribbean, although each had been born and brought up in England. But the talent pool that Capello was picking from was still considerably narrower than that available to Löw. England's squad was effectively monocultural, and its football was stuck in a rut of dour Anglo-Saxon predictability encouraged, ironically, by its Italian manager's increasingly outmoded dedication to a 4–4–2 system. Germany, once reviled for its attachment to racial purity, was using its football team to model its new multicultural face for the world.

If England often seemed like a group of players worn out by the trauma of previous disappointments, desperately trying to gather themselves for one last shot at the World Cup, there was an openness and a youthful optimism emanating from the German camp. It felt as if this was the same old England but an entirely different Germany. One was stuck fast in its stubborn assumptions of footballing superiority and clinging to the idea that its so-called Golden Generation of players could seize its last chance to deliver a big prize. The other was evolving quickly. It was hard to listen to Lahm and Neuer and central defender Arne Friedrich and not to feel impressed by their maturity compared to their English counterparts. They did not have the innate defensiveness that afflicts almost every England footballer. They were not suspicious or wary. They did not begin their answers to most questions with 'no', which was a habit several England footballers had fallen into. 'No' was a glimpse of the fear and uncertainty they felt when they were talking to the media, the desire to put up a barrier straight away. It was as if the England players felt that every question was a bad headline waiting to happen.

It was not necessarily because the German players were better educated than the English. Not academically anyway. Most of them were from working-class backgrounds (Klose's father had insisted he complete his apprenticeship as a tiler) and had left the education system before going to college or university. But if most England players were intimidated by their media, the Germans seemed comfortable sitting on a dais and talking into a microphone. Perhaps it was because they benefited from a different kind of education, the education given to them by their clubs. In the Premier League, players were bred to be suspicious of the media and to treat them as the enemy. In Holland and in Germany, as they rose through the system, players were encouraged to be open. It was expected that the media would have ready access to them, so the relationship between the two sides was not dominated by mutual antipathy as it was in England.

English football turned most players mute. When the Danish midfielder John Jensen arrived at Arsenal in 1992, he had been expecting to have an open relationship with English journalists because that was what he was used to in Denmark and Germany, where he had played his club football. He had even told one newspaper journalist that he would be happy to chat to him regularly because it would help him learn the language. But soon after he arrived in London his tone changed. He phoned the journalist and told him he had been warned by his English agent that he should not speak to the English media. It was the same when Jesper Grønkjaer, another Dane, arrived at Chelsea. He was told that if he wanted to survive in the Premier League, he should distance himself from the English press.

The relationship between the media and the England team had become dysfunctional too. Some (John Terry, Frank Lampard, Joe Cole, Matthew Upson, David James, Steven Gerrard, Jamie Carragher and Peter Crouch) had friends among the media and generally felt comfortable and confident talking to them in press conferences. Most of that group, to its credit, would also stop to speak to journalists after matches whether England had won or lost. Others (Ashley Cole, Aaron Lennon and Shaun Wright-Phillips) generally gave the impression that they would rather be dragged across hot coals than speak to the press.

But it also went beyond individual distrust. The mutual suspicion between media and professional football was systemic. Problems that could have been avoided were allowed to develop into festering resentments. The week before England's game against the USA, the England squad had been taken on safari in the Pilanesberg Game Reserve an hour's drive from their Royal Marang Hotel. They had been followed by a large group of English photographers and news crews. When the media asked, quite reasonably, if they could be allowed a staged shot of the players at the start of the safari to satisfy demand at home, Fabio Capello refused. So the news crews and the photographers followed them around the reserve.

The players were irritated by their presence and gave the impression that the level of intrusion had spoilt their day. The pictures backed that up. They did not look like a group of young men relaxing and enjoying themselves on a rare excursion from Camp Capello. They looked thoroughly fed up and irritated. One image of a group of them in a jeep was particularly striking. Beckham, Lampard, Upson, Carrick and Rooney were all glaring into the lens with looks of barely concealed hatred on their faces. It could all have been avoided if Capello had agreed to the request for a couple of simple shots. It would have taken five minutes and then the players would have been free to continue their outing unmolested. A day after the trip, when Joe Cole came to the England media centre to speak to the press, he mentioned the resentment the players felt. Cole was one of the few who enjoyed a bit of banter with the newspaper writers, so he made a joke about the photographers. 'A few of the lads would have liked to have seen a couple of them eaten by some lions,' Cole said.

England players rarely looked as if they were enjoying themselves at major tournaments. Many of the players marched through the mixed zone with scowls on their faces and headphones over their ears, headphones that screamed 'Don't talk to me'. And that was when they had won. But when Germany lost to Serbia in the second of their group games in South Africa, every player still stopped to give interviews afterwards. They dealt with their disappointment and they moved on. Many England players did things differently. When they suffered a wound, they let it fester and suppurate.

The Dutch, like the Germans, were another example of a team that seemed determined to enjoy the World Cup in South Africa. Early in the tournament a group of English journalists in a minibus had stopped at a set of traffic lights at the busy junction of Maude Street and Rivonia Road in Sandton. They noticed a line of smiling young men in football training kit strolling along the pavement towards the Hilton Hotel a few hundred yards away. Wesley Sneijder, Arjen Robben, Robin van Persie, Dirk Kuyt, Mark van Bommel and the rest of the Dutch squad waited at the lights until there was a break in the traffic and then ambled across the road. These were some of the best-known players in the world, superstars of the game, walking along city streets on their way back from training and looking as though they did not have a care. There was no security with them – none to speak of, anyway. There were no photographers running in front of them and taking their picture. There were no girlfriends tottering along beside them. None of them wore headphones. They did not insulate themselves. They seemed at one with their surroundings.

It was only a snapshot of the way the Dutch players lived their lives at the World Cup, but to English eyes it seemed an alien and marvellous sight. When England travelled anywhere, the levels of security were suffocating. Even the English football writers who were shadowing the team in South Africa and staying in the safe surroundings of Sun City had more security than the Dutch players. Adrian Chiles, the ITV presenter, who was staying in Sandton, was not allowed to walk across the road from his hotel to the local Pick 'n' Pay supermarket without being accompanied by armed guards. In fact, he was not even allowed to walk the aisles and buy groceries without his minders. The English had been suckered by the pre-tournament proliferation of scare stories about the grave dangers that faced them if they so much as sniffed the air outside the confines of a fortified compound in South Africa, so they lived in a state of siege.

Siege and isolationism have always been twin facets of an Englishman's natural state of mind. It is part of an island mentality, the need to have a barrier between a man and the rest of the world. It has always been the way with the football team too. At the World Cup in Japan and South Korea in 2002, England's footballers stayed on Awaji Island. To get there from Tokyo involved a three-hour journey to Kobe on the Nozomi, the fastest of all the bullet trains, and then another hour on a bus to England's base, the Westin Resort, on the island. The Japanese even had a submarine patrolling Osaka Bay to protect England from attack from the sea. In Germany in 2006 England stayed on their mountain-top outside Baden-Baden, as close to the border with France as you could get, and in South Africa they picked an isolated base amid a cluster of platinum mines not far from the border with Botswana. England's administrators seemed delighted with the Royal Marang Hotel, mainly because it was so far away from everyone else.

That was England's way. English players are closed off. Their mission, generally, is to shut everybody and everything out. It is the way they are bred. It is what they feel comfortable with. In Francis Ford Coppola's 1979 film *Apocalypse Now* the main character, Captain Willard, summed up his philosophy for avoiding trouble on his journey up the Nung River like this: 'Never get out of the boat'. Willard meant it as a metaphor for refusing to allow yourself to be seduced by native culture and heathen appetites. England took the advice. They never got out of the boat either. They never looked around themselves. They never tried to widen their horizons. It was as if they were scared of what they might find. In fact, when an England Under-21 squad was taken to view the Nazi death camp at Auschwitz before the England senior team played a match in Katowice some years ago, some of them distinguished themselves by giggling as they walked around. It was probably their way of coping with the horror of what they were seeing, but it was another illustration of just how immature and callow they were. Even in South Africa, when the England players were in Cape Town before their match against Algeria and had a day to spend with their families, they were offered the chance to visit Robben Island where Nelson Mandela was imprisoned for 18 years. None of them wanted to go. When the Dutch were offered the same opportunity, the whole squad took the trip. They got off the boat.

It was rare for English players to forge a career abroad too. The ones who have tried it since the turn of the century are collectors' items. Vinny Samways, Jay Bothroyd, Matt Derbyshire, Stan Collymore, Jermaine Pennant, Michael Owen, Jonathan Woodgate, David Beckham, Owen Hargreaves, Darius Vassell and Steve McManaman are just about the only Englishmen who have tried to make it abroad in an entire decade. It is hardly an expeditionary force. McManaman was the most successful. He won two Champions League winners' medals with Real Madrid. He was a rare example of an English player who embraced a foreign culture. He loved it in Spain. He learnt the language, he made Spanish friends, he kept Spanish hours. He saw his years in Madrid as the best of his career.

McManaman was in South Africa too. He was working as a World Cup analyst for the TV channel ESPN and he was saddened more by what he saw of the atmosphere surrounding the England squad than the standard of their performances. McManaman saw the England players come through the mixed zone after matches, heads down or eyes averted, headphones on and scowls primed. 'There's always a bad vibe around the England squad at major tournaments,' he said, 'and it's the same here.' He pointed out that Thomas Müller, the German midfielder who was on his way to becoming one of the players of the World Cup, had stopped to talk to ESPN a few minutes after a game had finished. And he conducted the interview in English.

McManaman saw these contrasting attitudes to the press as significant. To him, and to many others, they represented contrasting attitudes to responsibility. If somebody such as Lennon did not have the courage or the confidence to stop and talk to journalists after a match, there was a probability that he would also turn away from responsibility on the football pitch. That certainly happened in the match against Algeria. When Capello needed him to have a big game, he was anonymous. When the pressure was on, Lennon folded. He did not play for England again in the tournament. He did not need to worry about being asked to stop in the mixed zone any more. Nobody wanted to speak to him.

It all contributed to the sense that the England team was in stasis. There was no evolutionary change. The side and the players were standing still. They were deeply suspicious of change and, most damning of all, they seemed to struggle to think for themselves. Several times during the Word Cup, Martin Samuel wrote in the *Daily Mail* about the paralysis that had crept over English players in recent years. Samuel was a friend of former England manager

Terry Venables, and he knew that when Venables had worked as Steve McClaren's assistant with the England team, he had been surprised at how difficult some of England's players had found it to make even small positional alterations to their game.

Samuel argued that, for all the vibrancy and youth associated with the new Germany side, the real lessons for English footballers came from the senior players in Löw's team. He pointed to Bastian Schweinsteiger, who had once been a left-sided player and had reinvented himself as a creative holding midfielder. He pointed to Arne Friedrich, a right wing-back who had become the linchpin of Germany's central defence. And he mentioned Lahm, who switched between left-back and right-back and played both with equal flair. The comparison with England players was striking. It was more usual to hear where they could not play than where they might. Ashley Cole struggled when he was asked to play wing-back against Croatia in Zagreb in 2006. Gerrard and Lampard could not play together in midfield. Our centre-backs struggled to play in a back three rather than a back four. And so on. 'It is not just that England play in straight lines,' Samuel wrote. 'We think in straight lines too. Fabio Capello might as well try to place an English player on the moon as ask him to adapt. It is not Germany's kids that are our problem, but England's arrested adolescents.'

In the Germany camp that Friday before the game in Bloemfontein, everything seemed so different from being around England. Before Lahm and Löw started talking, the Germany press chief, Harald Stenger, announced that the players had been to a wildlife sanctuary called Lion Park near their hotel that morning. He said that a photographer had accompanied them and that the pictures would be pooled among all media outlets. It was that simple. English newspapers had a lot of fun with the pictures, particularly the one that showed the Germany squad peering through a metal grille as a trio of lions prowled past their vehicle. 'Look Who's Afraid of the

Three Lions' was the headline on the front of the *Daily Mirror*. But that didn't bother the Germans. Unlike England's players on their safari, the Germans had enjoyed the trip. It had been a hassle-free break. 'It was a bit of a petting zoo, so we had the lions in our hands,' Lahm said with a smile. 'On Sunday the treatment we give to these lions will definitely be more aggressive.'

By then, of course, the newspapers in both countries were working themselves into a frenzy of anticipation about the match. Some of the headlines two days before the latest World Cup meeting carried allusions to the war, but they were more subtle than the last time the nations had met in a major tournament in 1996. More time had passed. But in Germany the atmosphere was as febrile as ever. The morning after Germany beat Ghana, the *Berliner Zeitung* carried a headline that read: 'Yes. Now We Are Going to Sort out the Little English Girlies'. The mass circulation daily *Bild* described England's goalkeepers as 'nincompoops' and ridiculed Wayne Rooney's contribution to the World Cup so far. However, the *Nürnberger Nachrichten* took the honours by saying that England had been troubled by prominent Germans through the decades. It mentioned Franz Beckenbauer, Karl Marx and Adolf Hitler. For once, the British press looked restrained.

At the Germany press conference past military conflicts got a mention too. The world wars were raised not by English or German journalists, but by representatives of a Swedish television station, who seemed unusually preoccupied by it. They were given short shrift by Löw. 'It is high time to forget these things,' he said. 'This is 2010 with a unified Europe, and reverting to these old war themes is absolutely out of place.' He pointed out that many of his players did not even remember the 1990 World Cup semi-final between England and West Germany, let alone the Second World War. They were children of an era of friendship and harmony between the two nations. War references meant little to them.

Other areas of history were more relevant. Some argued that the fierce footballing rivalry between England and Germany was wishful thinking on England's part. England had not beaten a major footballing nation in the knock-out phase of a World Cup since 1966. In the 44 years since then, England had made it to the semi-finals of two major tournaments – that 1990 semi-final in Turin and the last four of Euro 96. England lost both times to Germany. In the same period, the Germans had contested 11 major tournament finals and won five of them. England had beaten them in the group stage of Euro 2000, when both teams were mediocrities, and of course there was the 5–1 thumping England meted out to them in Munich in 2001 in a World Cup qualifier. But the aftermath of that match said everything about the mental strength of the players on both sides. England duly qualified for the 2002 World Cup and went out in the quarter-finals. The Germans recovered from their humiliation, qualified for the tournament via the play-offs and then reached the final, losing to Brazil in Yokohama.

So our occasional triumphs had done little to camouflage the reality of the rivalry. J. Alfred Prufrock measured out his life in coffee spoons; English football fans measured out their lives in defeats to Germany. They were part of the scenery. An English boy born in the autumn of 1966 might have vague memories of England blowing a two-goal lead against West Germany in Mexico in the quarter-finals of the 1970 World Cup and losing 3–2 in extra time. He would have been in the first flush of mad enthusiasm for the game when Günter Netzer taught England a football lesson at Wembley in 1972 in the first leg of the quarter-final of the European Championships. When he was a young man, in his prime, he would have been in the pub with his mates watching Paul Gascoigne's tears in Turin and the penalty shoot-out defeat that followed in the 1990 World Cup semi-final. And when he was nearly 30, maybe married by now, he would have seen Gareth Southgate's penalty saved at Wembley in the semi-finals of Euro 96 to give the Germans victory in another shoot-out. And four years later, perhaps with children of his own, he would have watched the last game at the old Wembley and seen Didi Hamann score the goal that condemned England to a 1–0 defeat and led to Kevin Keegan, the England manager, resigning in the toilets after the game. Now, as England and Germany headed south into the heart of South Africa, he was deep in middle age and probably divorced.

Writing in the *Guardian* on the eve of the match in Bloemfontein, Marina Hyde put everything that English boy had seen into tart perspective. 'We are rivals with Germany,' she wrote, 'in the same way Christine Bleakley is rivals with Oprah.'

20 LOST IN BLOEMFONTEIN

BY the time they arrived in Bloemfontein the day before the game, England and their supporters had convinced themselves that the worst was behind them. The tension within the squad had been dispelled by the cathartic victory over Slovenia and Fabio Capello's new willingness to soften his regime a little. From the England training camp came stirring reports that the players, lethargic and listless until so recently, were finally beginning to look like themselves again. Wayne Rooney was crashing goals in from all angles during shooting practice on Friday to the extent that David James shouted: 'We've got to stop here. We've got a game on Sunday.'

The players had been entertained by Zulu dancers at a barbecue on Thursday night, and those whose families or partners had travelled to South Africa were allowed to make the short trip to Sun City to visit them. Just as in Port Elizabeth, the players would be allowed to make the journey from the team hotel to the stadium in tracksuits rather than their official three-piece suits. The feeling was that Capello had mellowed just in time. He had seen the warning signs, realised that his stringent regime was not working in the peculiar confines of a World Cup campaign and put things right. When Danny Fullbrook, the chief football writer of the *Daily Star*, organised the 100 rand per person sweepstake for correct score and first scorer, most English journalists picked England to win. Many had Rooney down as first scorer.

It was dangerous not to back England in the sweep. Martin Lipton, the *Daily Mirror*'s chief football writer, whose knowledge of football statistics and unfailingly generous nature made him everybody's best friend when his colleagues were writing against deadline, had tipped Denmark to beat England when the two teams met in the second round of the 2002 World Cup in Niigata. The other journalists sensed the opportunity for a wind-up. They told Lipton that the *Sun* had found out he had backed the opposition and were planning to turn it into a major news story. The wind-up became more and more outlandish to the point where Lipton was told that the then *Mirror* editor, Piers Morgan, was intending to release a statement apologising for Lipton's actions. When one of his colleagues finally took pity on him just before the kick-off and placed a note on his desk to let him in on the joke, he looked at it, scrunched it up and chucked it away.

But there were other reasons for backing England. They were not particularly rational but, in the search for hope, they were all that England fans had to clutch at. When they were distilled, they amounted to a belief that England could not be as bad as they had been against Algeria, and that the modest signs of improvement against Slovenia had been only the beginnings of the team's true potential emerging. There was still an awful lot of room for improvement. Surely players such as Gerrard, Lampard and Rooney, players who were giants for their clubs, players who were the faces of the Premier League, the best league in the world, could not sink into anonymity again. Surely England v Germany, the international equivalent of Manchester United versus Liverpool or Arsenal versus Tottenham, a match loaded with history and enmity, would shake them all out of their lethargy.

The English had also persuaded themselves that the Germans might be vulnerable. They had thrashed Australia 4–0 in their first group game, but they had lost to Serbia in their second match and squeezed into the last 16 with a nervous 1–0 victory over Ghana. Lukas Podolski had even missed a penalty against Serbia, which caused much merriment among the English. There were doubts about whether Bastian Schweinsteiger would be fit to face England, and Jerome Boateng was also struggling to shake off an injury. The siren song of their coach, Joachim Löw, about Germany being a team in the early stages of development and in awe of England's star names had also had an effect. It was what England supporters wanted to believe, so they believed it. English journalists started looking forward to the build-up to a quarter-final against Diego Maradona and Argentina in Cape Town the following Saturday.

Optimism reigned. More than 20,000 England supporters converged on Bloemfontein, which was in the centre of South Africa and known as the City of Roses because of the thousands of rose bushes that flourished in its Kings Park. The fans came from Cape Town in the south and Johannesburg in the north. Many of those staying in Johannesburg set off before dawn on Sunday morning for the 400-kilometre trip down the N1 motorway into the Free State. They saw the sun rise over the rolling hills, and watched field after field of maize rush past their windows. Some were caught in a long traffic jam after a light plane made an emergency landing on the carriageway, but England fans still outnumbered Germans by about two to one in the Free State Stadium when the match kicked off in bright late-afternoon sunshine.

The last time the two teams had met, England dominated a friendly international in Berlin in November 2008 and won 2–1. But only three of the Germans who started that night had been on the teamsheet in the game against Ghana. Capello and his staff felt they were well prepared. Added to his general knowledge of the German players, Capello had watched DVDs of Germany's group games twice and had detected weaknesses. He was particularly encouraged, apparently, by the travails of central defender Per Mertesacker, and felt he would be uncomfortable defending against the pace of Jermain Defoe. Franco Baldini had scouted Germany's

2–2 friendly draw with Ivory Coast the previous November, and Stuart Pearce had bitter first-hand experience of the excellence of the players who were in the German Under-21 squad that won the European Championship in Sweden during the summer of 2009 and had graduated to the senior set-up in South Africa.

Many believed that the key to an England victory was stopping Germany's full-backs, Lahm and Boateng, marauding down the flanks. If Gerrard drifted away from his left midfield role into the centre again and left Ashley Cole exposed, there was a danger that Lahm and Thomas Müller could run riot. Similarly, there was concern that Glen Johnson's defensive limitations would be exposed if Podolski and Boateng were allowed to get at him. Johnson and Cole needed to push Lahm and Boateng back and make them defend. And Gareth Barry, sitting in front of the England defence, would have to pick up Mesut Özil, who liked to operate in the space between the opposition defence and midfield. If those assignments were carried out successfully, the argument went, England would be able to give Rooney, Gerrard and Lampard the chance to shine. Whether they took it, of course, was a different matter altogether.

Others thought Rooney's performance would be decisive. If the real Rooney walked on to the pitch at the Free State Stadium, if he banished the impostor who had been wearing his shirt in the group games, if he even got close to playing the way he was capable of playing, then England would win. But if the zombiefied version of England's most talented player showed up, the player who had trudged through the game against Algeria in a daze, then England were destined for defeat. The full-back battle was one thing, but Rooney at his best was good enough to blow the best-laid tactical plans apart. He was that important to England. The pressure on him could hardly have been any greater.

One omen was not good. An octopus called Paul, who lived at the Oberhausen Sea Life Aquarium, had achieved a certain celebrity in Germany by predicting the result of each of Germany's group games correctly. Before every match, he was confronted with two jars, each containing a mussel and each bearing the flag of either Germany or their opponent. If Psychic Paul swam to the jar emblazoned with the Germany flag, flipped the lid off it and dived inside to eat the mussel, it heralded a Germany victory. The day before the Germany–England game, Paul ignored the mussel in the jar decorated with the Cross of St George and headed straight for the Germany jar.

Nor did England's stay in Bloemfontein begin well. Some journalists who had made the long journey to the city for Capello's press conference were outraged when the England manager answered questions for only five minutes and 12 seconds. There was a storm of protest. It was portrayed as arrogant and discourteous. The story ran on Reuters. The FA were forced to put out a statement saying that they had complied with Fifa regulations. It was also pointed out that Löw had not bothered to turn up at all. He had done his press conference the previous day at the Velmore Hotel.

Capello offered little other than platitudes. When the day of the game came, there were no surprises in his starting line-up. Many were sceptical about his continuing faith in Matthew Upson, particularly now that Jamie Carragher was available again and Ledley King was close to returning to full fitness, but Capello had had a blind spot about the West Ham central defender for some time. There was a strand of opinion arguing that Upson should not even have been in the squad, let alone the first team, but he had made that crucial late tackle against Slovenia. The main German threat was expected to come from midfield rather than attack, and Capello clearly believed he needed Upson's pace to buttress central defence.

It should have become evident to Capello by then that Upson struggled at international level. Although he had been dragged into mediocrity by West Ham's problems the previous season, Upson was good enough to hold down a place in a mid-table Premier League side. But when he played against strikers of international class, he was exposed time after time. When he was picked to partner John Terry against Egypt in March, he slipped as he tried to intercept a pass midway through the first half and allowed Mohamed Zidan the time and space to place a shot past Robert Green and put Egypt ahead. Upson blamed the Wembley pitch, but it was a familiar pattern. Capello ignored Upson's failings, but Löw did not. Before the game the Germany coach identified Upson as a weak link, and formulated a plan to try to lure Terry out of central defence and isolate Upson against Miroslav Klose. It worked beautifully.

England did not start quite as miserably as they had done against Algeria, but nor was there any sign of the magical transformation everyone had been hoping for. England's passing was still poor, Rooney was still subdued, Lampard could not find his passing range and Ashley Cole was still searching for the energy that was his trademark. Germany looked more assured. It had been billed as men against boys, but Germany turned that prediction on its head. Their young players looked like masters of their trade. England looked like novices. Özil, in particular, oozed elegance and style. It was immediately apparent that he possessed the rare gift of always seeming to have time on the ball. He was never hurried, never shaken out of his stride. He was not yet quite as accomplished as the young Paul Gascoigne, to whom he had been compared, but it was clear he was an outstanding talent.

Then there was Müller. The Bayern Munich midfielder was only 20 and had made his full Germany debut just a few months earlier, but he tormented England almost from the kick-off, running between the lines, dragging defenders out of position. David Walsh, the *Sunday Times*'s courageous and meticulous chief sports writer, is a good judge of a footballer, and as he sat in the press box, he mentioned Müller straight away as the man who might destroy

England. 'He is like Teddy Sheringham with pace,' Walsh said. And Müller was. Ashley Cole rarely struggles to contain the man he is marking, but he could not get anywhere near Müller. Müller taught Cole a lesson in movement and speed of thought. His darting runs from right midfield made early incursions, and Schweinsteiger, who had shaken off his hamstring problem, orchestrated the game from the centre.

It was a surprise when Germany opened the scoring midway through the first half, but only because of the direct nature of the goal and the particularly amateurish England defending that allowed it to happen. Neuer hoofed a goal-kick deep into the England half, and Terry was drawn forward to try to win it against Özil, just as Löw had hoped he would be. Barry should have been marking Özil. That should have been the only thing on his mind that afternoon. But Barry was not there, and when Terry rushed forward, the ball sailed over both him and Özil and bounced towards the England area. Suddenly it was a race between Klose and Upson. Upson looked about as sure on his feet as a kid having his first ice-skating lesson at the local rink. He possessed neither Klose's instinct nor his acceleration. Klose brushed past him and Upson tried to drag him back. It would not be the last time an England player tried unsuccessfully to take out one of his opponents during the game. If Klose had gone down, Upson would have been sent off, but he stayed on his feet. David James, who had been slow to react to the danger, came out to meet Klose, but as Klose stretched, the Germany forward reached out his right boot and guided the ball expertly past the England goalkeeper and into the corner of the net.

Ten minutes later, Germany went further ahead. This time the goal was well worked and beautifully crafted, but England's defending was even worse. The back four was a disorganised shambles, an anarchic unit that made a mockery of Capello's supposed talent for organising a defence. When Özil picked the ball up midway inside the England half, there was no apparent danger. But Barry, once again, had neglected Özil, so Terry was drawn out to him. Ashley Cole had also been sucked out of position, following Müller towards the halfway line. But when Özil played a simple pass wide to Klose on the right touchline, and Klose flicked it over Upson, Müller sprinted on to it and into open space. Cole, who had always been England's Duracell Bunny, a man who could not stop running, a man who could keep up with any opponent, a man whom right midfielders hated playing against, trailed forlornly in Müller's wake. He was nowhere near close enough even to attempt a challenge on him. Upson was hopelessly out of position on the touchline. Terry had been dragged out of defence too.

Barry, who seemed to have forgotten that he was meant to be a holding midfield player, a position that demanded enough discipline to be able to stay behind the ball, was hopelessly out of touch. The defence took most of the blame afterwards, but Barry, who was supposed to be sitting in front of the back four and snuffing out danger at moments like this, had gone missing. His role was to be an auxiliary defender when Germany broke, but he had lost concentration and moved too far forward. Freeze-frame the action at the beginning of the Germany move and there is Barry on the halfway line, standing next to Sami Khedira, Germany's deep-lying central midfielder. Barry did not need to be there. It was not his job to be there. By the time he turned and realised his mistake, it was too late. His absence was the first event in the chain that destabilised the England defence. Barry had lost Özil, so Terry was drawn out to him. Upson was wide, marking Klose, while Cole had been duped into following Müller and then could not track his run. So there was a gaping hole at the heart of the England defence. Glen Johnson came across from right-back to try to stop Müller, so Müller lifted the ball across the goal to Lukas Podolski, who was unmarked.

There was still time for one final England defensive mistake.

Podolski's first touch was not a good one. It took the ball away from goal and made his angle more acute than it might have been. But as James came rushing out to meet him, rather than making a solid obstacle, he flung his legs wide and Podolski smashed the ball in between them. It went in off the far post and Podolski wheeled away in triumph. Barry, Cole and Upson jogged back into the penalty area with the guilty air of a trio of law enforcers arriving too late at a crime scene. They hung their heads apologetically. If this Germany team was supposed to be a collection of kids, England were little boys lost.

'Jubeln, chillen, England grillen' (Celebrate, chill out and grill England) the *Bild am Sonntag* newspaper had written that morning as Germans prepared for a summer's day by the barbecue. Everything was going according to plan. But then, for the first time in the World Cup, England displayed some real defiance. Not just posturing or talking into a camera, but defiance on the field, during a match. Five minutes after Podolski's goal, England took a short corner from the right. It was worked to Gerrard, who swung a curling cross into the box, and now it was Germany's turn to look uncertain in defence. Mertesacker watched the ball sail over his head, and when Neuer came to punch it clear, Upson rose ahead of him, hung in the air and planted a fine header into the empty net. It brought him a small measure of redemption for his culpability in both Germany goals.

Suddenly, England were back in a game they thought they had lost. Hope flickered faintly. Maybe this could yet take its place among the great England–Germany matches. Maybe this was just the beginning of a rousing fight-back, the start of England doing to Germany what Germany had done to England in León in 1970. Then the fates, and the human frailties of a linesman and a referee, intervened: England were about to fall victim to one of the greatest controversies of the 2010 World Cup.

21 WHEN NOT TO BLAME A URUGUAYAN LINESMAN

THE Germans were disconcerted. They had been in total control, but now they were in a match again. Their lack of experience was being tested at last and they were wobbling. England were infused with the energy they had been lacking, and in their next attack Defoe tried to turn past Arne Friedrich on the edge of the Germany area. The ball cannoned off Friedrich's legs and rebounded to Lampard. Lampard reacted superbly. In the split second the ball bounced off him, he saw that Neuer had strayed a few yards off his line, and as the ball fell, the Chelsea midfielder lifted it goalwards from the edge of the box. His chip was so perfectly judged that it beat Neuer's leap and flailing hands, hit the underside of the crossbar and bounced down behind the line. It was a brilliant piece of improvisation from Lampard. It was one of the best goals of the tournament.

Everyone knew it was in. Neuer certainly did. He had twisted his body while he was in the air and was staring at the ball as it came down off the bar. He saw it bounce at least a foot behind the line. But when the ball bounced down and out, the Germany goalkeeper leapt up off the ground, caught it and ran out with it, keen to throw it to a colleague and move play on. In the aftermath of the game, Neuer largely escaped censure, but he cheated that day every bit as blatantly as Uruguay's Luis Suarez cheated when he handled on the line in the dying seconds of his country's quarter-final against Ghana at Soccer City, and prevented the goal that would have put Ghana into the semi-finals and made them the first African side ever to reach the last four at a World Cup. Suarez, quite rightly, was vilified. Neuer's reputation survived untainted.

Lampard was celebrating with Rooney, but a look of horror crossed his face as he realised that the Uruguayan linesman on the far side, Mauricio Espinosa, had not raised his flag to signal that the ball had crossed the line. Capello was up off the bench, dancing in celebration as well. A look of disbelief creased his features too when he realised what was happening. It was hard to understand how the officials could have got it so wrong. The trajectory of the ball was familiar to anyone who knew football. A ball that hits the underside of the bar is often so heavily loaded with spin that it bounces down and back out. In the press box, high in the stand behind the dug-outs, every journalist knew it was a goal. It was visible with the naked eye, even from there. Espinosa was well enough placed, level with the edge of the Germany penalty area, and still he got the decision wrong. Somehow the Uruguayan referee, Jorge Larrionda, did not see the ball cross the line either.

The game continued. England protested wildly, but they had little choice other than to play on. Boos rang around the Free State Stadium, drowning out the vuvuzelas. When half-time came, England's players trudged towards the tunnel. Their flash of defiance had come and gone. They wore the look of men who believed the world was against them again. David Beckham waited by the entrance to the tunnel for the referee. As Larrionda drew near, Beckham approached him and held the palms of his hands wide apart to illustrate just how much the ball had crossed the line by. Larrionda waved him away, but when he saw a replay of Lampard's shot on the television in his dressing room, the colour drained from his face. 'Oh, my God,' he said.

Espinosa must have been worried too. English fans did not have a reputation for being forgiving towards officials who made decisions that went against them. The Swedish referee Anders Frisk retired in 2005 because he and his family had been deluged with death threats from Chelsea fans after he sent off Didier Drogba in a Champions League tie against Barcelona. And a year earlier, Urs Meier, the highly rated Swiss official, received more than 16,000 abusive e-mails and death threats from England fans after he disallowed a late goal from Sol Campbell in England's Euro 2004 quarter-final with Portugal, which England went on to lose on penalties. Reporters from the *Sun* travelled to Switzerland and placed an oversized English flag on a field near his home. He was branded 'Urs Hole' by the English press and had to go into hiding for seven days. Espinosa must have thought he had just entered a world of pain.

Fifa's refusal to use any form of video replay or modern technology to aid its officials made football's refereeing system uniquely anachronistic in the world of big league modern sport. Cricket used video-replay to help umpires rule on run-outs, stumpings, doubtful catches and whether a ball carried for six. Grand Slam tennis tournaments used the Hawk-Eye computer system to track the path of a ball and display a record of its path so that its players could challenge contentious line calls. Basketball, hockey, ice-hockey, American football, rugby league and rugby union all used forms of video replay to aid their officials. Football, the wealthiest member of the sporting elite, was also the Luddite of the family.

There was a particular piquancy to the fact that Lampard's goal had not been allowed to stand. In 1966 Geoff Hurst had shot against the underside of the crossbar in extra time of the World Cup Final between England and West Germany at Wembley with the score tied at 2–2. Modern research suggests that the ball did not cross the line, but the Azeri linesman, Tofik Bakhramov, told the referee that the goal should stand. The Germans still harboured a sense of injustice about the incident. Even though their World Cup victories in 1974 and 1990 had eased their pain, a dubious goal is still often referred to as a 'Wembley-Tor' in Germany. For the Germans, the mistake over Lampard's goal was a delicious combination of sweet revenge and belated justice.

It also made football a laughing stock. In the years since 1966 there had been quite a few advances: man had landed on the moon, torn down the Iron Curtain and abolished apartheid, but he still did not possess the technology to help decide whether a football had crossed a white line in a World Cup match between England and Germany. Actually, that is not quite accurate. He possessed it but he would not use it. Only a few months earlier, Fifa president Sepp Blatter had set himself up for a fall by saying that the use of even goal-line technology in football was off the agenda. 'Let it be as it is and let's leave soccer with errors,' Blatter had said. 'The television companies will have the right to say the referee was right or wrong, but still the referee makes the decision – a man, not a machine.' So Fifa, an organisation that would make £3.2 billion from the World Cup, would not invest in simple goal-line technology that had been available for years.

Many felt squeamish about the use of instant replay in football. They argued that it would disrupt the flow of the game. They tried to throw up as many scenarios as they could where instant replay would be problematic. It was clear, though, that if football adopted a system akin to the one used in American football, disruption would be minimal. The National Football League (NFL) system allowed a coach two challenges per game. The challenge had to be made within a few seconds and if it was not successful, the coach's team lost a time-out. The equivalent penalty in football would be a manager losing one of his three substitutions. It was a good, simple system. If Blatter had introduced something similar for football, Capello could have challenged the linesman's decision that the ball had not crossed the line, the referee could have checked the replays on a pitch-side monitor and awarded the goal. It could all have been done in less than a minute.

Mike Pereira, the architect of the NFL's video replay system, had spoken the previous year about the improvements that technology had made in the gridiron game. Much of what he said exposed the emptiness of the arguments that football purists used to counter the use of technology. 'Video replay has baled us out of making mistakes that would have had a major impact on game after game,' Pereira said. 'I would rather give up the three minutes it takes to make the right decision with video replay than spend the next three months talking about a wrong decision. We don't want people talking about officiating. Our goal is to talk about the game and the players, not the officiating. The game changes. Athletes change the game. They are bigger, more skilful, stronger, faster. That makes them harder to officiate. When any sport first takes on video replay, you are going to have the purists who say it ruins the flow of the game and stuff like that but, like everything else, when you get into it, it is forgotten about. Technology is a challenge but we should not be afraid of it. We have to improve it and keep pace with it. We are more exposed than we have ever been, so embrace it and use it to your benefit. We need to do everything we possibly can to make sure the integrity of the game is unquestioned. If that means a system that allows you to correct clear mistakes, then adjust and do it because there is too much involved in the game to pretend it won't work.'

That was far too radical for Fifa, but the proponents of goal-line technology knew they had hit the mother-lode the moment Larrionda waved play on in Bloemfontein. The momentum for some form of change, even it was just the introduction of goal-line technology, was becoming too great to resist. The previous November, the France forward Thierry Henry had handled the ball several times in the process of laying on a goal for William Gallas that put the Republic of Ireland out of the World Cup in a qualification play-off at the Stade de France. There was an outcry about it, but still Blatter remained unmoved. Then, on the same day that Lampard's strike was not allowed to stand, a few hours later and a couple of hundred miles to the north at Soccer City, another linesman failed to spot that Carlos Tevez was standing a few yards offside when Lionel Messi played a ball through to him to nod in Argentina's first goal against Mexico.

One of the things that angered proponents of the use of video technology was that, even though Fifa opposed its deployment publically, it was obviously already using it informally. When Zinedine Zidane was sent off for head-butting Marco Materazzi in the 2006 World Cup final, it was clear that neither the referee nor his assistants had seen the incident. There was a delay, presumably while the fourth official studied television replays on a touchline monitor, and then Zidane was shown the red card. What was that if it was not the use of video technology? And if Fifa recognised its worth on an ad hoc basis, why were they not willing to formalise its use? The only logical answer was that Blatter was afraid of losing face after making himself a high-profile opponent of its implementation.

In the midst of the uproar, it was easy to forget that England still went in at the break only one goal down. They knew Germany had been flustered by their fight-back. Now it was a question of how they reacted to the injustice that had been visited upon them. Their misfortune when Rob Green had allowed Clint Dempsey's shot to squirm through his hands in their opening game against the USA had drained them of confidence, but there was a chance that they would use this new moment of adversity to their advantage and feed off the resentment to drag themselves level with their opponents. For a few fleeting minutes, it seemed as if the linesman's mistake had acted as the catalyst for a transformation in the team's play that the nation had been waiting for. Rooney finally began to drop between the German defence and midfield, picking the ball up in dangerous areas and prompting others to attack. Lampard had raised his game to a level he had not produced in the tournament until then. He was even starting to look like the same player who starred for Chelsea. Gerrard's confidence was coming back.

Seven minutes after half-time, Lampard, who had been struggling to control the flight of the Jabulani ball during the tournament, hit a free-kick with pace and swerve from 25 yards that crashed against the face of the bar and flew away to safety. Neuer had not got anywhere near it. England sensed they had the advantage, but then they overplayed their hand. There were still 23 minutes to go when Lampard lined up another free-kick on the edge of the Germany box, but England poured men forward as if they were searching for an equaliser in the dying seconds of injury time. When Lampard's shot slammed into the wall and bounced out, Barry tried to dribble it through the massed German defence. It was a fatal error.

Barry was dispossessed immediately, and Jerome Boateng, the man-mountain of a left-back who was to join Manchester City when the tournament was over, clipped the ball to Müller. Suddenly, Germany were counter-attacking at lightning speed. Müller swept the ball out to the Germany left to Bastian Schweinsteiger, who tore towards goal. England's players tried to get back, but they had been caught hopelessly out of position. Their failure to leave any cover at the back was desperately naive. Glen Johnson did his best to rein in Schweinsteiger, but the midfielder angled his run so that he cut in front of Johnson and made it impossible for him to make a tackle without fouling him. Schweinsteiger looked up, saw Müller unmarked at the far post and the slid the ball out to him. Ashley Cole had managed to get back, but he was covering Schweinsteiger's run. Lampard was the closest man to Müller, but he had been sucked towards the ball too. He tried to close Müller down, but Müller had time and space to compose himself. He hammered his shot at James, and even though the England goalkeeper got a hand to it, it beat him at his near post and nestled in the back of the net. It was a beautifully constructed goal that exposed all England's limitations in a devastating 15-second burst of pace, power and precision.

Three minutes later, Germany put the game out of reach. When another England attack broke down, Khedira cleared the ball down Germany's left wing towards Özil. England were over-committed again as they searched for a way back into the game, though this time Barry was in position to cut the ball out. But as it bounced, it became clear that Barry was struggling to make the interception. Özil is not particularly quick, but the duel between the two of them was like watching Usain Bolt race a pub landlord. Barry actually appeared to be going backwards. Özil got to the ball first and knocked it down the wing into England's half. Barry knew the ball had gone, but he tried to take Özil out anyway. He wasn't even quick enough to do that. That moment summed up the game. Tired old England, clueless and demoralised, chasing a young, eager Germany full of energy and ideas. It was a depressing image. Barry gave up the chase, Özil raced on down the wing, saw Müller accelerating like a Mercedes on the autobahn into the penalty area, and slipped the ball through Ashley Cole's legs into his path. Müller did not need to break his stride as he smashed the ball past James.

Barry's humiliation was a symbol of something else too: Capello's flawed selection policy. At his best, Barry gave the England midfield balance. He was an anchor, a platform to allow Lampard and Gerrard to excel. But Barry was not at his best. He was, quite palpably, far from fully fit. Capello had said he would not take half-fit players to the World Cup, but he brought Barry even though he was still struggling with the after-effects of the ankle ligament injury he had sustained late in the season with Manchester City. He was utterly ineffectual in South Africa. Betrayed by his lack of fitness and unable to operate properly as a holding midfielder, he was a liability at the World Cup. Capello had broken his own rules and he was paying dearly for it.

England never learnt. It had been the same with Beckham at the 2002 World Cup, and the same with Rooney in 2006. Now it had happened with Barry. All fine players, but all unable to justify themselves at a World Cup because they were hobbled by injury. Capello had fallen into a familiar trap. It was one thing saying he would take only players who were fully fit, but when it came to the crunch, he decided that a half-fit Barry was a better bet than a fully fit Tom Huddlestone or Scott Parker. The way Barry played in South Africa showed that taking him was one of Capello's biggest mistakes. Michael Carrick, who had made the squad, must have felt particularly aggrieved at being overlooked for a place in the starting line-up.

There was no way back for England after Germany scored their fourth goal. Neuer made a fine diving save from Gerrard late in the game, but England were well beaten. The Germans were running riot. They could have won by five or six. It was still England's heaviest-ever World Cup defeat. When the final whistle went, the England players did not even bother to harangue Larrionda and Espinosa. They knew they had been outclassed. They knew the way they had been outplayed had turned the decision about Lampard's goal into an irrelevance. They shook hands meekly with their German conquerors and sloped away towards the tunnel. The England fans did not have the energy to boo them. They were too stunned by the manner of the team's capitulation and the realisation that another World Cup dream had been snuffed out so brutally. There was not even any appetite to vilify Espinosa. The Uruguayan linesman had got lucky. England's players had been so inept in the second half that they had got him off the hook.

As fans streamed out of the Free State Stadium, Harry Redknapp, whom many would have liked to take over from Capello, spoke to some English reporters as they walked down the stairwell on their way back towards the Media Centre. Redknapp was appalled by what he had just seen. 'England played football from 20 years ago,' he said. He mentioned how predictable England had been, how boring, how stolid. They had played in straight lines, he said. Germany had played between the lines. Redknapp talked about Müller and Özil, and how England had not had a player who was in their league. Capello's team was one-dimensional and scared to death, he said. The people he was talking to nodded sadly in agreement.

A hundred or so journalists streamed into the marquee in the lee of the stadium to wait for the managers to appear for their press conferences. Müller beat them both into the tent because he was man of the match. He spoke a little about how happy he was and then made a joke about needing a shower. Löw was next. He was generous in victory, but he was keen to point out how well his plan to draw Terry out of the centre of defence had worked. He was entitled to that. As he spoke, Capello came in through a door in the corner and stood with his back pressed against a wall, out of sight of Löw and facing away from the media, flanked by Adrian Bevington and Ray Whitworth. He looked weary. There were still hints of the exasperation he had shown on the touchline. But he did not look surprised.

By then he had already given television interviews to English broadcasters, which had angered viewers watching at home. Rather than admit England's failings, he had blamed the Uruguayan linesman for England's defeat. Everyone knew that Espinosa had made a terrible mistake, but they also knew that this was a classic attempt to pin an England loss on a scapegoat. England had not lost to Germany because Lampard's goal had not been allowed. They had lost to Germany because Germany were the better team, with better players, better tactics and a better manager. Everything else was just empty excuses. Capello should have been honest about England's failings, but he could not bring himself to do it.

That was the time for some home truths. It was the time to say how badly England had played throughout the tournament. It was the time to admit how completely things had fallen apart. Instead, Capello hid behind tired excuses. He even had the gall to say that England had played well. That just provoked bitter laughter from everyone who heard it. 'The disallowed goal was one of the most important things in the game,' Capello said. 'The goal was very important. We could have played a different style if it had stood. We played well. Germany are a big team. They played a good game. We made some mistakes when they played the counter-attack. The referee made bigger mistakes. Little things decide the result always.'

The obvious question was whether Capello would announce his resignation. He had failed miserably, after all. There was no way of sugar-coating that. England had been abysmal from the start of the World Cup to their sorry end. If Steve McClaren had been in charge, he would have been sacked before he got back to the dressing room at the Free State Stadium. But Capello had two advantages over McClaren: he had a reputation as one of the great coaches of European football; and he had a newly water-tight two-year contract worth £12 million awarded to him by his new boss, Sir Dave Richards. If Richards sacked him now, he would look like a fool.

The days of managers quitting on the spot after defeats had gone. Capello might have been a combustible character, but he was not about to ape Kevin Keegan, who had resigned in the Wembley toilets after defeat to Germany in October 2000. There was £12 million to think about. As vuvuzelas blared forlornly outside, Capello was evasive when he was asked whether he wanted to stay on. He said he would have to talk to the chairman – he still seemed to be having problems remembering Richards' name – to see if he still had his confidence. One interpretation of what he was saying was that it was the first gambit in a negotiation for a pay-off. As usual when the heat was on, Capello seemed to be having problems understanding many of the questions.

But when someone asked him if he would resign, he did not need the interpreter to help him out. He became animated. He puffed out his chest. 'Absolutely not,' he said.

22 A DEAD MAN LIVES

AN hour or so into their retreat from Bloemfontein, some of the England fans heading north on the N1 motorway thought they saw the lights of a city away in the distance to the northwest. It was too far north for it to be Kimberley, the city of diamonds, and way too far south for it to be the beginnings of the conurbation around Johannesburg. The lights grew brighter the further they travelled, and soon it became clear that it was not a city at all. The lights were alive. It was another grass fire, like the ones that burnt in the fields on the way to the Germany camp. But this time it was a great conflagration, with a front line extending several miles. It was sweeping across the veldt, purging the ground of all that was old and withered, and readying it for a new crop.

The next day, back in Phokeng, Capello walked into the white media tent in the middle of the dusty field a few hundred yards from the Royal Marang Hotel for the last time. He was accompanied by Adrian Bevington, the managing director of Club England, who was grim and unsmiling. Bevington was not a press officer any more. He was one of a few men who held Capello's fate in his hands. Many expected an announcement that the FA and the England manager had reached an agreement over his departure after a night of negotiations. But that announcement never came. Instead, Capello and Bevington sat side by side at a table surrounded by newspaper journalists and Capello listened while Bevington said the FA had not made up its mind whether it was going to sack him or not. They were going to think about it for a fortnight and then let Capello know.

One interpretation of the plan was that the FA was going to do its sums and see whether it could afford to pay Capello off – and maybe they hoped while they procrastinated that a leading European club might intervene and take Capello off their hands. Many people speculated that was the subtext of what was being said. When Capello was pressed, he said it was his preference to stay and manage England through to the 2012 European Championships in Poland and Ukraine. There was an obvious interpretation for that too: his lawyers had told him to say it. Now that the dust was settling and everyone was coming to terms with the bankruptcy of the campaign Capello had just masterminded, no one could quite believe that he would be allowed to stay on for another two years. Or, indeed, that he would want to stay on.

Bevington insisted that the FA did not want to be forced into any knee-jerk decisions, and, from the governing body's point of view, there was some sense in taking a couple of deep breaths while it stood with its finger on the trigger. There was no need for the FA to make an instant judgement. After all, it had paid £12 million to keep its man under lock and key for another two years. For that kind of money, it was entitled to make him wait while it discussed whether to sack him or not. But even those who believed Capello shouldered most of the responsibility for England's pathetic showing in South Africa felt uneasy about his treatment. He was, at the end of it all, one of the great managers of his generation, and this was an undignified conclusion to a desperately disappointing World Cup campaign. 'The end of World Cup finals for England teams are, generally speaking, pretty brutal occasions for the hapless managers involved,' Sam Wallace wrote in the *Independent*. 'But this one was the equivalent of execution by a firing squad commanded by Emile Heskey.'

Capello sat and listened as Bevington spoke, nodding his head occasionally, saying he thought the two-week wait to find out whether he still had a job or not was a good idea. Capello looked exhausted. He looked beaten. He looked broken. His face was drawn and lined, and he sounded almost hoarse, as if he had not had much sleep during his last night in South Africa. It was a shock to see that his defiance seemed to have left him. Suddenly, he looked every one of his 64 years. He did not look a man who was going to have the energy or the drive to lead a bunch of dispirited, disillusioned England players forward into a difficult qualifying campaign for a tournament that was a poor second to the World Cup. He did his best to maintain a façade of optimism, but spoiled it with a rather feeble attempt to identify new young talents who might be able to reinvigorate him and his ageing, failing squad if he were allowed to stay on and guide the team towards Poland and Ukraine.

He succeeded only in suggesting the cupboard was bare. He mentioned Manchester City's Adam Johnson, Arsenal's Kieran Gibbs, Theo Walcott and Jack Wilshere, and Aston Villa's Gabriel Agbonlahor. But then he started to struggle. He said he hoped Owen Hargreaves recovered his fitness and that Michael Dawson would remain involved. Then he mentioned Bobby Zamora. The journalists in the room looked at each other and raised their eyebrows. It became obvious then that Capello was clutching at straws. Zamora had had a fine season with Fulham. He was a decent Premier League player, but he had done nothing to suggest that he could make the leap to the international stage. He was also 29 years old. He would be 33 by the time of the next World Cup finals in Brazil. It seemed absurd to be mentioning him as one for the future.

It was hard not to feel sorry for Capello. He was reaching out for what was left of his credibility, but it was difficult to avoid the conclusion that his position as England manager had become untenable. There had been too many mistakes and the team had played too badly for it to be any other way. There were other, deeper-lying factors at work too, other long-term trends that were contributing to the steady demise of the England team, but the point of paying Capello £6 million a year was that he was supposed to arrest that demise. Instead, he seemed to have accelerated it. England had good players, but for the duration of their short involvement in the World Cup, Capello turned them into talentless, passionless, brainless, listless drones. The term 'dead man walking' appeared in plenty of English newspapers the next day.

The legend of Capello had turned into a myth at the 2010 World Cup. Fabio the Tyrant, Fabio the Great Dictator, Fabio the Scourge of the Baby Bentley Brigade, Fabio the Anti-Sven, Fabio our Saviour: lost in a fetid pool of disillusion and dismay. In the place of the man who led England's qualifying campaign so authoritatively and smoothly appeared an ageing, out-of-touch England manager whose team played football out of the Dark Ages, an arrogant, stubborn man who could not adapt to the demands of tournament football, a man who was fêted as the best England boss since Sir Alf Ramsey when he got the easy part right, but who got the hard part spectacularly wrong.

His failure raised questions about a range of subjects, not least England's recent predilection for hiring foreign managers. Even many of those who had previously believed that England should get the best man for the job, irrespective of his nationality, were starting to have second thoughts in the light of what had happened in South Africa. Deep down, there had always been unease that the 11 players on the pitch were English while the manager was Italian. Deep down, there had always been a feeling of guilt that none of the other major footballing nations had ever looked outside their own country for a coach, but England had. Putting someone of another nationality in charge of the England team was the first step in diluting the spirit of international competition.

England's experience in South Africa also showed that there were significant practical obstacles to overcome with a foreign manager.

Capello could barely speak the language for a start. When he had become England manager, he had boasted he would learn English in a month, but after an initial flurry of lessons, his English had been getting gradually worse, not better, for some time. His suggestion to the press before the tournament that he had to finalise his squad by May 34th was a worrying sign that he was heading deep into parody territory. He had discarded his usual translator before England left for the World Cup, but another one, Christian Lattanzio, who was also the team psychologist, had appeared at his shoulder in press conferences once England arrived in Phokeng. The YouTube package of his touchline antics during the game against Algeria proved that Capello had learnt to say 'Pass the f***ing ball', but beyond that, his ability to communicate was limited to a series of extravagant hand gestures.

There was a culture clash at work too, that extended beyond the obvious contrast between the England manager's fondness for ballet and his players' attachment to their PlayStation consoles. The most obvious reason for England's failure in South Africa was that Capello and his players simply did not understand each other. Capello did not understand that the *ritiro* (retreat) system, with its strict, isolationist, disciplinarian approach, would not work with a group of players that was used to being consulted and included in at least some of the decision-making processes surrounding issues such as travel and accommodation, and reacted with sullen resentment to the quasi-army regime they were expected to submit to in Phokeng. When Terry sought to broach the subject with Capello, he was slapped down.

In his critically acclaimed book *Inverting the Pyramid*, Jonathan Wilson analysed the reign of the great Inter Milan coach Helenio Herrera, the man widely credited with inventing *ritiro*. It brought great benefits to Herrera's side, but sometimes it got too much for the players. Many of the Inter team that lost the 1967 European Cup final to Celtic in Lisbon blamed an extended retreat in Portugal for their listless play. Inter's *ritiro* in Portugal was so claustrophobic that many players couldn't sleep. Herrera's invention had been so successful that he had forgotten another of his maxims: 'Avoid monotony in speeches, training and meals.' Capello had forgotten that too.

The World Cup exposed what many of the England players already knew – that Capello and Baldini were poor man-managers. Their failings ran deeper than the unyielding regime in Phokeng. When Ashley Cole and David James had spent long periods of the previous season out through injury, for instance, others players had urged Baldini to telephone them to offer support and let them know they were still in the thoughts of the England management team. Cole, in particular, was at a low ebb after breaking his ankle at almost the same time as his marriage was disintegrating. He felt alone and isolated as he began the long period of recovery and rehabilitation. But Capello and Baldini were not big on support. They didn't provide shoulders to cry on. Some players warned them that one day they might need Cole to go the extra mile for them. They said that if Cole remembered a time when he had needed encouragement and they had provided it, it might help Cole and help the team. But when it was suggested to Baldini that he should phone Cole and let him know he was in his thoughts, Baldini was baffled. 'But he is not in our thoughts,' he said. 'He is injured.'

Capello realised his mistake too late. Only after Terry had spoken out did Capello attempt to relax his regime, but even then his response betrayed a fundamental misunderstanding of what his players needed when they were agitating for more freedom. When he told them they were free to have a beer on the eve of the make-or-break group game against Slovenia, the players still avoided alcohol that night. They appreciated Capello's gesture, but they felt that it was essentially empty. England's players were modern professionals. They did not drink the day before a game. They had not been badgering Capello to relax restrictions because they wanted to go on some kind of bender. Maybe Capello had read too much into reports of their night-time antics in between matches during the Premier League season, but the alcohol issue was not particularly important to his England players. Some of them were teetotal anyway. All they were asking for was that the psychological intensity of the preparations be turned down a little bit, and that instead of being confined to their rooms for long periods of the day, they be allowed to spend more time in the communal areas of the hotel and, in the periods between matches, perhaps wander down to the bar to have a quiet drink with their teammates.

There were plenty who leapt to Capello's defence. They wanted to blame the players, not the manager. They saw the attacks on Capello as examples of ill-disguised xenophobia and lazy scapegoating. They pointed out, quite reasonably, that when England had a libertarian manager, such as Sven-Goran Eriksson, the country and the media craved an autocrat like Capello. And then, as soon as the FA appointed an autocrat like Capello, the country began to crave a libertarian like Eriksson. Maybe somewhere there was a manager who was a happy medium. Maybe somewhere there was someone who neither allowed England's World Cup to become a sideshow for a Wags' shopping and sunbathing extravaganza, nor found it necessary to keep his players locked up in solitary for most of the day so that they played like whipped curs afraid of their master.

The theory that it was all the players' fault was particularly bleak. Maybe blaming Capello was so popular because it did at least leave room for the thought that the players could have achieved more if they had been managed better. The idea that, actually, Capello had got the best out of them and that they had nothing else to offer was too depressing to contemplate. It meant that English players, journalists and fans had been guilty of over-estimating Wayne Rooney to an almost criminal extent. How many of them had said Rooney was one of the best in the world? How many of them had said he was up there with Lionel Messi and Cristiano Ronaldo? As a microcosm of his World Cup, statistics showed Rooney lost the ball in possession 32 times during the Germany game, more than any other player in a single game during the World Cup. Yet if Capello had got the best out of him, England had to come to terms with the idea that Rooney was not worthy of being mentioned as one of the world's elite and that we had attributed qualities to him that he simply did not possess.

The same went for Steven Gerrard, Frank Lampard, Ashley Cole and John Terry. Had the praise that had been routinely showered upon them by coaches of other countries and rival international players just been perpetrating a big illusion? Were the reputations of the best England players founded on nothing more than empty words and hollow deeds? Was Capello working with shadow men, with a bunch of overblown, overpaid kids who had lived such sheltered, cosseted, protected existences within their Premier League clubs that their emotional and psychological development had been stunted and they had never grown up? Was the standard that they produced in South Africa all they had to offer? Was there nothing at the end of the rainbow? Were they such poor players that Capello was always destined to fail at the World Cup in 2010? England had suspected for some time that its Golden Generation was more like a Silver Generation, even a Bronze Generation. But what Capello's defenders were asking everybody to believe was that they were actually base metal and that Capello's only failure had been a failure of alchemy.

The truth was that the explanation for England's execrable performance in South Africa spread far wider than just Capello and the players. The inexorable advances of club football and the heavy demands of the Premier League and the Champions League were encroaching more and more on the international game. Players from Spain and Germany might have played as many league matches as their English counterparts the season before the World Cup, but they did not play at the same breakneck tempo as English players did in the Premier League. Both the Bundesliga and Primera Liga players benefited from winter breaks too, a point that was given great prominence in the days after England's defeat in Bloemfontein. By the end of an English season, even one where none of the leading clubs had progressed beyond the quarter-finals of the Champions League, England players were mentally and physically exhausted.

Club football meant more and more to English players. International football meant less and less. It was impossible to ignore that conclusion. Many of them, particularly the Manchester United, Chelsea and Liverpool players, had come to associate club football with success and their time as England players with failure and mediocrity. It was almost a taboo subject, but the brutal fact was that if United played England, United would win. If Chelsea played England, Chelsea would win. The same with Arsenal. Probably the same with Spurs, Liverpool and Manchester City too. The standard of club football in the Premier League was higher than anything the top players experienced with England. If Rooney sometimes looked uninterested and disillusioned in an England shirt, that was part of the reason why.

These analyses of the reasons for England's failures happened every two years, and every two years the only thing that changed was that the outlook became darker and darker. Every two years English journalists wrote their own version of What Is to Be Done, and every two years the list of reforms needed to drag the England football team out of its depression grew longer and longer. The revolution never came. No one ever stormed the Winter Palace. Some recommendations cropped up again and again. Building the long-awaited National Football Centre at Burton was one, investing in more youth-team coaches for 5–11-year-olds was another. The introduction of a winter break was a favourite, as was trying to encourage the Premier League to adopt a more enlightened approach to releasing players for national team duty. Then there was the familiar lament about there being too many foreign players in the Premier League and not enough opportunities for English players. The Bundesliga, once again, was held up as an example of where the Premier League was going wrong. The academies at German clubs operated under rules that insisted at least 12 players from each annual intake must be eligible to play for Germany. It meant that the percentage of German players in the Bundesliga had risen to 62 per cent. In the Premier League the percentage of English players was around 38 per cent.

England and Capello flew back to Heathrow Airport to be met with a hail of abuse. The *Sun* devoted its front page to a spoof weather map. 'Sunny outlook in many areas,' the forecast read, 'but depression over Heathrow as shower drifts in from South Africa.' The *Daily Mail* front page was dominated by a quote taken from Richard Littlejohn's column inside: 'If the Few had defended as badly as England, we'd all be speaking German now.' Several newspapers printed pictures of Ashley Cole and Ledley King in fits of laughter, which were taken when they arrived back in Phokeng a few hours after the defeat to Germany. They provoked particular outrage. 'What a Joke' said the headline on the front page of the *Daily Mirror*.

Actually, England had been the butt of jokes since midway through the tournament. They had started after the Algeria game. One told of the England team visiting an orphanage in Cape Town. '"It's heartbreaking to see their sad little faces with no hope," said Jamal, aged six.' Others targeted individual players. 'David Blaine is reportedly furious after England crashed out of the World Cup – his record of doing absolutely nothing in a box for 42 days was broken by Wayne Rooney.' And, of course, Capello was the butt of many: 'Fabio Capello was wheeling his shopping trolley across the supermarket car park when he noticed an old lady struggling with her bags of shopping. He stopped and asked, "Can you manage dear?" To which the old lady replied, "No way. You got yourself into this mess. Don't ask me to sort it out."'

But despite the widespread disillusion with Capello, despite the fact that he had fallen woefully short of his own stated goals of leading England to the World Cup final, despite his failure to motivate the players, despite all the mistakes he had made in the build-up to the tournament, the FA quickly backed away from the idea of sacking him. They denied it, but maybe their decision was influenced by the £12 million they would have had to pay him to go away. As they were deliberating over his future, it also became evident that Roy Hodgson, who would have been one of the leading candidates to succeed Capello, had agreed to become Liverpool manager. So Hodgson was out of the running, and the popular choice for the job, Harry Redknapp, was facing charges of tax evasion.

So when the Bolton chairman and FA Board member Phil Gartside said on the day that the England squad returned home that Capello was 'the best man for the job' what he really meant was that he was the only man for the job. Sacking Capello would have meant FA finances took an instant £12-million hit. It would also have made Club England chairman Sir Dave Richards look particularly foolish for agreeing to scrap the break clause in Capello's contract before the World Cup. In tough economic times, and with the FA facing an immediate future dominated by low Wembley crowds and disillusion with the England team, it made financial sense to avoid a massive pay-off to Capello.

The official announcement that Capello would remain as England manager came on 2 July. It had taken the FA five days after the defeat to Germany, not two weeks, to make its mind up. 'Fabio went into the World Cup with a reputation as one of world football's finest managers,' Richards said, 'and we are confident he will benefit from his first international tournament experience, and this will undoubtedly make us all stronger for the Euro 2012 campaign.' There were leaks from the FA promising that Capello had changed, that he had vowed to pay more attention to younger players with potential, that he had promised to add another Englishman to his coaching staff, that he had said he would learn from his mistakes in South Africa. The only problem with those assurances was that Capello had not actually admitted to any mistakes. And he was a bullish, successful, stubborn, 64-year-old man. People like him did not change.

There was another, even more cynical, view of the course of action the FA had taken. They realised, the argument went, that England's Golden Generation was through. Rio Ferdinand probably would not make it to Poland and Ukraine, Frank Lampard would turn 34 during the tournament, John Terry's injuries might have caught up with him by then, Michael Owen had been exiled by Capello, and Steven Gerrard would be a fading force. Unless Theo Walcott could be revived, there were no special talents coming through who could give England new momentum. So England might struggle to qualify for Euro 2012, let alone be realistic contenders to win it. The next two years were probably going to be a write-off anyway, so it did not matter who the manager was.

By the time Capello's reappointment was confirmed, anger and dismay over England's performance in South Africa had faded to apathy. The news that Capello had survived was met with dull fatalism. No one seemed to care much who the England manager was any more. Enthusiasm had been crushed. Even if England sailed through qualifying for the European Championship, it would not change things. Especially not if Capello was in charge. Because under Capello, England had sailed through qualifying for the World Cup in South Africa too.

And look what happened when they got there.

23 THE DAYS AFTER

EMILE Heskey retired from international football. Jamie Carragher re-retired.

Other England players weighed up retirement. Some retired without realising it.

David Beckham did not retire. He said he wanted to play at the 2012 Olympics and the 2014 World Cup.

Joe Cole signed for Liverpool and said he wanted to play for a manager who believed in him. His daughter, Ruby Tatiana, who was four months old when the World Cup finished, landed her first modelling shoot as the face of Huggies Little Swimmers.

The Capello Index published its World Cup markings online and included the England players in its rankings, despite earlier assurances that it would not.

Robert Green was the worst-rated England player, with a 51.67 rating. Jermain Defoe was the best with 62.47. None of the England squad made the top 50.

Fabio Capello was said to be threatening his Index collaborators with legal action. 'He appears 97.43 per cent incapable of getting even his business partners to do what he wants,' Marina Hyde wrote in the *Guardian*.

The England Under-19 side competed in the European Championships in France. They played four games and made the semi-finals. Capello did not go to watch any of the matches.

The Under-19 squad did not just get further than the senior team had done in the World Cup. They took an interest in their surroundings too. They learnt something. They went to the Normandy beaches and saw where the World War II landings that claimed so many young English lives had taken place. The team captain, Manchester United's Matthew James, spoke movingly about what it meant to the players to have seen the site.

Ashley Cole and Shaun Wright-Phillips returned from South Africa and went to Los Angeles on holiday. Cole was pictured leaving a nightclub with two girls. 'This has ruined our lives,' one of them, Elle Hartley, said. 'We've been made to look like slappers.'

Wayne Rooney and Steven Gerrard pulled out of the A:3K skills face-off with Cristiano Ronaldo, David Villa, Didier Drogba and Cesc Fabregas that was scheduled to take place at the 02 Arena less than a week after the World Cup final.

'Both Steven Gerrard and Wayne Rooney have made it clear they believe it would be inappropriate for them to participate in A:3K at this time,' event organiser Terry Byrne said.

Sir Alex Ferguson said Rooney had not been able to handle the pressure at the World Cup. He said he would be fine next time.

Rooney defeated an attempt by his former agents Proactive to sue him for £4.3 million.

Manchester City spent over £100 million on summer signings before they bought an English player.

John Terry, his wife, Toni, and their children went to Disney World in Florida.

Fifa released their team rankings for the 2010 World Cup. England were 13th, their lowest ever placing. Fifa also revealed their new world rankings. England rose from eighth to seventh.

France suspended all 23 of the players who brought shame upon the nation at the World Cup. England let all theirs off without punishment.

The FA said they wanted to hire another English coach to work in Capello's set-up.

Paul Gascoigne arrived in Rothbury, near Newcastle, with a can of lager, some chicken and a dressing gown to try to mediate between the police and his friend, the murderer Raoul Moat. A couple of hours later, Moat shot himself.

Manchester United put 4000 season tickets on general sale for the first time in decades.

On the same day that the *News of the World* ran a front page exposé claiming that Peter Crouch had paid a prostitute £800 for sex, the paper announced Gary Lineker had become its new star columnist.

Adrian Bevington announced that ticket prices would be slashed for the England friendly against Hungary at Wembley on 11 August, England's first match since the World Cup. 'We accept it is going to take time to rebuild the trust with the fans,' Bevington said.

On Saturday 7 August, Capello picked Paul Robinson and Wes Brown in his squad to face Hungary. On Sunday 8 August, Robinson and Brown announced they were retiring from international football.

Capello told ITV he would never pick David Beckham for a competitive international match again. When it was suggested to him that should have phoned Beckham to tell him in person, Capello laughed. Capello tried to soothe the outrage over his treatment of the former England captain by offering him the chance to appear in a farewell friendly at Wembley. Beckham rejected the offer. He said he wanted to be picked on merit or not at all.

England beat Hungary 2–1. Theo Walcott was man of the match until he was taken off at half-time. Wayne Rooney was booed by the Wembley crowd. So were John Terry, Frank Lampard and Ashley Cole.

The Royal Marang Hotel reopened to the public. The books the FA had provided for the players' relaxation were still there. One of them was *The Damned United*.

ENGLAND'S RESULTS UNDER FABIO CAPELLO

UP TO AND INCLUDING THE 2010 WORLD CUP FINALS

ENGLAND'S RESULTS UNDER FABIO CAPELLO

Key:
WC-Q – World Cup qualifying match
WC-F – World Cup finals match
F – Friendly match

6.2.08 Switzerland (F) (Wembley) Won 2–1

26.3.08 France (F) (Paris) Lost 0–1

28.5.08 United States (F) (Wembley) Won 2–0

1.6.08 Trinidad & Tobago (F) (Port of Spain) Won 3–0

20.8.08 Czech Republic (Wembley) Drew 2–2

6.9.08 Andorra (WC-Q) (Barcelona) Won 2–0

10.9.08 Croatia (WC-Q) (Zagreb) Won 4–1

11.10.08 Kazakhstan (WC-Q) (Wembley) Won 5–1

15.10.08 Belarus (WC-Q) (Minsk) Won 3–1

19.11.08 Germany (F) (Berlin) Won 2–1

11.2.09 Spain (F) (Seville) Lost 0–2

28.3.09 Slovakia (F) (Wembley) Won 4–0

1.4.09 Ukraine (WC-Q) (Wembley) Won 2–1

6.6.09 Kazakhstan (WC-Q) (Almaty) Won 4–0

10.6.09 Andorra (WC-Q) (Wembley) Won 6–0

12.8.09 Netherlands (F) (Amsterdam) Drew 2–2

5.9.09 Slovenia (F) (Wembley) Won 2–1

9.9.09 Croatia (WC-Q) (Wembley) Won 5–1

10.10.09 Ukraine (WC-Q) (Dnipropetrovsk) Lost 0–1

14.10.09 Belarus (WC-Q) (Wembley) Won 3–0

14.11.09 Brazil (F) (Qatar) Lost 0–1

3.3.10 Egypt (F) (Wembley) Won 3–1

24.5.10 Mexico (F) (Wembley) Won 3–1

30.5.10 Japan (F) (Graz, Austria) Won 2–1

12.6.10 United States (WC-F) (Rustenburg) Drew 1–1

18.6.10 Algeria (WC-F) (Cape Town) Drew 0–0

23.6.10 Slovenia (WC-F) (Port Elizabeth) Won 1–0

27.6.10 Germany (WC-F) (Bloemfontein) Lost 1–4

ENGLAND'S RECORD UNDER FABIO CAPELLO

Key:
F – Goals For
A – Goals Against

World Cup finals	P 4,	W 1,	D 2,	L 1,	F 3 – A 5
World Cup qualifiers	P 10,	W 9,	D 0,	L 1,	F 34 – A 6
Friendly matches	P 14,	W 9,	D 2,	L 3,	F 27 – A 14
TOTAL	P 28,	W 19,	D 4,	L 5,	F 64 – A 25

ENGLAND APPEARANCES UNDER FABIO CAPELLO

(Maximum 28; substitute appearances in brackets)

Rooney, Wayne 24

Barry, Gareth 22 (+ 1)

Terry, John 22

Lampard, Frank 21 (+ 1)

Cole, Ashley 21

Gerrard, Steven 20 (+ 1)

Johnson, Glen 19 (+ 2)

James, David 17 (+ 1)

Ferdinand, Rio 14

Heskey, Emile 12 (+ 5)

Upson, Matthew 12 (+ 2)

Green, Robert 9 (+ 1)

Walcott, Theo 9 (+1)

Brown, Wes 9

Defoe, Jermain 8 (+ 9)

Lennon, Aaron 8 (+ 2)

Beckham, David 6 (+10)

Wright-Phillips, Shaun 5 (+ 11)

Milner, James 5 (+ 6)

Bridge, Wayne 5 (+4)

Crouch, Peter 4 (+ 12)

Carrick, Michael 4 (+ 4)

Downing, Stewart 4 (+3)

Cole, Joe 3 (+ 6)

Lescott, Joleon 3 (+2)

Agbonlahor, Gabriel 3

Jenas, Jermaine 2 (+2)

Bent, Darren 2 + 1

Foster, Ben 2 (+1)

Hargreaves, Owen 2 (+1)

Barnes, Leighton 2

King, Ledley 2

Young, Ashley 1 (+5)

Bentley, Darren 1 (+4)

Carragher, Jamie 1 (+3)

Huddlestone, Tom 1 (+ 2)

Jagielka, Phil 1 (+2)

Woodgate, Jonathan 1 (+1)

Ashton, Dean 1

Cole, Carlton 0 (+ 7)

Hart, Joe 0 + 3

Carson, Scott 0 (+1)

Johnson, Adam 0 (+1)

Owen, Michael 0 (+1)

Warnock, Stephen 0 (+1)

Total number of players used = 45.

GOALSCORERS

Rooney 11; Defoe 9; Crouch 7; Lampard 6; Gerrard 5; J Cole 3; Terry 3; Walcott 3; Wright-Phillips 3; Barry 2; Heskey 2; Upson 2; Brown 1; Ferdinand 1; Jenas 1; G Johnson 1; King 1; own goals 3. (Total 64)

CAPTAINS

Terry 15; Gerrard 6; Ferdinand 5; Beckham 1; Rooney 1.

INDEX